Kitty's story cont'd.

He was discharged to home while K in Fla. for her b'day. On May 15 I went to Densons to show the pix of my trip & they knew my host in Fla. from his being in Old Hickory St. John's J

"Kitty" "Where's your walker?"
"I can walk around house + use a cane otherwise".

FYI
Elizabeth (Liz) Brecht McKee
died 12-25-1988.
Lane officiated at service and her burial.

Eliz. Roess (Betty) McKee
b. 2-4-1925
d 12-2-2010.
I phoned Lane about her impending death. "Would you participate in service at St. Mark's, Antioch". 12-11-2010
He gave a fine homily and mentioned the mutual b'day.

with love from
mckee

3. paid for books.

Grace Notes

Volume Two: Preachments
The Insight, Irony, and Imagination of

Lane Denson

ta Brian & Mary

— Lane

GRACE NOTES: THE INSIGHT, IRONY, AND IMAGINATION OF LANE DENSON

PUBLISHED BY WESTVIEW, INC.
P.O. Box 210183
Nashville, Tennessee 37221
www.publishedbywestview.com

Volume One: Essays ISBN 978-1-935271-26-0
Volume Two: Preachments ISBN 978-1-935271-39-0

First edition, March 2011

For beloved CP
(aka Caroline Phillippe Stark)
Wife, Mother, Grandmother, Musician, Reference Librarian, Gardener

One of the highest compliments I ever got was someone saying I write like Frederick Buechner. One of the more articulate theologians of our time, he has his unintentional mark all over this book, hopefully under the protective custody of forgiveness rather than permission. Where I have been blatant, I have quoted him. Where I've been unconsciously marred but nevertheless borrowed, it has always been unintentional. In lieu of a dedication, I simply emblazon at the outset one of my favorites of his many quotable sayings:

"All theology like all fiction is at its heart autobiography, and what a theologian is doing essentially is examining as honestly as he can... his own experience... and expressing in logical abstract terms the truths about human life and about God that he believes he has found implicit there."

– Frederick Buechner

PROGRAMME

We are made and named in the image of God, that is,
as God imagines us to be... to love, to create, to reason,
to live in harmony with all of creation and with God,
to serve as God's windows (BCP p 845).
But, of course, the irony is not only that we are so imagined,
but that we are set free simply to say Yes... or simply to say No.

Prelude

THE BAPTISMAL COVENANT*

Do you believe in God the Father?

I believe in God, the Father almighty, creator of heaven and earth.

Do you believe in Jesus Christ, the Son of God?

I believe in Jesus Christ, his only Son, our Lord. He was conceived by the power of the Holy Spirit and born of the Virgin Mary. He suffered under Pontius Pilate, was crucified, died, and was buried. He descended to the dead. On the third day he rose again. He ascended into heaven and is seated at the right hand of the Father. He will come again to judge the living and the dead.

Do you believe in God the Holy Spirit?

I believe in the Holy Spirit, the holy catholic Church, the communion of saints, the forgiveness of sins, the resurrection of the body, and the life everlasting.

Will you continue in the apostles' teaching and fellowship, in the breaking of bread, and in the prayers?

I will, with God's help.

Will you persevere in resisting evil, and, whenever you fall into sin, repent and return to the Lord?

I will, with God's help.

Will you proclaim by word and example the Good News of God in Christ?

I will, with God's help.

Will you seek and serve Christ in all persons, loving your neighbor as yourself?

I will, with God's help.

Will you strive for justice and peace among all people, and respect the dignity of every human being?

I will, with God's help.

*from the Book of Common Prayer (BCP)

WORK

My beloved fellow churchers and I up country celebrated St Patrick's Day one Sunday with after-Mass Irish foods — stew, breads, cheeses, and other goodies. Time and place are no challenge for them. Like the month when Valentine Day bumped Epiphany's swan song, the scheduled lections were replaced with more appropriate ones on hearts (Jeremiah, eg) and love (Paul), and the text for the homily was George Gershwin's "Love is Here to Stay." If you can't be with the theme you celebrate, celebrate the theme you're with or some liturgical something like that.

The remarkable thing about liturgies is that they can be flexible all the while yet ordering our time and place in a way that helps us remember through cycle and crisis who we are and God is and what we're up to together. They cycle us through Jesus's life and teaching, through ours, and through the seasons, leaving no time unturned, and take the crises in stride — baptizing, marrying, ordaining, dying, all the major turning points in our maturing that enhance along our remembering. Liturgy means the work of the people, but around its edges, it can mean our play, as well.

One of the more reliable ways to evaluate the health of a congregation is to observe whether it takes its service more seriously than its services, whether it gives more attention to its ministry than to itself, whether its *Book of Common Prayer (BCP)* stays in the pews all week or leads its pray-ers out into the world where the real liturgy is, where the rite gets celebrated. It's rarely ever all that hard to find out. If you can turn up a copy of the parish budget, take a look. (I know a priest who when a nominee for an open episcopate asked for a copy of the diocesan budget. He couldn't find one. He got elected anyway, found one, and was shocked, for then he discovered why it had been kept under wraps.)

Churches that never seem to think twice about singing by the book sometimes have a hard time with us Anglicans praying by the book. Just like it might be useful to keep the hymns on track and theme, the chord changes in place and between the curbs, it's sometimes altogether orderly to keep our praying about something other than just what pops into our and the parson's mind. There's plenty of time for that the rest of the week.

Have fun.

Second Set: Imagination

*To be created in the image of God means, at least, to be imagined into being by God,
to be the creature of God's imagination, to be told into being,
to be God's "once upon a time."*

PREACHMENTS ON
THE REVISED COMMON LECTIONARY*

The letter A, B, or C following an asterisk (*) delineates the year of the lectionary cycle in which each scripture passage is found.

First Sunday of Advent *A

Lookout

"Keep awake therefore, for you do not know on what day your Lord is coming." (Matthew 24:42)

It's Advent, and away we go! It's that fork in the road again. Like Bishop Yogi said, When you come to it, take it. Don't just stand there counting up the Pentecost.

And remember, Matthew said that Jesus said, "Watch... for you don't know from nothing..."

Lookout! Look for the signs. To understand the times, to read the seasons, to grasp the moment and how it fits into all the other moments... Watchout.

Look at something else besides yourself. When we promise in the Baptismal Covenant to seek Christ in all persons it doesn't mean just those comfortable ones around you. It means look everywhere for the hand of God and while you're at it, get a notion of what God's hand looks like. Watch. And don't stop to count the fingers.

To understand our lives, we must see other lives. To understand events, we must see the ways those events impact other people. To understand our children, in spite of the confusion, we must see and listen to them. To understand our mates, we must step outside the shelters of our desires, our perceptions, our feelings, our needs, and see what kind of flag they're flying and whether it's upside down or not.

"Dying to self," even "I feel your pain," has become so trite and oversimplified a phrase that we've got ourselves blind to what a messy job it can be. So easily can it escape us that it's actually a way to God and to God's point-of-view. It means stepping away from self-reference, from self-determination, from self-expression, not because they are wrong, but because they keep us from seeing over the next hill. It means to be surprised over and over again to find out that the gospel is not about how to live. The gospel, like the First Step of the Twelve, is about how to die.

If we see life only from the vantage of self, we hurt others even if we want only to love them. We diminish ourselves. We trespass on community. We turn away from God. Before we know it, we become as parched and sterile as last summer's backyard. So we look. What makes a difference? When it comes to planning our days, it's easy to presume the time's already used up. It's not all that easy to realize that the point is more like the old Duke Ellington tune, "It ain't whutch yew do, it's the way whutch yew do it." It's the way we come and go, stay and return, meet and greet.

And don't forget, there's more to our lives than putting one foot in front of the other even though we'll never get anywhere if we don't. As we go, listen to the talk and then walk the talk. Tune in to the laughter and the crying, and then guffaw and shed a few yourself. Take somebody's hand. Listen to somebody's story. Honor somebody's journey. It never is and never could be parallel to ours nor is it all that different. Unlike in geometry, our paths will intersect long before we get to infinity.

"In God's economy, all of life is connected in a way that we can neither create nor stop. So far as we know, we may be the only part of life even halfway self-conscious. The universe needs us for a voice. God made us for an audience that would talk back, and, as well, figured rightly how important it might be that we'd have each other to talk about. The commitment to be aware of this and to see it as it is remains an essential part of our being, our privilege, our responsibility, our vocation, our Advent." *(Buechner again.)*

Advent has Christmas by the tail and probably won't let go until it gets half as much press.

Second Sunday of Advent *A

Reverence

In those days John the Baptist appeared in the wilderness of Judea, proclaiming, "Repent, for the kingdom of heaven has come near." (Matthew 3:1)

When the last British soldier present in the trenches of World War I on Christmas eve in 1914 died, he was one hundred and six years old. It was on this night that the Germans, only a few yards away, laid down their arms, began singing Silent Night, their Fatherland's carol, as they climbed out of their trenches, then came over and exchanged gifts with the Allies.

The next morning at sunrise, they began once again the killing. Merry Christmas.

Almost one hundred years later, that extraordinary holy and silent moment we call Christmas is about to happen again. It is matched only by the extraordinary silent and holy moment just before it happens. Advent is the name of that moment, this moment. I like to think that if only the world knew these things, if only we knew these things, really down deep knew these things, we might hold our breath — and listen.

For one, we might listen to how Wendell Berry, farmer, philosopher, poet, talks about Place as the "informing ambience of one's mind and imagination." We might listen to how the church can be such a place, not just a latitude and longitude, but a true place, a metaphor of attention, a parable where truth trumps logic, an environment where the absurd happens, where the Word becomes flesh. A place that so informs our minds and our imaginations, that so gives shape to them, that once again in these times we might come out of our trenches to embrace our enemies, not only to bring presents to them but to be present to them.

Hovering now over all my thoughts with increasing frequency and poignancy in these times is this question: How might a human economy be conducted with reverence? How might we therefore show and practice due respect and kindness toward everything involved in such an economy — not only an economy of wealth or the lack of it, but more importantly, an economy of ourselves and our neighbors, and all that we are — our health, our education, our homes, our work, our environment, our religions, our many systems which we value so deeply and by which we live so intently? How might we show reverence for all the displaced persons in the world?

Reverence seems somehow the password for this season. The reverence of Blessed Mary before God's wishes for her. The reverence of garrulous old John Baptist when he beheld what for him was the Lamb of God. The reverence of the alien kings at the Epiphany. The reverence those World War I enemies had for one another.

We lack sorely this reverence. One only need to drive the interstate system or to walk in the shopping malls or to stand in the interminable lines of waiting to experience it. One only need attend to our government's budgets to discover where is the reverence for the poor. There is no shame in the poverty Americans suffer today. The shame adheres to those who do nothing to change it. One only need observe the unilateral arrogance of our leaders toward other cultures and other languages, other voices and other rooms, the Other in whatever shape or form to ask "where is the reverence."

Is it any wonder that, lacking such admiration and esteem, we are soon succumbed by fear? When we are afraid, we become angry, and we inevitably turn to violence and war. War. It is only a strange and simple little three-letter word that means not only strife and confusion, but quaintly enough, means as well to sweep away, to wipe out the other like some stain, with total disregard and even blindness for the fact that we never seem to learn that in war there are no winners, only losers.

Reverence. An Advent sound of gentle stillness, a silent and holy moment can prepare us once again for such due respect and kindness toward all of life — and toward ourselves, for we are God's beloved. The church can, the church must have a hand in this. We must turn from our crippling narcissism to the practice of reverence. We must pray about it. We must pray for it. We must wish for it, for what is prayer, but such wishful thinking?

This, of course, if ever it happens, will be the ultimate maturation of our culture. Then we will no longer need preëmption if, indeed, we ever did. For when we build such reverence, truly they will come.

Third Sunday of Advent *A

Risk

When John heard in prison what the Messiah was doing, he sent word by his disciples and said to him, "Are you the one who is to come, or are we to wait for another?" (Matthew 11:1-2)

There is always an element of uncertainty in a life of faith.

For this, faith must have an open mind. And open minds are not only marked by curiosity, they are also marked by risk. Curiosity and risk are two of the hallmarks of a faithful life. To make faith into a closed system, nailed down in some century long past and for all time, is not faith, but dogma. It has its place. It is orderly. Above all, it is safe, for there is little or no risk. It is the life blood of religions. But it is not faith.

Even John Baptist, as certain as he once had been, finally had his moment of zen there in the dark of that prison when he sent his followers to ask Jesus, "Art thou he that should come? Or do we seek another?" Are you the one? Or do we have to keep waiting — and looking? If we're to believe that meeting between Mary and Elizabeth, their moms, John spent his entire life pointing to Jesus and walking and talking and preaching the risk of faith.

When the Baptiser finally got prison for his reward and entertained his greatest moment of doubt, Jesus understood. Jesus answered John in effect with what John already knew. He answered him with the only truthful answers that can ever be given to certify the presence and work of Jesus, the Christ.

The work you have already witnessed, he said to John, continues. Be assured. The blind see. The lame walk. The deaf hear. The poor and hungry are fed and finally know justice and peace. A broken world is being mended. And you know, as I, that wherever such healing takes place, there is present the kingdom of God.

We make covenant in our baptism to "seek and serve Christ in all persons…" And we can fairly ask, "Yes, but how will I know this Christ?" It is the same question John asked. Our baptism not only commissions us to be Christians, it commissions us to a ministry altogether, like John's, as well… a ministry to witness, to point, to say Here is the Christ… There is the Christ… in this event, in that healing, in that judgment, in that moment of truth.

Civil rights leader Howard Thurman set the stage for us to know this Christ when he wrote of Advent and Christmas as seasons of hope. "When the song of the angels is stilled," he said. "When the star of the sky is gone. When the kings and princes are home. When the shepherds are back with their flocks. The work begins… To find the lost. To heal the broken. To feed the hungry. To rebuild the nations. To bring peace among people. To make music in the heart."

But it's no promise of a rose garden. There are "false Christs," Jesus said. There are those who in his name would justify war, who would substitute piety for service, who would put orthodoxy before sacrifice, who would make of the gospel a system or a philosophy rather than the Way of life, who would claim me and then turn their backs on me, who would elevate doctrine before faith.

When we make that vow in our baptism to seek and serve Christ, when we ask that question with John, Are you the one? we're soon, to take C S Lewis's great phrase, surprised by joy to discover that we are not only *part* of the answer, we *are* the answer. In this present time in the church… we cannot just be handed out the answer by some prelate, we must *be* the answer by our faith. For it is the Christ in us that will always recognize and know the Christ in others — and in all.

Fourth Sunday of Advent *B

Magnificatharsis

In the sixth month the angel Gabriel was sent by God to a town in Galilee called Nazareth, to a virgin engaged to a man whose name was Joseph, of the house of David. The virgin's name was Mary. And he came to her and said, "Greetings, favored one! The Lord is with you." (Luke 1:26-28)

It was when Gabriel told Mary about the fix she was about to be in that the venerable old trumpet player's unswerving loyalty to God was faced with a major challenge and test. StoryTeller Frederick Buechner imagines the scene this way:

"She struck the angel Gabriel as hardly old enough to have a child at all, let alone this child, but he'd been entrusted with a message to give her, and he gave it.

"He told her what the child was to be named, and who he was to be, and something about the mystery that was to come upon her. 'You mustn't be afraid, Mary,' he said.

"As he said it, he only hoped she wouldn't notice that beneath the great, golden wings he himself was trembling with fear to think that the whole future of creation hung now on the answer of a girl" *("Peculiar Treasures," Harper & Row, 1979, p 39).*

Gospeler Matthew's accounting is not quite so colorful. He starts with a kind of biblical once-upon-a-time plainly and almost with resignation when he says, "Now the birth of Jesus took place in this way."

And then he tells the story through the medium of Joseph's dream and about how it took the power and authority of Joseph's angel to turn him away from abandoning his young betrothed altogether as he had every traditional right to do. But for us, the Annunciation is more than "the medium is the message," no matter how profound. For the medium is also the answer.

First, there's Mary's answer. Her Yes, and her subsequent paean that we call her Magnificat *(Lk 1:46-55; BCP 91f).* And then, there's our answer. These antiphons combine to model for us what God expects from all his children and his church as they gather, now and in every generation past and future. God wants a Yes from us in whatever way we can say Yes with the most integrity. And our souls, as well, are called to a Magnificat in however and whatever way we can proclaim the greatness of the Lord. It is ours, as well, again in our way, to magnify the Lord, to rejoice in God. It is our calling to show God's strength. It is our ministry to scatter the proud in their very heart of hearts. It is our responsibility and, indeed, privilege to put down the mighty from their thrones and exalt those of low degree, to fill the hungry, and to empty the rich.

In a very real way, this, our Magnificat, is what we call our Baptismal Covenant. When we take up that vocational commission to give birth to this Christmas Jesus in our way, we're asked to respond ever so much as did Mary in her way. "Yes. Let it be to me according to your word."

We enter now into a season marked by great expectations. These hopes are of the ways in which this season's joys are informed, given shape and expression — and become flesh. The pulse of Christmas that courses through us may be in this entire coming year as near as we can ever an approach to our own Christ-in-us-and-others character that we confess and seek in the Baptismal Covenant.

We know the pattern, we know the evidence. It's the same evidence that Jesus sent to an emprisoned John Baptist — "the blind receive their sight and the lame walk, lepers are cleansed and the deaf hear, and the dead are raised up, and the poor have good news preached to them. And blessed is he who takes no offense in me" *(Mt 11:5f)*. And we know the ways this brokeness in our society can be mended, can take shape, can become a reality. Once again, we've got the Twelve Days, the partridge and all the rest, the better part of a fortnight to load and lock the arsenal of grace that we'll proclaim in Epiphany.

Once again, the Yes.

Once again, the Virgin's cry, that magnificatharsis for the church.

Christmas Day *Proper III

Place

In the beginning was the Word, and the Word was with God, and the Word was God. He was in the beginning with God. All things came into being through him, and without him not one thing came into being. What has come into being in him was life, and the life was the light of all people. The light shines in the darkness, and the darkness did not overcome it. (John 1:1-5)

T S Eliot suggested that the real meaning of exploration is to get back to the starting point "and know the place for the first time."

His counsel seems altogether appropriate for Christmas. We always know, of course, or think we know exactly how this exciting story turns out. But it is still always an exploration into the unknown of ourselves and of tomorrow, for we really have never the foggiest notion about how all that will turn out.

Most of us heave a sigh of relief when Christmas is "over." But Christmas is never over. It remains the most profound mystery for the life of faith and it is always a starting point to which we return and risk knowing "the place for the first time."

But what kind of mystery is it? "There are mysteries which you can solve by taking thought. For instance, a murder mystery whose mysteriousness must be dispelled in order for the truth to be known.

"There are other mysteries which do not conceal a truth to think your way to, but whose truth is itself the mystery. The mystery of yourself, for example. The more you try to fathom, the more fathomless it is revealed to be. No matter how much of yourself you are able to objectify and examine, the quintessential living part of yourself will always elude you, that is, the part that is conducting the examination. Thus you do not solve the mystery, you live the mystery. And you do that not by fully knowing yourself, but by fully being yourself.

"To say that God is a mystery is to say that you can never nail God down. Even on Christ, the nails proved ultimately ineffective." *(Frederick Buechner, "Wishful Thinking," Harper & Row, p 64, 1973)*

For this "light shines in the darkness," John wrote of Christmas in the prologue of his great gospel, "and the darkness has not overcome it" *(Jn 1:5).*

When he wrote this about Jesus, it's safe to say he probably knew from nothing about light in the terms we call the quantum principle. (It is also safe to say that neither do I. Homiletic license, however, is often a sure route into indeterminacy and arrives there with the very best of them.)

Light, say the astrophysicists, can be either particle or wave, but never both at the same time. It always depends on the way you look at it. So does Christmas. So does Jesus. Both are always a matter of the mystery, an altogether holy ambiguity. One cannot stop Jesus and make him into a bangle on the Christmas tree and also follow him as Lord at the same time. This Jesus Light shines, as well, into the darkness of our own uncertainties, our own mysteries. We can bring that dark path of our experimentation with life, disappointed as we often are, and even lay it before the bedecked and garnished Christmas altar. Standing there, we are free to look away from the often blinding light into another year of resolutions, another year of planning, another year of expectation… and only find more darkness.

Or we can embrace that Light to lead us forth into this new year, exploring with love and faith and all those other great risks of grace. We well remember in these days that questioning apostle Thomas, the one whose faith and doubt made him something of an amalgam of himself, and perhaps a mirror of ourselves. Jesus confronted him not as some orthodox system of thought or doctrine, nor some attempt to freeze and manipulate reality, nor some institution, but that he was, instead, "the way, the truth, and the life," the very pattern for being human as God imagined all of us to be.

Christmas allows us and sometimes even inspires us that in returning to it again and again, we might quite possibly come as T S Eliot reminded us, to "know the place" and even know our Lord — "for the first time." Perhaps we will. And then may we discover how awesome, indeed, is the gracious and mysterious ambiguity of the holy set down here in our midst.

First Sunday after Christmas

Silence

But when the fullness of time had come, God sent his Son, born of a woman, born under the law, in order to redeem those who were under the law, so that we might receive adoption as children. And because you are children, God has sent the Spirit of his Son into our hearts, crying, "Abba! Father!" So you are no longer a slave but a child, and if a child then also an heir, through God. (Galatians 4:4-7)

Once upon a time near Christmas, a teacher asked a group of first-graders what love means. A seven-year old answered: "Love is what's in the room with you at Christmas if you stop opening presents and listen."

I can hardly think of a more exciting time, especially when I was a youngster, than opening presents on Christmas morning. The larger the family, the noisier, the more laughter — the clatter of new things, the music, the shouts of joy. Think of the contrast if everyone stopped for a moment, everyone in the house and especially around the tree. The electric train at a standstill. The horns set aside. The dollies not crying. Remember the song, "The Sounds of Silence"? Such silence as this does indeed make a sound.

When the teacher asked his students what love means, one said, "Love is what's in the room with you at Christmas if you stop opening presents and listen." When we listen to that silence, maybe we can hear all the thought, all the shopping, the wrapping, the cooking, all the pleasant remembering of friends and loved ones, for now and in other Christmases past. Perhaps someone may realize in the silence that there's a reason we call gifts "presents." They are certainly not "pasts."

They are not "futures." They are presents. They are gifts in the "now," not in the "then" and not in the "when," but in the "now." They are presents.

Ever so often, you'll remember that in the liturgy, in the words we say and hear, the music we listen to and sing, there's a time for silence. That short reminder usually comes after a reading or after a sermon or in the prayers of the people. It says "Silence may be kept." It does not say that silence shall be kept. It says that silence may be kept.

One meaning of that is that silence — here and now — is yours to keep. You can do with it what you will, what you wish. Silence is a gift, a present, for you. You can even take it with you and use it whenever you need it. For most of us, there's always a time when silence, even a little silence, will be welcome. It can be a time to remember, maybe even to remember love, that God loves us right here and now in the present. Every time we gather here in this place, silence is given and silence is kept. We take and keep these silences. Sometimes, visitors here are so surprised by the silences that they think the priest has "somehow lost the place."

There are gifts here and presents every time we come together. They are God's gifts of bread and wine and story, of sound and music, bells and horns and violins, of our choir, of words, of signs and symbols. When we are reminded that silence may be kept midst all this, as with the first-grader's answer about love, perhaps if we stop "opening" all these gifts, love may be, love can be especially noticeable. The love of your family, of your friends, of your neighbors, if we will but listen for it.

And remember midst all this that God is love. God is the love in the Christ child whose birth we remember as God's present "to" us. God is the love in our hearts as God's presence "with" us. God is love in Mary's and Joseph's puzzled joy. God's love in this place is yours. With the silences, it, too, may be kept. Of all the gifts in this life, said St Paul, love is the greatest, the one that lasts forever, the one that you "can" take with you, that you can keep.

Please take the silences. When you can, fill them with love. And one day, perhaps, you may bring them back. You are always welcome here... and loved.

January 1 / Feast of the Holy Name *ABC

Name

And he was called Jesus, the name given by the angel before he was conceived in the womb. (Luke 2:21b)

Perhaps more than any other season in the year, Christmas inundates us with its great repertoire of symbols, plowing and enriching our thoughts and feelings and visions with its universal time, its universal language of liturgy and music, its universal message of peace, good will, and joy. The same is true of all the other symbols we use to communicate with one another. It is no different with art and the dance, with poetry and prose, with all our myths and the language myth requires for its telling. But it seems especially true of Christmas.

No wonder, the Wonder of it all.

It is common religious practice often to think of such symbols as icons, as windows through which one may prayerfully discover and perhaps experience a greater depth and power. We speak of sacraments in that way, as "outward and visible signs of inward and spiritual grace... [and] as sure and certain means by which we receive that grace." *(BCP, p 857)* As well, it is not uncommon to make icons into idols, to admire — or to be offended by — only the window and to remain completely blind to the view, failing to discover any possible deeper meaning altogether.

On the First of January in the very middle of these twelve days of Christmas, the church keeps a day whose symbol, indeed, whose icon is for Christians perhaps second only to the cross.

We call it the Feast of the Holy Name. It recalls for us that this child of manger and miracle became through his flesh a son of the Old Covenant. And it recalls that through his naming as Jesus, he became a symbol and bearer of the New. Thus Jesus is a name above every name that, like the cross, anyone can use or misuse, but that is always rendered superficial until we can read through and beyond it, until we can read behind the symbols.

The power, place, and understanding of icons and especially the icon of Jesus himself has not been nor has it ceased to be the least source of great division in the Christian tradition. The study of this person and his work in our own time in the so-called "Jesus Seminars" creates likely some of the most controversial scholarship since the great credal councils themselves.

For in and through the historical Jesus, there is shaped the discovery of the Christ of faith and the possible reconciliation of all humankind. Through the icon of his holy name and his identity with it is revealed the profound irony of the Word made flesh, Christmas. But Christmas, like anything else that ever happens, including you and me, enters history through this peculiar event and its peculiar people with whom we share our lives. If it is not a miracle, then it is such an exception that it might as well be.

Frederick Buechner said that God's sense of humor is perhaps no more apparent than in his creating human being so that the universe will have something to talk through, so that God will have something to talk with, and so that the rest of us will have something to talk about. That irony of God, that reversal of events by surprising us with the most familiar, is perhaps never more apparent than in his choosing our human being for a window through which we can see not only ourselves, but beyond that to God's very presence.

We are occasions, you and I, opportunities, if such were needed, for all sorts and conditions of things. Just look at the way the universe fits itself around us. For doors and doorknobs and dishes. For mattresses and motorbikes. For books and bathtubs. For poems and posies. For pulpits and pews. For each other. Forever.

We are made and named in the image of God, that is, as God imagines us to be... to love, to create, to reason, to live in harmony with all of creation and with God, to serve as God's windows *(BCP p 845)*. But, of course, the irony is not only that we are so imagined, but that we are set free simply to say Yes... or simply to say No. That we're given this choice calls forth preëminent imagination and reminds us that we may be nearest God's will for us when we are most imaginative. It should be no surprise, as well, that it is then that we are also most faithful.

In the name of Jesus, are we named. In the name of Jesus, do we pray. In the name of Jesus, are we made whole. What a remarkable way to begin a new year.

Second Sunday after Christmas *ABC

Mountain

Listen, nations, to the word of Yahweh. On the farthest coasts and islands proclaim it, say, He who scattered Israel is gathering him, will guard him as a shepherd guarding his flock. (Jeremiah 31:10)

Blessed be God the Father of our Lord Jesus Christ, who has blessed us with all the spiritual blessings of heaven in Christ. Thus he chose us in Christ before the world was made... (Ephesians 1:3-4a)

Today I want to preach about Taking Back Christianity and maybe Christmas with it. I don't know about you, but I'm embarrassed to death to call myself a Christian these days. And I resent that. The name "Christian" has been hijacked, taken over, and practically patented by a particular sect of Christianity, and it's been stolen right out from under me. The opportunity of being a peculiarly Anglican kind of Christian is being stolen out from under us right here in this diocese, as well, and I especially don't like that. How dare they!

I read that a recent presidential election was decided by something called "moral values." That is, specifically, opposition to abortion and to gay marriage. We are told that those were the two moral issues that made all the so-called Christians stand up and be counted. Christian values, Christian morals. We are told that this sort of thing won out in this election. (There've been polls to the contrary since then, polls that show a deeper sense of morality, the kind I want to talk about, but electoral results don't show much evidence of their influence.)

Well, the ones that are claimed to have won the election are not my Christian morals, and I don't want to be that kind of Christian. I don't want a name that implies that I think or feel or believe like people who make these their highest values or fears. There are many kinds of Christianity out there, some actually in contention with one another, and there always have been. The Religious Right wing, the fundamentalists, the zealots, the anti-intellectual evangelicals, the creationists, the biblical literalists have a lot of nerve trying to claim that their very narrow brand of Christianity is the only one.

I say that it is time that Christians who believe in and follow and actually live by the teachings of Jesus and frame their lives by the Baptismal Covenant or a reasonable facsimile — that it's time these Christians reclaim the name "Christian" and stop being coöpted by persons who have little knowledge, understanding, or practical application of Christian principles in their own lives.

Real Christians have to stand up and say, "Morality? This is what you call morality? You've got to be kidding!" Real Christians have to point out that "Christian" means "someone who follows the example and teachings of Jesus," not "someone who will swallow whatever a preacher will tell them." Real Christians have to take this book that everyone keeps referring to, this *Bible*, and actually read it and find out what those teachings are.

In the book, Jesus never said a word about abortions. Some Christians oppose aborting a fetus that cannot even live on its own, but this deeply held conviction did not prevent millions of good, life-respecting Christians from voting to continue an unprovoked and falsely justified war of aggression that has killed tens of thousands of perfectly innocent men, women, and children who were already living. I think Jesus for sure would not have liked this. In this book that none of us read often enough, Jesus never says one word about homosexuality. It probably never even crossed his mind. As a matter of fact, Jesus very seldom talked about "thou shalt nots," about terrible things you weren't supposed to do. His morality was about what you were supposed to do. He was crystal clear about the "thou shalts."

According to Jesus, this is morality: Feed the poor. There are about twelve million people in our country who worry daily about whether they will have food, not just enough, but any. Jesus said, comfort the prisoners — and that probably includes not torturing or shooting them or hooking them up to the base plug. He said, accept the outcast — the alien, the different, the single mother, the street person, the Muslim. He said, shelter the homeless and stop creating more of them. He said, be good stewards and shepherds and stop raping the environment. He said, depend on God, not on wealth and don't greedily collect it at the expense of the poor. He said, treat others as you would have them treat you. And he said, fight for justice.

This is the morality Jesus taught. This is Christian morality. This is what "good" Christians endeavor to do. Everything else is self-righteous claptrap and proof-texting of the old Hebrew Scriptures and unworthy of the adjective "Christian."

Morality? Murder and violent aggression are immoral. Allowing people to wallow in poverty is immoral. Raising children to hate others for any reason is immoral. Rewarding the rich and greedy is immoral. Lying is immoral. Suspending basic human rights is immoral. Torturing prisoners is immoral. How dare the supporters of a list of atrocities like these claim to be voting for morality?

I'll tell you why they claim it. They think they're "moral" because their priests and pastors and preachers and bishops tell them they are. These insecure and often power-hungry leaders feed on people's basest fears, they prey on the weak, they threaten true believers with hell on earth and hell afterward. Now, that's immoral! It doesn't matter that most of it is lies. It doesn't matter that the preachers and priests and pastors and bishops have proven to be a dismally badly behaved bunch themselves. It doesn't matter that the churches are temples to greed and self-indulgence and self-righteousness and fancy silken vestments.

These people have been allowed to claim the title "Christian" because we have done nothing to stop them. Too many of us have chosen good manners over fighting for justice, and now we have to face the fact that we have lost Christianity. We have handed it over, lock, stock, and barrel.

We act viscerally, we are easily swayed, we don't want to look too closely at the consequences of our actions. We find it hard to follow Jesus's commands — and rightly so. We pick and choose our moral positions to make ourselves most comfortable. But since there's one thing we're always moral about — being polite — we don't speak out against the theft of Christianity right here under our noses, we don't want to tell the harsh truth about the hijackers of morality, we don't dare mention that the emperor has no clothes. We think we have taken the high road by doing this when what we have taken is a dead-end to nowhere.

Read the book. Listen to what Jesus says. Do the right thing. And speak out. Rise up and take back Christianity, so that we can be proud to be Christians again. Talk loudly and often about real Christian morals. Practice them conspicuously. Incarnate the Baptismal Covenant in your lives. Refuse to be intimidated when bigotry and fear and power-hunger drape themselves in the robe of morality. Apply your morality to your life and your votes. It is not just a nation and a system of constitutional government at stake, it is the future of Christianity and the ethical face of tomorrow's world. If we don't stand up and take back Christianity, we can hardly expect our children to.

It's time to take it back! And to do that we're going to have to "get real." A small example: Look around you. You probably cannot find a single soul in this congregation who doesn't have more than a passing acquaintance with suffering or with serving another in any number of selfless ways or who has not been judged unfairly for who they are or who has not given sacrificially or who has not thought of leaving in disgust over some of the church's self-serving shenanigans, but has vowed and prayed to stay and give and serve, anyway.

Now go, and tell it on the mountain!

January 6 / The Epiphany *ABC

Show & Tell

When they saw that the star had stopped, they were overwhelmed with joy. On entering the house, they saw the child with Mary his mother; and they knelt down and paid him homage. Then, opening their treasure chests, they offered him gifts of gold, frankincense, and myrrh. And having been warned in a dream not to return to Herod, they left for their own country by another road. (Matthew 2: 10-12)

As the story goes, they were very wise, even smart enough to be kings. On top of that, they must have had an unlimited personal line of credit. Surely they spent a bundle on the gifts they brought and then left in hardly the kind of place where they usually stayed overnight. In addition, they read stars altogether well enough to find their way across a perilous desert and all the way back home again.

It's when they got home that makes me wonder what on earth they must have said.

That they found the one who made the very star they followed, the Ruler of the Cosmos, helpless on a bed of straw in a manger? When they began telling something like that around the courtyard, being a king and having executive privilege and all must have come in mighty handy. No offense. But somehow, the record carefully neglects letting us know how it all came out back in their own precincts, save that history shows the Orient waited a lot of centuries before it ever heard the Good News.

You and I go to the manger every year and don't seem to find it all that hard to locate. Just now, we've been once again. We've seen the star and borne the gifts, even if we do have a way of giving them to everybody but the one whose birthday we claim to be celebrating. We've made a lot of the usual fuss, often with considerable inconvenience and at great distances, and, heaven knows, we've spent a wad ourselves.

Like the three kings, we're back on familiar turf, settling down pretty much to normal. Yet if we will, we, too, have a whale of a story to tell all about what we found in a manger.

But unlike those royal magicians, we don't have executive privilege. We can't expect people to believe what we say just because we say it. We learned long ago — or should have — that nobody believes much of anything until they are shown.

We've found the King of the Universe at Christmas, we tell them, and by the way, he's that baby in the cow stall. He's the Word, the Prince of Peace, and he became flesh and moved into the only overnight place he could find. But nobody much listens. Nobody pays attention. Nobody, that is, until all our talk and song and tinsel and light itself becomes flesh. That's when God's peace and justice and good will and joy to the world comes alive in our time… in us.

First Sunday after Epiphany / The Baptism of Jesus *A

American Jesus

Then Jesus came from Galilee to John at the Jordan, to be baptized by him… And when Jesus had been baptized, just as he came up from the water, suddenly the heavens were opened to him and he saw the Spirit of God descending like a dove and alighting on him. And a voice from heaven said, "This is my son, the Beloved, with whom I am well pleased." (Matthew 3:13-17)

Perhaps nothing so identifies Jesus with us, nor us with him, as does his baptism. The tender and touching nativity stories of Christmas evoke in us a warm and universal, but often distant compassion for him and his family. John Evangelist's brilliant philosophical apologetic that the Word became flesh stuns us with awe. But Jesus's baptism reveals for us how deeply he identified with his people… how he crossed the Red Sea out of slavery with them, how he entered into the Promised Land with them. In his baptism, he accepted their heritage and their hopes as his heritage and his hopes. So, in our baptism, do we identify with him in this same heritage and with the hopes of all those who have followed him down through the centuries to this very day. In his baptism as in ours, the rubber meets the road and we fast-forward into this new season called Epiphany. Here we are, alongside the three kings, riding camelback across the desert on the way home. What in God's name do we say about where we've been and what happened to us there? Yes. It's show and tell time in the neighborhood.

Stephen Prothero has written a book which tells some of the ways we've answered that question. It's called *American Jesus: How the Son of God Became a National Icon.* We've covered the spectrum with our answers, he says — from the second-person-of-the-Trinity Christ of the Creeds to Thomas Jefferson's Enlightened Sage shorn of miracles, resurrection, and divinity, from the amiable, countercultural hippie-cum-rock-superstar fostered by the "Jesus freaks" of the 1960s to the willowy "sweet savior" given us by Currier and Ives and described by Dorothy Sayers as the "household pet" of little old ladies and pale curates.

One worries, he suggests, with all these assaults on the Christian tradition together with the disintegration and misuse of the biblical foundation, that this Jesus, the Lord of the marginalized and forlorn, may soon become the man nobody knows in 21st century America *("NYTimes," 8i04, p B9).*

With those in the church in these times who are so imprisoned by their obsessions, with their squeamish uneasiness about the "lifestyle" of some of their own colleagues, and with their lashing back in anger and judgment, fear and denunciation of the very tradition that has nourished them through the ages, we, ourselves, may well be distorting the image of Jesus.

This Jesus of ours could soon become the man nobody knows not only in 21st century America, but in 21st century Christianity, as well. It is, indeed, show and tell time. Let us return to his baptism for a moment and listen to what God's commanding Spirit proclaims to the world — "This is my beloved son; with whom I am well pleased" *(Mt 3:17).* Jesus is what God means not only for the fulfillment of human being but by the very being and becoming of human. Here is the image as God intends it, the image in which we share in our own creation, and the same freedom which we are given as Jesus was given to accept

God's calling as the church, the Body of Christ in the world. To wrestle with it in our own wilderness. To question it in our own garden of Gethsemane. Or, of course, not.

We, by grace, freely receive that commission, just as we, by grace, may freely reject it. Will it be the Gospel's Jesus or the American Jesus? Will Jesus become the man nobody knows and we the people everybody knows as empty, introverted narcissists, navel-gazing our way into eternity?

We pray in today's collect, God… "grant that all who are baptized into [Jesus's] Name may keep the covenant they have made, and boldly confess him as Lord and Savior" *(BCP p 214)*. We embrace that in our Baptismal Covenant. There is no holier order and there is no more strategic evangelical commission than this and the way it gathers into itself all the dimensions and hallmarks of Christian life and mission.

Listen again to the great verbs. Continue in what the apostles have begun. Persevere in resisting evil, and failing, return to the Lord. Proclaim the Good News in both word and example. Seek and serve Christ in all persons. Strive for justice and peace. What does it mean to be a Christian in any time and place? There's the answer in our Covenant, quite as clear as can be. May the primates take notice. We need no other. We've not made a contract to carry that out. We have made a covenant. A contract is by law entered into with clear and equal understanding and agreement as to the terms or conditions, results, consequences, and implies not only cooperation, but compromise. If broken by either or subsequently abolished, it no longer pertains. A covenant is by grace initiated by one with others and even if broken, yet endures. A broken contract ends. A broken covenant lives on and by grace is renewed. Our Baptismal Covenant is a relationship initiated by God, to which we respond in faith. Once made, it is eternal, broken or not, and may always be healed and restored by forgiveness, reconciliation, and return. In such healing there is present the kingdom of God.

This church we embrace is founded on that covenant with God, not on a contract made with the Windsor bishops. It is founded on a promise not to make life easier or more orthodox, God knows, but to make life more purposeful, more meaningful, not for self-serving, but for serving selves. When we are baptized, we say "Yes" to that covenant. Just so, did Jesus. So how do we use such freedom? By hoarding it or by giving it away?

We shun political action in the church at our own peril and destruction. As most frequently practiced, politics is about power — who has it, who doesn't, and over whom it is exercised, with rewards to the shrewd and the strong. It can and often does become a natural nursery for greed. From this does it get its scarlet name. Not often do those who practice it remember that the very word means "of the people" and that therein is the true authority that can be led to implement the community which grants it to be utilized for the fulfillment of God's purpose.

Our mission, our authority is not about *telling* people how, but about *showing* people how, not only about answering and providing, but also about creating an environment in which we and others can become and fulfill God's image within us. Will it be the American Jesus or it will it be the Jesus with whom we are baptized into new life?

Second Sunday after Epiphany *B

Guileless

When Jesus saw Nathanial coming toward him, he said of him, "Here is truly an Israelite in whom there is no deceit!" (1John 1: 47)

Whenever I drive by one of those churches with a big marquee or standing sign out front and see somebody's name on it in four-inch letters followed by the word "Minister," I cringe a little (maybe with a touch of envy, as well!). There's a lot of theology in such a billboard. There's theology about leadership, theology about vocation, theology about servanthood, not to mention expectations about who does what in that place the sign is telling about, maybe even who's in charge. Or who's not in charge.

"Minister." It's a common mistake we make all the time. To call the leader of a congregation its minister as if he or she is not only the only one and there are no others, but is also to relegate that great vocation to one person whom for all intents and purposes contains, represents, and includes the ministry in that place.

Now, I'm pretty sure that's not what is meant by such a sign. The folk there in that church might be quite surprised to discover that anybody would interpret it that way. Yet, there it is for all to see. And there it is maybe even for that congregation to explain and in the explanation to discover all the richness in why they are there at all on that corner with those big buildings and all that choice, tax-free real estate.

The story of Samuel and Eli *(1 Sam 3:1-20)* is all about ministry, and it's one of the more charming bits of Old Testament lore. Eli's practically blind, staying pretty much to himself, leaving Samuel to keep watch in the temple over by the ark of God, maybe the same one Indiana Jones went looking for a few centuries later. It's a story about ministry, about Samuel's wondering who's calling him and then finding that God is calling him to be a priest and a prophet and subsequently one day to take Eli's place in the succession and have the dubious honor of naming Israel's first king.

And then over in the gospel, there's that story about Jesus and Nathaniel which is also a story about ministry *(Jn 1:43-51)*. Philip brings Nathaniel to meet Jesus and tells him along the way that Jesus is the real thing, the Messiah they've been waiting for all these centuries. Then he adds, almost as if to apologize, that Jesus is from Nazareth, of all places. Hearing this, Nathaniel blurts out the question we've all used at one time or another about somebody we think of not much worth. "Can anything good come out of Nazareth?"

Well, yes and no. We get the answer to that later as the Jesus narrative unfolds. But for now, it's something of an exchange between the two. Jesus overhears Nathaniel, of course, just like he seems to overhear everything whether we like it or not. And Jesus says, "Behold, an Israelite indeed, in whom is no guile." Nathaniel finally comes to his senses, realizes in whose presence he stands, and the story moves on. His name doesn't appear in any of the lists of the twelve apostles. Some say he was also called Bartholomew, and as you know, that name does show up. At any rate, he probably never forgot his gaffe about Nazareth and may never have known what a memorable phrase he left for our continued use.

We'd like to think that ministry hasn't got a lot to do with where one comes from, though there seem to be exceptions now and then. But it is useful in its practice to have little or no guile, no deceit, though from the looks of things, some would probably argue that point.

"Who are the ministers of the Church?" our Catechism asks, then answers just as forthrightly: "The ministers of the Church are lay persons, bishops, priests, and deacons." Then as the query goes on asking what is the ministry of each of these, the answers all begin with the same definition before moving into particulars: "The ministry of [fill in the whomever] is to represent Christ and his Church." *(BCP p 855)*

We'd do well in the church to set aside for a time the notion that deacons, priests, and bishops are "holy orders," somehow to be taken as more blessed and sanctified than the laity. And we'd do well to remember that no order nor ordination vow is holier than that by which we are commissioned and will to embrace and follow in our Baptismal Covenant. All Christians share that holiest of orders, and any subsequent "refining" of it is quite another matter.

As Nathaniel came toward Jesus in all earnestness, maybe with his yarmulke on crooked and his dog-eared Torah under his arm, Jesus said, "Behold, an Israelite indeed, in whom is no guile." One could look far afield to find any better qualifications to meet the *Prayer Book* Catechism's notions about ministry — "to represent Christ and his Church." — than a commitment to one's *Bible* and tradition and a life without deceit and, as Nathaniel reminds us, realizing that not every vision is what it seems.

Third Sunday after Epiphany *A or B

Organize

And [Jesus] said to them, "Come after me and I will make you fishers of people." And at once they left their nets and followed him. (Matthew 4:19-20, Mark 1:17)

God and the devil are walking along the road together. God sees something lying there and picks it up. The devil says, "What's that?" God says, "It's the truth." The devil says, "Give it to me, and I'll organize it."

Today's gospel tells the story of Jesus selecting his disciples. It's a story of both good news and bad news. The good news is to witness the apparently willing surrender of all that these men held dear — work, family, perhaps even their lives — for the uncertainty of whatever it might mean to follow Jesus. This kind of an act is one that might embrace us all. The bad news is to witness what are probably the first steps, albeit it nascent ones, in the organization of truth, an act that does for sure embrace us all.

A colleague of mine once introduced himself. He said, "I am a member of no organized religion. I am an Episcopalian." I wish this were true, but of course, it is not. Nevertheless, there is a strange and uniquely Anglican spin on the Gospel that we might just remind ourselves of from time to time. It would go something like this: Perhaps our most important and distinguishing mark is corporate prayer, with thanksgiving (we also call it Eucharist) at the center of our worship. All that we do and the way we attempt to understand what we do grows out of this, our corporate worship, powered by grace in gratitude.

We discover God's will for us in Scripture. But also in tradition, as says one of our prayers, "joining with the heavenly chorus, with prophets, apostles, and martyrs, and with all those in every generation who have looked to [God] in hope."

We take this Scripture and this tradition and through our rational capacities we strive to understand these things. They are brought together for us in the shape of the liturgy, that is, the work of the people, so that we can share mutual trust with our inheritance.

We distrust judgmentalism, biblical literalism, election, predestination. These ideas lead to division, then hatred, alienation, and even killing. We embrace inclusiveness, moderation, and toleration. To follow these leads to collegial and spiritual enrichment.

We live comfortably with ambiguity in our tradition, and we do not require certainty in all things. We argue. We fight. But then, we come together once more for Common Prayer and Eucharist. This is our way. We seem actually and rather quaintly to prefer vagueness and imprecision. We practice a generous and forgiving orthodoxy, an ordered freedom. We are the oxymoron of the Christian view of things.

Don't we wish. But there is hope.

There's an Episcopal parish that, so I've heard, includes among its actively pledging, attending, and serving people, a group whose members have one other thing in common — they do not believe in God. That's a pretty good step in the direction of inclusivity, might we say? For whether or not it is, what better place for atheists to be? It is good not only for them, but also for the rest of us in all our many stages of belief and disbelief.

A congregation at its best is a place where atheists may not only freely challenge theology by their mere presence, but where, as well, they may learn enough about theology to provide real substance for their disbelief and fend off a few challenges, themselves. Then, there's always the outside chance that they may be loved so much they'll have to wonder why on earth why.

Our sciences show us over and over with convincing and commanding evidence the great biblical truth that we human beings and all of creation for that matter are members one of another, whether we choose to be or not. What we believe, that is, what religion we may or may not practice has very little to do with it. That we cannot know absolute truth and certainty and, as the devil would have it, cannot organize it, is an idea that's next to impossible for some folk to accept.

Nevertheless, it's a model of community to which we all might well aspire. It's part of this Anglican Communion's "ordered freedom." It is a delightfully redundant diversity with a graced pragmatism about it all. We proceed, do we not, by the way of "probable persuasions."

Frank Griswold, the former presiding bishop of the Episcopal Church, claims as his rule of life these words once spoken by a Roman Catholic archbishop from South America: "The bishop belongs to all. Let no one be scandalized if I frequent those who are considered unworthy or sinful. Who is not a sinner? Let no one be alarmed if I am seen with compromised and dangerous people, on the left or the right. Let no one bind me to a group. My door, my heart, must be open to everyone, absolutely everyone."

This, of course, must not only be true for our bishops, but it must also be true for ourselves and thus for the church. For it is our fear that prevents us from being such a community, not our welcome and affirmation of diversity. If I must choose, and I hope never to have to, I would choose without question an uncertain church that is loving over a loveless church that is orthodox.

Fourth Sunday after Epiphany *B

Walk

"And the people were astonished at his teaching, for he taught them as one who had authority, and not as the scribes. And immediately there was... [in his

audience] a man with an unclean spirit; and he cried out... "I know who you are..." (Mark 1:21-24)

"He taught them as one who had authority."

There is a confounding ubiquity about spirit, a simultaneous and inclusive presence one simply cannot avoid, no matter where one turns or where one attempts to run. Furthermore, one can never quite be sure whether that presence is good or bad, for spirit is inherently neutral, that is, until one engages it, embraces it, incarnates it. It is then that the rubber meets the road.

One who has authority knows that reality intimately. For it is the very nature of authority to embrace and engage and elicit spirit, indeed, thus to inspire, and furthermore, to order, shape, and in the classic sense and meaning of the word, inform. The daemons in Jesus's world do us a great service, for they are often the first to know this authority about him. They already know it about us and how vulnerable we are. In our blindness, they frequently have their way with us. But they've met their match in Jesus — and ultimately in all those who truly serve God.

This marvelous little story in the early verses of Mark's gospel illustrates his urgency in telling the Jesus saga by starting right off with the truly critical effect of Jesus's presence. There's no beating about the bush here, and the rest is downhill in the rush to climax.

The people in the synagogue are almost instantly "astonished at his teaching... [with] authority," but they are only "amazed" and driven to murmuring among themselves. Whereas the "man with the unclean spirit" who was also there at worship knew instantly in abject fear of who confronted him and, I should hope, to his relief at the demise of his possessors. This scene recalls for me C S Lewis's Wormwood in *The Screwtape Letters* and his out-of-balance churchiness. It, too, is about the confrontation of power with authority. See how authority meets and elicits, draws forth the spirits of those it would lead and incorporates them in accomplishing their goals? Whereas power commands and overrides the other's spirit with its own. One need but recall the World War II leadership of a Churchill or a Roosevelt to discover a brilliant illustration of authority. And then to lay it over and against the dictators of the Axis to find the momentary clash and destructive results of authority when construed as power.

Authority reaches out of its own spirit into our spirits and enjoins us to its cause. Power manipulates our spirits and cripples them. One remembers the story of the lame man lying by a pool at the Sheep Gate for decades, waiting for someone to take him to the waters to be healed. When Jesus saw him there, he simply asked the man the obvious question, "Do you want to be healed?" (If so, then) "Rise, take up your pallet and walk" *(Jn 5:1-9)*. Jesus met the man's will with authority, not power at the weakened implement of his lagging spirit. The man stood and walked.

Some confuse authority with power and, as well, construe teaching with manipulation. This confusion muddles the church in our time. Authority, we often hear — and rightly so — is truly the critical turning point in the church's current demise within itself. It is no easy task to incorporate or rather perhaps incarnate grace and justice into law, if, indeed, it can be done effectively at all. And yet that's what any creative legal system must attempt. It is true of our American Constitution and its call for the balancing of powers to achieve authority. It is true of the way the church strives to be faithful to its commandment to do justice and to love and to its commission to baptize and enlist disciples. It is true of any attempt to order holiness.

We are inherently like this. For we are spiritual beings by virtue of God's having created us. How we enlist and incarnate that spirit determines the ultimate effect and maturity of our humanity. The church is the place where we can undertake this process. The daemons know who we are, and they know that for they are pure spirit, lurking to become incarnate in us, to elbow Jesus's presence off center with their own. On the other hand, Jesus simply asks us if we want to be healed, if we want to walk. And to walk is to cast out the daemons.

Jesus says simply, "Get a life — and walk."

Fifth Sunday after Epiphany *B

Daemons

[Jesus] would not permit the daemons to speak, because they knew him.
(Mark 1:34b)

Two little daemons were having an argument of sorts. One of them was saying, What is it with humans? I heard the other day that they actually prefer the lesser of two evils.

One should exercise great care in making light of evil. Equally so, in labeling things as evil, or even as an axis or an empire of evil. Something like this is afoot in that part of our family history that Mark recounts in today's gospel lection *(Mk 1:29-39)*. It takes place midst a plethora of daemons, evil's special name for its emissaries or, if you will to be more biblical, its disciples.

Simon's mother-in-law was sick abed, thus putting out of service anyone to manage the kitchen. Apparently, that would never do, so the first thing Jesus did was to heal her so that the first thing she could do was to begin to serve them. Pretty soon when the word got around, "the whole city was gathered around the door," not for supper but for healing. The daemons were stirring up mayhem. So he shut them up and "would not permit [them] to speak, because they knew him" *(Mk 1:34b)*.

This is not the only place in the gospel recounting that makes reference to the fact that the daemons know Jesus and that he shuts them up. Maybe it's because he's not all that proud of their company, but maybe also, it's because spirit always recognizes spirit, evil or no. In one story, Jesus casts daemons out of a deranged man and sends them packing to a herd of swine, showing, perhaps, less concern for other people's livestock than for other people. Spirit knows spirit, spirit is the means whereby we recognize one another, spirit makes a collage of community. Spirit is what makes us human. It is that energy about us that we can use either for good or for evil, that esprit de corps by which Jesus communicated wherever he was, preaching on the mount, walking on the water, or healing Simon's mother-in-law so she could stir up some nourishment. Ministry, you know, is not always as impractical as one might think.

"Wherever two or three gathered together in my name," Jesus once said, "I am present." That's as good a definition of church as one might imagine. If there is evil spirit there, Jesus shuts it down, just as if there is good spirit there, Jesus commands it to heal and casts out its malaise so that we can become who it is God intends us to be, an axis not of evil, but of good.

An old preacher was telling a class of young homiletic upstarts about how to structure a sermon. First, he said, You tell the people what you're going to tell them. Then, he said, You tell them. Then, he said with considerable enthusiasm, You tack a rousement on it.

However this preachment followed or did not follow his counsel, here's anyway a rousement:

Spirit is always present in us and in our communities because that's the way God imagines us into being human. And God sets us free to use that gift in anyway we choose, either to worship him or worship ourselves. Perhaps one of the better ways we can worship him is to become more like the humans, the persons, he wishes us to be, more human, I suspect, rather than more spiritual. Then, like Simon's mother-in-law, we can take up our beds and walk — straight to the kitchen where we might do some good.

Sixth Sunday after Epiphany *C

Congratulations

"Blessed are you who are poor, for yours is the kingdom of God. Blessed are you who are hungry now, for you will be filled. Blessed are you who weep now, for you will laugh. Blessed are you when people hate you, and when they exclude you, revile you, and defame you on account of the Son of Man. Rejoice in that day and leap for joy, for surely your reward is great in heaven" (Luke 20b-23a)

As he was checking out for the day, a workman pushed a wheelbarrow full of sawdust up to his company's security gate. The guard took special care to poke around through the sawdust, then cleared the man to pass. Day after day, the two went through this same routine.

One day, the guard said that he had been transferred, that his curiosity about what was being smuggled out was driving him bananas, that he would keep strict confidence if only the workman would tell him. So, cautiously, looking over his shoulders both ways, the workman whispered, "Wheelbarrows."

The Beatitudes occur in two places in the New Testament. In Luke's Sermon on the Plain and in Matthew's perhaps more familiar Sermon on the Mount. I can't speak for you, but whenever I think of the Beatitudes, I nearly always envision those whom Jesus blessed — the poor, the mourners, the hungry, the peacemakers.

There, plainly before us, is our Lord's handbook for pastoral ministry. It's been the church's model for centuries and rightly so. We may not always have measured up, but there it is, anyhow, reminding us to whom we are called so that we never lose sight of our purpose.

So it is that this remarkable and inclusive Jesus-sermon challenges any preacher. It certainly makes me wonder what more can be said or even needs saying about church and world. But then, like the curious company security guard, the obvious hits me smack-dab in the pulpit.

Wheelbarrows! Blessings! It's the blessings, stupid! And further, it is not so much who or what the church blesses, but that the church blesses, and that the church itself be a blessing. What a moment of Aha!

Strange is it not that the act of blessing is at the very heart of the schism over which we anguish in these times. The blessing of a priest to make one a bishop. The blessing of a loving relationship to make a commitment sacramental. The cry of thousands ringing in our ears to claim that blessing.

It is not only the church's primary vocation to bless and to be a blessing for its own and for its neighbor, but it is also the calling of each and every one of us. What is our worship in this place, our service, but to bless God? At the end of every reading of the Daily Offices, there it stands.

"Let us bless the Lord! Thanks be to God!"

The circle of blessing is completed when we bless God, when we offer grace for God, that God's blessing of us does not return empty. For the church ever to withhold blessing may be the gravest of the ways we separate ourselves from God and from each other, for that is a judgment call that only God can make.

It must and should be clear that blessing does not always mean approval or that it is merited. God's grace is always free and unearned. We who by that same grace are commissioned as God's servants dare not risk the peril of standing in its way for another. We cannot claim thus to comprehend grace and not, as well, extend it, nor finally define the means for its giving as if it were some possession that we alone can certify. It is precisely when we are so addicted to our past or to Holy Scripture or to our fixed ways and take ourselves more seriously than we take our work that, for a pity, we become graceless and we are no blessing at all.

Now, I should like to add something of a postscript or actually something that is called a *lagniappe*. A lagniappe is a kind of grace, itself, something given or obtained gratuitously or by way of good measure. It is rather like the thirteenth cheese Danish in a baker's dozen.

In the matter of blessings, the scholars of the Jesus Seminar have suggested that the word "blessed" in the Beatitudes may well be translated as "congratulations." Indeed, one has offered that the phrase, "Blessed are the poor in spirit," might be translated, "Congratulations, you bums!"

"Congratulations" is a word we often use, sometimes just a throw-off without much thought behind it. Somebody will say it to somebody else surely before this day is out. So let me then suggest that we may be blessing folk when we're not even aware of it, and that, of course, is the best way, the least pompous way of all. For to "congratulate" literally means to "wish grace" to another, to hope for them joy for the time of their life.

When we share the peace in a moment, maybe we should say, "Congratulations! God loves you."

Seventh Sunday after Epiphany *B

Faith

And when they could not get near him because of the crowd, they removed the roof above him; and when they had made an opening, they let down the pallet on which the paralytic lay… And when Jesus saw their faith… he said to the paralytic… "Take up your pallet and go home." (Mark 2:4-11)

As Mark tells this short story about Jesus, one cannot but wonder at the bumptious chaos of the scene. The room is packed so that even the door cannot be opened. A preachment is underway, the audience is surely intent on every word. And suddenly somebody starts taking the roof apart.

Some scholar from the Jesus Seminar or the like would surely know about roofs in Capernaum at the time of Jesus and even how to dismantle one. I know nothing, but I am sure that when those four guys with a gurney came through, it must have made one helluva mess.

It is said that Mark wrote his gospel with urgency and almost as a brief. Perhaps that's why he goes into no more detail in this tale about any damage control. All that aside, he surely means to remind us of the great power of faith, not only of our own personal faith, but of the faith of the community of which we are a part.

When we bring a child to baptism, such faith is in effect. When we sponsor someone to be confirmed, such faith is at work. When we promise to envelop and help sustain a marriage, a celebration of a new ministry, an ordination, such faith is always in play. As well, in the laying on of hands, in a simple phone call to a shut-in, in the intercessions in the prayers of the people, there is the kind of faith that can also raise the roof in the name of God.

It has been said that a sacrament is God offering his holiness to us, and that a ritual is our raising up the holiness of our humanity to God. This healing in Mark's gospel, our next time that we gather around the Holy Table with our parish, is, as well, such an exchange.

Eighth Sunday after Epiphany *A

Mister Rogers

Thus says the Lord: In a time of favor I have answered you, on a day of salvation I have helped you; I have kept you and given you as a covenant to the people, to establish the land, to apportion the desolate heritages; saying to the prisoners, "Come out," to those who are in darkness, "Show yourselves." (Isaiah 49:8-9a)

Fred Rogers of TV's "Mister Rogers's Neighborhood" was asked once why it is people so often seem afraid to talk to one another.

He sat quietly for a moment, then he answered. "Perhaps we think that we won't find another human being inside that person, and how sad it is to think that we would give up on any other creature who's just like us." I wonder how he might feel about those who have made it altogether clear that there are not only certain folks they won't talk to, but with whom they won't even stay in the same room or at the same table. If Mr Rogers is right, there's a lot of fear at hand at work.

Maybe we're missing what is perhaps one of the most distinguishing characteristics of Mister Rogers's Neighborhood: His recognition of our common humanity and how that seemed so often almost inseparable from our fear. What a sight it would be to see him now. There he is, inviting us in, taking off his suit jacket and putting on his sweater, taking off his loafers and putting on his sneakers, feeding his fish, suggesting we change out of our dress clothes and let the air out of our puffery, while always listening respectfully to whomever might be talking about their craft or their concerns or their big responsibilities somewhere around the world.

Maybe he would gently introduce topics likely troubling to a four-year-old, maybe even to them. Are scary things on television really real?

Will I be sucked down the bathtub drain with the water? Will people who leave come back? Is it all right to get angry? Such questions in one form or another are not all that far off the mark for many of us.

And I can especially see Eddie Murphy's parody, his Mister Robinson lamenting with embarrassing accuracy, "I hope I get to move into your neighborhood someday. The problem is that when I move in, y'all move away."

Rogers once told of his often puzzling over a verse in one of Martin Luther's more popular hymns, *A Mighty Fortress is Our God.* The verse says, "The prince of darkness grim, / We tremble not for him; / His rage we can endure, / For lo! his doom is sure, / One little word shall fell him." He asked one of his favorite seminary teachers, then retired, with whom he had studied for the Presbyterian ministry and with whom he visited often, "What is that one little word that would wipe out all evil?"

"Forgiveness," said his professor. "Evil disintegrates in the presence of forgiveness. For Satan would prefer that you look with accusing eyes at your neighbor, thus extending the accusing spirit, the greater power of evil. On the other hand," his professor continued, "if you can look on your neighbor with the forgiving eyes of the one who is our Advocate, those are the eyes of Jesus, himself."

Fred Rogers was of certain a pastor. His compassion was prophetic, as well. His clear, almost palpable caring could often challenge one into a nourishing reflection and resolution. The neighborhood he created and welcomed us into as fellow advocates was literally permeated with forgiveness and acceptance, reconciliation and the banishment of fear. It knew nothing of judgment.

It's not easy for us to discover the human in the other person and not succumb to our fear of the unknown. The church struggles with this very problem now and not all that successfully. We seem to prefer keeping our distance. When there comes an opportunity to open ourselves to everybody or even to somebody, perhaps unconditionally as healers, including these "others," we pass. We say "No, thanks."

We make covenant in our baptism to seek and serve Christ in all persons, loving our neighbors as ourselves. For this Christ — this other human being of whom we seem to be so afraid, who seems so often elusive and unknown — is in fact God's beloved son in whom he is well pleased, to whom God would have us listen, the very same image in which we are all uniquely created.

We err when we so often would make the church a remote shrine above it all for our protection. Mr Rogers's Neighborhood is as good a metaphor for the church as I can imagine. If it's not, may it pray to become a neighborhood where we can discover not only our own humanity and begin to fulfill it, but where we can discover the humanity of others. May we there dare to become more human precisely as our fear is dispelled, and to do so by the grace God gives us to love our neighbors as ourselves.

It is a pastor's work to lead people into reconciliation and truth. Fred Rogers was a pastor and prophet, perhaps one of the finest. As we now leave this Epiphany time, this time of telling others where we have been and what we have seen, may we enter into this more introspective Lent to become now such a Mister Rogers neighborhood where fear is no more.

Last Sunday after Epiphany / The Transfiguration *A

Listen

And [Jesus]was transfigured before them, and his face shone like the sun, and his clothes became dazzling white…While he was still speaking [with Moses and Elijah] suddenly a bright cloud overshadowed them, and from the cloud a voice said, "This is my Son, the Beloved; with him I am well pleased; listen to him!" (Matthew 17:2-5)

When the prophet Elijah was called by God, he searched for the evidence of that call in some spectacular sign — earthquake, fire, wind, thunder, lightning. His answer came, instead, not nearly so grandiose, but in the familiar King James Version's "still, small voice" and in the later American Version's far more poetic and lovelier "sound of gentle stillness" *(1 Kgs 19:12 AV)*.

That may often be the same for us. Like Elijah, we look for signs, rather than simply listen for them.

The Transfiguration tells such a story. No noise, just a super wardrobe malfunction. It would be hard to imagine a more brilliant scene than that of Jesus's consort with Moses and Elijah and having his garments suddenly lit up like half-time at a rock concert. We can't fault Peter, James, and John for being overcome and wanting to negotiate a more permanent arrangement. It was only natural. It is only natural with us churchers. Majestic cathedrals, fancy vestments, great music and liturgy, all pointing to us in the hope that maybe like those disciples, the world will want to negotiate and join up.

The Voice from the clouds up there on the mountain says, simply, "This is my beloved son with whom I am well pleased." These were God's words at Jesus's baptism. But the Transfiguration story seems to suggest that there's been an attention deficit in the meantime, as if that simple recommendation was not enough. There on the mountain, the Voice adds a simple command… "Listen to him."

Perhaps this story is about witnessing. Witnessing that takes at least two forms. The obvious and more common one is telling the story of our experience as a people with God, enacting our story, making it as attractive as we possibly can. The perhaps less obvious way of witnessing is to listen to the other's story, the neighbor's story, the world's story, listening for God's presence, for Christ in the other. Listening, giving audience, paying attention may be, after all, a most profoundly magnetic and winsome way of witnessing. Listening for the "sound of gentle stillness."

"This is my beloved son with whom I am well pleased; listen to him."

In his little monograph, *Reaching Out*, Henri Nouwen rings changes on the Great Commandment to love God and neighbor as self. He calls our growth in fulfilling this commandment "spiritual maturity" and describes it as offering audience to self and to neighbor and to God.

That we don't listen to ourselves, he suggests, results in our profound loneliness. There's a saying around Alcoholics Anonymous circles that "boredom is a personal insult." Whereas, to give ourselves unrestricted, unconditional audience, Nouwen says, defines the difference between loneliness and truly creative solitude.

As well with our neighbors must be our gift of audience, of truly listening without condition, without planning our next speech, opening from hostility to a true and welcome hospitality. And finally does Nouwen say, we must offer such audience to God without condition, by opening up from mere illusions about God to attentive prayer. Or put another way, by attending not to God as we understand God, but prayer as searching, enquiring of God to discern how God understands us and the ways in which he has imagined us to become.

Deafness comes in many forms… arrogance, vanity, compulsive talking, dismissiveness, aloofness, and, so much more subtly, through an obsession with always having to be right (and just happening to have the biblical text on hand to prove it). The church is called to be a listening community, a community where the deaf can be healed. There is much in our corporate worship to hear. Great stories of our long family history. Thoughtful prayers. Better than average hymns. And, of course, each other with mutual and peaceful greetings, exchanges, and catching up. But our good liturgy also offers us moments in certain of its parts when we can simply be silent, listening, reflecting on what or who we have just heard or seen, surely awed by the majesty of the possibilities of access to God's grace.

The prophet Isaiah once admonished us in one of his more provocative ways to "Seek the Lord while he wills to be found…" *(Is 55:6a)* Thankfully, God was more gently gracious to those who waited for Jesus on the Mount of Transfiguration and for those who wait for him here when he said, "This is my Son, the Beloved; listen to him!" *(Mk 9:7)*

Ash Wednesday *ABC

Ya gotta have…

"Where your treasure is, there will your heart be also." (Matthew 6:21b)

Only a few years after my seminary days, I had the privilege of serving on a conference staff with one of our church's outstanding theologians by name of Norman Pittenger. Even more impudent then than now, I played a game of stump-the-professor with him. Never mind who won. I asked him a question I was hearing more often than I could answer. "How does one ever know the will of God?" Rather than stumble around, pondering and harrumphing, as I had hoped he might, he quipped instantly, "Just trust your hunches."

That's a hard charge for those of us "from Missouri," who have to see the evidence, and who think intuition is for the birds. But it wasn't for Jeremiah.

Jeremiah stood in the biblical tradition that one's heart is the seat of knowledge, the place where the hard choices are made, that one's heart is the source of spiritual energy and courage and the ultimate storehouse where fundamental allegiances are kept. And he was apparently giving this tradition a lot of thought.*

But be that as it may and rather like today, alongside that notion was this other tradition that gave immutable certitude, as well, to an external law of life and covenant given by God to Moses and developed over the centuries, both literally and virtually graven in stone.

On the other hand, Jeremiah's hunches about God's will were keeping him up at night. He was already convinced that nobody ever invites a prophet home to dinner more than once. And he knew full well that the old legal, hard-nosed approach never did much good, anyway, and that God was suggesting a radical change as is often said about God, making all things new, if only he'd listen. So he stood up in the marketplace, took the risk to threaten his already shaky reputation, and shouted...

"Behold, the days are coming, saith the Lord, when I will make a new covenant... not like the covenant which I made with [your] fathers... my covenant which they broke..." But now, "I will put my law within [you], and I will write it upon [your] hearts; and I will be [your] God, and [you] shall be my people" *(Jer 31:31, 33b)*.

Well, we apparently got the word.

On Ash Wednesday in every Lent, the special collect asks God to "create in us new and contrite hearts" *(BCP p 267)*.

And Matthew's gospel reminds us that where our treasure is, there will our heart be also *(Mt 6:21)*. And as if all that is not enough, one of our Lenten collects prays that "our hearts may surely there be fixed where true joys are to be found" *(BCP 219)*.

In Lent, we are called once again as followers of the Way and reminded to search even more deeply into our hearts where love and God's law are inseparable, into our hearts where love is commitment, not mere disposition, and into our hearts where love is a deliberate act of the will, a choice, not a mere responsive feeling. And where most importantly — if Jeremiah is to be believed — God's covenant with us is written and can nourish and grow.

In these same hearts, we all pray fervently for peace. Some, not without considerable risk, march and demonstrate for peace. The covenant God makes with us, together with the Incarnation that brought that covenant to fulfillment in his son, not only calls for peace on earth, but in its shocking scheme of things, asks us, as well, both to love and to pray for our enemies — one thing in peacetime when our enemies may sort of come and go, quite another in wartime when they may be wearing a dynamite corset with their finger on the trigger.

I thought, how refreshing to be reminded in a time of so much ill will that we truly are called to be people of good will who strive for a government of good will, and how dare we not take notice of the irony that these enemies for whom we now pray, together with so many of us, are also children of Abraham, and that we are systematically killing each other and decimating the very spiritual homeland that God gave to us all.

After 9/11, the mystic Thomas Keating spoke of an "ocean of grief" that swelled out in its wake. And what is grief, but a broken heart, not broken only over our loss, but even more deeply perhaps broken over the covenant which God writes inside us in our very being. On the death of John F Kennedy, Senator Pat Moynihan spoke of the Irish words that apply, as well, to us Christians. "There's probably not any point in being [a Christian]," he said, "if you don't know that the world is going to break your heart eventually."

All this fear and grief only heightens our sensitivity to the horror and the hunger and the pain and the injustice that go on somewhere in our world every moment of every day. It only intensifies the need for what we do as the church all the time. If what we are doing here day by day is not relevant, even more relevant now, then it is never relevant at all.

We are people living in this covenant community trying to discern and to do God's will. We are not of one mind. We have not a common understanding of these complex issues. Nevertheless, we come here again and again to be shaped by the gentle touch of God's peace.

Let us, then, realize that our hunches and our hearts are often one and the same. Therefore, let us remember that in every choice we face we must steadfastly will the good as we understand it and put ourselves into the hands of God to be shaped at God's pleasure, then doing that it is altogether likely that trusting our hunches will indeed open our hearts and reveal God's will. Then will we know a peace that is not the mere absence of war, but rather the presence of love. And like Jesus said, "where your treasure is, there will your heart be also" (Mt 6:21b). After all, what is Lent but an affair of the heart?

In both Old and New Testament, the heart is the seat of wisdom (1 Kgs 3:12) and thought and reflection (Jer 24:7, Lk 2:19), the instrument of belief (Rms 10:10) and of will, the principle of action (Ex 35:21) which may be hardened so that it resists God (Dt 15:7; Mk 16:14). Heart is the principle both of virtues and vices, of humility (Mt 11:29) and pride (Dt 17:20), of good thoughts (Lk 6:45) and evil (Mt 15:19).

First Sunday of Lent *C

Compulsion

Jesus answered him, "It is said, 'Do not put the Lord your God to the test.' "
(Luke 4:12)

For Jesus it was finally show and tell time to decide what he would do with his life, what he would "be," and his annoying notion that it certainly wasn't carpentry and other kinds of woodworking. We go through that, especially in our youth, when we're pondering the same questions or when we're wondering what on earth we're already doing and have done with our life. Three things confront us: we want our lives to mean something, to be relevant. We want to have at least enough control over all and our environment to keep it, as they say, "between the curbs." And we want to be noticed, if even only for Andy Warhol's "fifteen minutes."

Anybody wrestling with vocation is probably influenced and even especially tempted at one time or another by these three great compulsions: relevance, control, and notice.

Naturally (perhaps even supernaturally), the daemons presumed these kinds of compulsions to be going on with Jesus, maybe even before he knew it himself. They seemed always uncannily to recognize him and what he was about before anyone else. There's no reason not to think that something like this may be true for us. The devil is, indeed, in these kinds of details. Those stages in one's life preoccupied with confusion about vocation and its relevant choices can be the neatest briar patches of details as to make the devil feel right at home. Like why else was the devil waiting out there in the boonies until Jesus was half starved to death before moving in on his puzzling vocational anguish?

You want to be relevant? Satan said. Then turn these stones into bread.

You want to be in charge? Here's a whole empire of kingdoms and all the power and glory that goes with it.

You want to be noticed? Then take a flying leap off the pinnacle of this lofty temple, surely the angels won't let anything happen to the Son of God, himself. *(Lk 4:1-13)*

No vocational headhunter could come up with better tests than these then or now for an individual or even for an institution. Yes, even for an institution. The church is not exempt from these same desires. Indeed, clear and strange parallels of temptation are going on in the church's life at this very moment.

But the gospel as Jesus understood it and as we've received it never fails to confront every one of such pretentious priorities. In this confrontation, the gospel asks us not whether we are relevant, or noticed, or powerful, but whether our ministries offer an occasion for justice and peace and a fair concern and respect for all.

Of all the answers Jesus gave Satan and of all the answers we must give ourselves and those who would dismantle us and make us a second rate and unwelcome cousin, one stands front stage center: "You shall worship the Lord your God, and God only shall you serve."

This major turning point in Jesus's understanding of himself and of his work became the furnace of his transformation to protect him from becoming a victim of society and from becoming entangled in the illusions of a false self.

We are faced now, as well, with our own furnace of transformation to protect us from becoming a victim of society and from continuing to be entangled in the illusions of a false church. In the face of these temptations, Jesus affirmed God as the only source and substance of his identity. In the face of these temptations, so must we, as well, affirm God as the only source and substance of our identity.

Ironically, what Jesus told the devil in the wilderness, he tells the church today. Religion's proud towers are for princes and tourists. Its intricate doctrines are for the angry and the arrogant. Its pretensions to power are just warmed over Caesar outlined in fancy script.

The kingdoms of this world are humanity's mistake, not its glory. Can you imagine Jesus vested in silks and sitting on a throne in a cockeyed hat or whatever demanding that we do him homage? Rather might he be here at table with us, if we would just think and pray to invite, erasing centuries of warfare, turning us to discover our common humanity, easing us out of our historic enigmas and into the shared language of love which makes this gentle, but no less firm demand of us — "You shall worship the Lord your God, and God only shall you serve."

Jesus gave the devil the right answer. So must we.

Second Sunday of Lent *C

Presence

"Jerusalem, Jerusalem, the city that kills the prophets and stones those who are sent to it! How often have I desired to gather your children together as a hen gathers her brood under her wings, and you were not willing!" (Luke 13:34)

If Jesus didn't love Jerusalem, he probably wouldn't bother to tell it that it's going to straight to Hell. He'd just let it go. For Jesus's quarrel with Jerusalem is a prophet's quarrel with the world. With all the zeal that he condemns, he, as well, yearns to embrace, as he himself said, with all the tenderness and security of a mother hen and her brood. For the prophet's quarrel is deep down a lover's quarrel. It is another example of the irony that pervades every church worth its salt. It can well be called the "prophetic presence."

Perhaps there's no better way to sum up the church's ministry than the old saying about good preaching, that it must both comfort the afflicted and, as well, afflict the comfortable. There must be no doubt about our caring. And there must be no hesitancy about our enduring demand for justice and peace from all and for all. This is the irony of the prophetic presence. With arms outstretched, the church must beckon all to come for both solace and sacrifice, for comfort and compassion, for recovery and reconciliation, and while we're at it, also keep the holiness God gives intact.

Only those subject to the worst kind of religious addiction, that crippling malaise ever so rampant today with all its denial and grandiosity, can fail to see these dimensions in Jesus's presence before Jerusalem. Just as only the very spiritually mature can possibly endure such moments of judgment and truth, the very moments that can keep us to be even more spiritually awake.

Jesus's ministry could not remain rooted in the tribal religiosity of Jerusalem and neither can ours in the tribal religiosity of our own narrow divisions. And just as his ministry came to be anchored in compassion and love and justice, so must be ours. Such ministry reveals that the gospel is meant for anyone who will listen, that its healing is there for anyone who truly desires it, and that the grace of its salvation is accessible to any who dare take the risk of faith.

Tribe (denomination, race, ethnicity, whatever) means nothing. Past affiliations mean nothing. The narrow-minded distinctions we impose on each other, as well, are simply silly, an insult to God. Any claim to be in the religious right is already by its very nature in the religious wrong. We have long since moved beyond the question of whether Jesus was Messiah only to Israel. We've already spent too much of our history in the opposite assertion that God cannot possibly love Jews. This, I suspect, is why the contention is at base fallacious that Mel Gibson's movie about the passion of Jesus is anti-semitic. We crucified Jesus, and if need be to settle the argument, we are all Jews and whatever else the current anthropologic traffic will bear. (Old Bishop Pike, bless him, once said on the Today Show that we can't be good Christians unless we're also good Jews. It came as something of a shock to Barbara Walters.) And yet, we continue to maintain our tribes within tribes, to erect barriers and lines across which Jesus supposedly doesn't go or worse, still, dare not go. Some still make it their business to say that Jesus loves this one, but not that one, that Jesus will accept this group, but not that group.

It is unlikely that we will ever stop seeing skin color or hearing accent or noticing behavior. Praise God for them. But we must no longer allow our perceptions — as important as they are to us — to be mistaken entirely for truth. For our ways are not necessarily God's ways. Virtually everything that people have fought over in the name of God is eventually proven to be meaningless, simply a token of personal rigidity, and hardly an expression of God's will at all.

Let us not lose sight that this gospel we profess is about conversion, about repentance, about returning, reconciliation, and renewal, about justice and peace, in short, about change. And that we, the church, are called to be primary stewards of all that both compassionately and prophetically.

Jesus sets for us one more splendid example of such spiritual authority in his prophetic presence at Jerusalem. Just as we must, in whatever place we are, be our own community of welcome and of explicit common sense by the power of a faith that can provoke for the world a renewed crisis in our way of seeing things.

The old hymn calls it well. "The peace of God, it is no peace, but strife closed in the sod. Yet let us pray for but one thing — the marvelous peace of God" *(1982 Hymnal #661)*.

Third Sunday of Lent *A

Irrational

The [Samaritan] woman said to him, "Sir, you have no bucket, and the well is deep. Where do you get that living water?" (John 4:11)

That pensive mystic and altogether lovely person Madeleine L'Engle once wrote about Christmas as "…the irrational season / When love blooms bright and wild. / Had Mary been filled with reason / There'd have been no room for the child."

The story of the Samaritan woman come to Jacob's well for a jar of water is about such an irrational season. Here's a woman who is surely down to her last nerve in monotony, dipping once more after countless times into that all-too-familiar well with its long and tiresome history. Suddenly, she's faced with almost a time warp in her history, a totally unexpected detour in her seemingly unending serial of one domestic and personal crisis after another.

In a rapid succession of shocks, a stranger, a Jew, a man speaks to her, a woman, a Samaritan. He speaks not only across religious and ethnic and sexual boundaries, but with an alarming candor and penetrating insight. Then he brings her back to earth and does a "guy thing." He asks for a drink of water. But then he speaks to her of a living water that does away with thirst forever. Step by step, he lays bare her past and her present and sees right through her into her future.

In one stroke, the rigid sanctions of the kind of worship and religion and custom that she and her people have embraced for centuries are abolished. Jesus proposes a revolutionary new liturgy based not on the usual male-dominated, retrogressive system of exclusion and judgment, but a worship grounded unpretentiously and candidly in spirit and in truth.

As if all this is not enough, he commissions her to be a disciple to her own people and does not send "a member of his staff" or some other man to accompany her to make sure she gets it right. Obviously, the ordination of women is not all that novel, after all. Those who oppose it could well do to meditate on this story.

The Samaritan woman dares to accept her charge and returns to her townsfolk to tell them her tale. Never did she have to say, "He told me how sinful I was." Rather could she say, simply, "He told me everything about myself." One can suspect that she'd never had such self-esteem before as in this altogether unreasonable assignment.

As well, there's nothing especially rational about the Gospel which is entrusted to us. Every occasion in which we embrace it is an "irrational season" in our lives. The love at its center which can cast out fear, even the fear of risking the acceptance of such a trust, is perhaps the most unreasonable of all that we've ever undertaken. For it means that we remember ourselves, and that we love ourselves, and that this comes before any other truly creative love we could give to others, the love that "blooms bright and wild."

At our baptism, we and those who sponsored us, stopped by a "well of living water" and received a bend in our own personal history. We made and continue to remake the Covenant that commissions us to go and to tell, not because of who we are, but because of who we can become.

***Note: May I suggest that the Baptismal Covenant be used in place of the Nicene Creed should the celebration include this preachment (BCP pp 304f).*

Fourth Sunday of Lent *C

New Creation

"If anyone is in Christ, they are a new creation; the old has passed away, behold, the new has come" (2 Corinthians 5:17).

"New creation." It is a careful, a cautious phrase. It has a ring to it of Genesis and of Eden. In these present times of churchly turmoil, it can be, it is, indeed, a refreshing insight into our remembering who we are, what our Baptismal Covenant calls us to be and to become, that "in Christ," the "old has passed away" and the new, as some say, has made the scene.

Is it possible that we've become so fond of the notion of being "in Christ" that we've lost sight of being *with* Jesus, who said that we are his friends, not his servants? That we are with him in our partnership with the one who spoke of himself as the Way to that new creation, as the Truth of it, as the very Life of it? Jesus himself questioned anyone calling him "good." He said that "no one is good but God alone" *(Mk*

10:17f). Yet he said, "When you have seen me, you have seen the father." Jesus is the icon of God, the window through whom we see God, even darkly as Paul said, the beloved son in whom God is well pleased and to whom God demands that we listen *(Lk 9:28-36)*. It is with Jesus that we share this life and this baptismal covenant we have made.

Maybe we should never have called this religion of ours "Christianity" in the first place. Strikingly, theologian Paul Tillich points out that this letter to Corinth says in effect that the message of Christianity is not Christianity. The message of Christianity is a "new creation." Like God and the Devil, when we came upon that truth in our path in those early days, almost the very first thing we did was to organize it, to make a religion of it. To turn it ultimately from The Way into of all things a denomination, from a life of faith into a religion, from a willful choice into a passive belief, from a covenant into a creed. For what is religion after all but a human endeavor to render faith — that is, the life in the new creation — both memorable and manageable, to make a mold of it out of which to cast even more religious followers? A noble task, and maybe even at times a necessary task, but never an end in itself.

Our belief in scripture as God's norm for us is inevitably shaped by our history and tradition and reason out of the past and into the present. It has been said that our tradition can best be understood as a mode of making sense of the experience of God, a particular approach to the construction of reality or to the building of a world. *(Holmes, "What Is Anglicanism?", Morehouse, 1982, p 1)*.

Satan would always organize God's truth, whereas God's truth revealed in Jesus as God's way and life, would always risk itself, in new creation, in being created anew, not so much by what Jesus would do or even how he would do it, but by what Jesus would be. Faith risking itself as God imagines us in the nature of our human freedom to choose to love, to create, to reason, and to live in harmony with all of creation — so very importantly with ourselves and with our neighbors — and most of all, with God.

Homiletic license alert: That we would take this truth to ourselves, organize and shape it to our own independence and pleasure, is illustrated in this Lenten parable of the Prodigal Son's assumption of his inheritance. It is interesting and I am sure of little or no significance at all how pigs figure in this story and the one of Jesus's confrontation with the Gerasene wild man. The Prodigal comes to his realization wallowing in a pig sty. The daemons enslaving the Gerasene come to theirs in a herd of swine.

We are the new creation by no doing of our own but by our human being as God imagines us to be. It took place in Jesus, and it is taking place in us, commissioned in our baptism, renewed in our prayer and in the Eucharist.

Look and reflect on us. Whatever our calendar time may be, we are each new creations. We are new beings. We are reconciled reconcilers. We are ambassadors through whom God is forgiving the world. And we will meet once again and finally in heaven. Paul would say that it is simply that simple.

Wherever such compassion and lack of understanding is absent, there in that place and time church is failing to be church. Instead, we must stand forth and offer it and embrace our Baptismal Covenant, for that is our mission, that is our servant leadership, that is what it means to be a "new creation."

Fifth Sunday of Lent *C

Always

Jesus said, "… You always have the poor with you, but you do not always have me" (John 12:8).

Lazarus and his two sisters Mary and Martha lived in a town called Bethany a couple of miles outside Jerusalem. They were among Jesus's best friends, the kind you just drop in on whenever you're in the neighborhood. It was from Bethany that Jesus took off for his parade into Jerusalem on Palm Sunday and it was to Bethany he went back to rest up for a few days before his final arrest. *(after Buechner, "Peculiar Treasures," p 89)*

John's Gospel and those who chose it for us in this Lent seem to suggest this is the time and place for this little story in our spiritual genealogy.

It's a dinner party. We're all familiar with those. Lazarus was there, he and his sisters and Jesus had gone through the terrible and shocking ordeal of Lazarus's death and resurrection and spared us having to confront those enormous problems again, a fact for which any preacher should be grateful.

It's a dinner party and none of us would be surprised to learn who is waiting on whom — Martha, of course, served. Mary is wasting the expensive perfume in her intuitive and open-ended ways. Or who is complaining — Judas, always the heavy, takes issue. He's not above stealing from the collection plate, but he can't stand to see Chanel Number Five being poured out on somebody's feet, even if it is Jesus, himself. That he would give the money from its sale to the poor is not all that clear and seems altogether out of character. But it does prompt Jesus's response which seems to me the point of this story.

Jesus said, "Leave [Mary] alone. She bought it so that she might keep it for the day of my burial. You always have the poor with you, but you do not always have me" (Jn 12:7f).

Strange. "The day of my burial" — a comment that seems rather out of place considering Lazarus's presence, and that would anyway cast a pall over an otherwise happy affair — as well as if Judas's doom and gloom hadn't already done enough. But no. It is followed by the bit about we always "have the poor" which everybody knows, "but you do not always have me," which everybody would rather not know.

What's going on here? Once we get past the obvious shock of that statement, there's always or there should always be a second thought. After all, for whom did Jesus come to minister? The poor, the downtrodden, the cast out. Why did he tell the parable of the Good Samaritan? Why did he tell the healing stories? To show his purpose, but also to show us our purpose. Why did he say that when we have done these things or not done these things, we have done them or not done them to and for him? And why were we so perplexed when he said that? Because sometimes it doesn't just take second thought, it requires what the comedians have learned so well — the double take.

Of course, we realize. I hope.

Our Baptismal Covenant reminds us to seek and serve Christ in the other. I don't know about you, but I always need reminding of that. Nothing so readily spoils a good scrap with anyone, especially someone you love as to be confronted with — Here's that Christ again, right in front of me.

Jesus says, Anoint me, sure, for all you know, I'm gone. But, "You always have the poor with you," he adds. And remember, that's why I came in the first place, and that's why I've chosen you. For the poor, the downtrodden, the cast out, the sick, the prisoner, the neighbor, for to do God's work, for to love God's love, for to do God's justice. For to do this in remembrance of me. Always.

Who else might you suggest?

But don't be surprised where it might get you. And don't forget where it got me. He might have added that, but didn't.

Palm Sunday / Liturgy of the Palms *C

Stones

As he was now approaching the path down from the Mount of Olives, the whole multitude of the disciples began to praise God joyfully with a loud voice for all the deeds of power that they had seen, saying, "Blessed is the king who comes in the name of the Lord! Peace in heaven, and glory in the highest heaven!" Some of the Pharisees in the crowd said to him, "Teacher, order your disciples to stop." He answered, "I tell you, if these were silent, even the stones would cry out." (Luke 19:37-40)

That cry and all its accompanying "king talk" was all the Pharisees needed to shift into red alert. They smelled treason, and they knew the consequences. If alone for their own sake, they warned Jesus to tell the people to cool it, only to hear him say in response...

"I tell you, if these were silent, the very stones would cry out."

That simple affirmation could be the most overlooked and unsung song of perceptive wisdom in all the events and words that surround us during our celebration of Passion Week.

Bennett Sims reminds us in his book on servant leadership that the quantum physics theorists are certain that there is a caring pulse of energy that animates and interconnects all the entities in the cosmos. Teilhard de Chardin, the French Jesuit paleontologist, outraged his time when he said that the "molecules make love." This, of course, got his books banned as a consequence. (The notion of "making love" and who or what does it and how and with whom never seems even now to sit all that well with the orthodoxers.)

In Jesus's time, it might have been — indeed, was — seen all along that the created order in all its facets always knew and recognized in their own way who and what was present in him among them. The daemons, the loaves and fishes, the storms, winds, and waves, the human maladies, the fig trees, Satan itself in the wilderness, all were on to what had happened and was going on to happen when the Word became flesh.

No wonder Jesus could say that if the crowds were silent, the very stones, themselves, the seemingly most inert and mute of all creation (and, by the by, the epitome of efficiency), would burst forth in adulation. We call it atomic energy, but by whatever name, it remains, *Benedicite, omnia opera Domini* — "O all ye works of the Lord, bless ye the Lord."

It was sound geology if it was nothing else. For every geologist knows that rocks talk. Every road cut, every creek bank, every well log, every pebble lying by the side of the road tells us that the earth has its own version of life and its own journal of life's past. The stones can teach us much about ourselves and our history.

Further, anyone who's ever paid attention to birth, be it of fire pinks or elephants or ferns or a grandchild, knows that life evolves from one or another kind of seed on its way to rooting and blooming. Every sermon needs at least one fancy scientific name about discovery. Even this one, and that is "Ontogeny recapitulates phylogeny." It's the geologist's mantra, elite for "Been there and done that."

Life is a gift. The irony is that it is often too easy to forget that life is so precious and that we really have so little to do with its presence that we arrogantly fight wars about it and all that it represents as if it were ours and we were not only stewards of it. Any thinking person knows that war is an insult to life, and not only an insult to life, but an insult to God. What has war ever proved? The historian Barbara Tuchman defined war as the unfolding of miscalculations. It is likely that she had in mind the kind of war that had nations at each other's throats hoping that the winner will be better off. Or maybe, at least, that the other fellows will be worse off, or maybe then settling for the satisfaction that they're certainly not any better off, and finally, surrendering to the great surprise that whaddya know? Nobody's better off.

Palm Sunday perhaps reminds us of that, even more than Easter. Jesus knew that. The crowds knew that. For Palm Sunday is more like life as we experience it than is the notion of resurrection. Palm Sunday is about war, and we know more about war than we do about empty tombs. I did not know this until the Jesus Seminar scholars told me that on that day we call Palm Sunday and Jesus was entering Jerusalem, at the same time so was Pilate arriving across town. The one riding on a jackass, the other on a stallion surrounded with all the hoopla of a police escort and uniformed armed guards. One came in on the back roads to be welcomed by discarded bushes, even old tires so far as we really know, the other on the parkway to be welcomed by richly-colored bunting and flags and choking with confetti from the office shredders. Imagine that scene for a moment. Remember that both Jesus and Pilate were plunging headlong into a cross of conflict. A conflict in which the church, if it is true to its commission, has been ever since. It is a conflict that may never be over. It is the conflict between God and empire. Palm Sunday is its symbol.

At the very heart of the *Bible* is a moral and ethical call to fight unjust super powers, whether they are Babylon, Rome, or even America. Mary's Magnificat sums it up as well: God "has shown the strength of his arm, he has scattered the proud in their conceit. He has cast down the mighty from their thrones, and has lifted up the lowly." The *Bible* is about land and economy, about violence and retribution, about justice and peace, and, ultimately, about redemption.

In contrast to the oppressive Roman military occupation of the first century there's the nonviolent Kingdom of God proclaimed by Jesus and the equality and inclusiveness advocated by Paul. These messages of peace stand in opposition to the apocalyptic vision from the Book of Revelation so often misrepresented by modern right-wing theologians and televangelists to justify our military actions in the Middle East. This is what Palm Sunday is about.

Jesus preached a peace not won by war, but a peace that passes all understanding, a kingdom not of Caesar, but of God, a peace that can only be won through justice and fair and equal treatment of all people. Pilate witnessed the very opposite.

We are fortunate to enjoy the separation of church and state which Jesus's entrance into Jerusalem implied. It is a separation that is essential to the health of any society in order that both may be faithful to their roles. Such a relationship is symbolized in Palm Sunday with the two entrances into Jerusalem, understood perhaps better by Jesus than by Pilate. Palm Sunday does not let us settle for the comfort of our priestly role, for it challenges us to our prophetic role, a role which is not only a privilege, but a responsibility, a vocation in a system whose founding dream is one based on peace and justice and freedom. The church may not be a paragon of witness to any of this, but no less it yet has a mandate to exemplify it and to understand and exercise its prophetic ministry both to the state and, as well, to itself.

It was Thomas Jefferson who said that if he had to choose between a government without newspapers or newspapers without a government, he would unhesitatingly choose the latter. He said that, I think, because even such a remarkable government as he imagined and actually helped shape, one that championed the individual and human rights as central to its purpose, would be impotent to its cause without a parallel and independent institution such as the press to be free to call such a government to its task whenever it fell for empirical illusions, to remind it of its glories and as well as of its failures, and to protect its citizens from the perils of greed and fraud and incompetence.

One of the tragedies of our present economic chaos is the possible loss of an articulate, powerful, and indeed prophetic press. But one of its blessings is to remind the church that it has always had such a role, such a social responsibility, and that we can no longer enjoy merely toying with and squabbling over our identity if ever we want to be taken seriously at all. Being a prophet is not a popular role in society. Prophets are never invited home for lunch twice. Nor should prophecy be relegated to the curious and diversionary task of predicting the future often only with all the accuracy of a Ouija Board. The classical Old Testament prophets, the Isaiahs, the Jeremiahs, the Micahs were first of all deeply loyal to the very tradition to which they spoke so devastatingly. For the prophet, far from being a predictor, was an indicter of both the state and the state's religion wherever and whenever they drifted into imperialism. A drift that never seems to end, a drift that is so very obvious and present in these perilous times, a drift that always brings God and empire into confrontation.

Palm Sunday is not just about flag-waving and parades. It is God's reminder that we become who she intends us to be. It is a message that not only the stones cry out but that the very universe literally shouts.

For the theme of this preachment, I am indebted to John Dominic Crossan's insightful book "God & Empire: Jesus aginst Rome, then and now," and to his and Marcus Borg's "The Last Week: a day-by-day account of Jesus's final week in Jerusalem," Harper, San Francisco

Liturgy of the Passion *ABC

Wholly

It is the Lord God who helps me; who will declare me guilty? (Isaiah 50:9a)

I trust in you, O Lord; I say, "You are my God." My times are in your hand; deliver me from the hand of my enemies and persecutors. Let your face shine upon your servant; save me in your steadfast love. (Psalm 31:14-16)

At the name of Jesus every knee should bend, in heaven and on earth and under the earth, and every tongue should confess that Jesus Christ is Lord... (Philippians 2:10-11)

While they were eating, Jesus took a loaf of bread, and after blessing it he broke it, gave it to the disciples, and said, "Take, eat; this is my body." Then he took a cup, and after giving thanks he gave it to them saying, "Drink from it all of you; for this is my blood of the covenant, which is poured out for many for the forgiveness of sins." (Matthew 26:26-28)

Our cathedral in Our Town offers a splendid regular program on a Friday night that centers on the arts as instruments of worship. It is a welcome and mindful diversion from the usual Music City fare that holds forth only a few blocks away and has for decades set us apart. One evening, the Cathedral's offering was a "Bachanalia" which featured numerous of the great master's compositions played by as diverse ensembles as a jazz quartet, a bassoon octet, a clarinet choir, a solo violin, and a brass quintet.

In the thoughtful and stewardly doing of these thing, the cathedral refers to itself as a "sacred space" for the city. It is a splendid piece of public relations and, some would say, not all that inaccurate. CP and I have frequently enjoyed it and inevitably have come away refreshed by the remarkable capacities of the performers and, of course, the intuitive skills of the composers and writers and the thoughtful planning of all those who make these things possible.

As for the space being somehow sacred or, better said, implied as being more sacred than the rest of downtown or uptown or wherevertown, we surely should not lose sight that there is another cathedral of another Christian community a few blocks away that surely thinks of itself as sacred, let alone the real estate of any number of different religions across town. Our Town has not been called the Buckle on the *Bible* Belt for naught. Even the big international publishing house of one of them is often called their Vatican.

We do that, don't we, at least out of respect for where we may be more certain of God's presence in places and things, for where we expect her to show up from time to time, at least for where the prayer wheels are spun and where we might presume better to get her attention. After all, God made Moses take off his shoes if he was going to stand around gawking at the burning bush for he was on holy ground, at least holier than the rest of the farm. But it was God, not Moses, who made that designation out of all creation as if the rest of it had not yet made the cut.

We don't stop, however, with spaces. We do it with people and time and things. We continue to set apart and discriminate by saying that some things are holy implying as if others are not. Holy Orders for the deacons, priests, and bishops as if they are somehow holier and even more reverend (right, most, very) when others are not and as if any order could be a holier order than that, for one, to which baptism commissions us.

We call this week Holy Week. Granted, major events once took place in these few days. The Entrance. The Last Supper, and Good Friday which is not called holy, but the interim Saturday, for lack of a better name, is. Our precursors on the spiritual family tree, as if they had worn out the word and the times and the places long ago and in order somehow to make it even more special, set aside a space in the Temple in Jerusalem and called it the Holy of Holies. I suppose there couldn't be anything holier than that, and so must have they, for they set it even more apart by screening it off with a veil. Then it was that only special people might view or enter the space, holy people, I suppose, holier than the average run-of-the-mill pew-sitter from whose view the veil shielded the spot. We have a word today for them, the laity, and they dare not touch some holy things left for the clergy, especially those who when outfitted in their ecclesiastical drag. seem to be "holier than thou."

Let it not to go unnoticed that when Jesus died on the cross, it is said that the very veil of this holier than holy place in the Temple was "rent in twain." This holiest of all places was exposed for all to see. Was this rending God's intention? Had she now bypassed her encounter with Moses? Does this suggest finally that no place in all God's creation, no ground is holier than another? That all of creation is a sacrament, and if not, most certainly sacramental? Could there be a holier order, a holier command than our stewardship of its care, than for to be its caregiver, to receive the "gift of joy and wonder in all [God's] works"? *(BCP p 308)*. Let the EPA beware and maybe rejoice.

William James wrote: "Common sense and a sense of humor are the same thing, moving at different speeds. A sense of humor is just common sense, dancing."

Which prompts me to wonder whether common prayer and a sense of humility might be the same thing, moving at different speeds. A sense of humility is just common prayer dancing.

That so seems so much so, maybe it is.

Epilogue: One Lent, one of my associates dropped fatigued into a chair in the sacristy following his participation in the three-hour Good Friday liturgy. A placard was hung about his neck. He turned it over slowly. It read, Wholly Weak.

Monday in Holy Week *ABC

Dignity

Jesus said, "Leave her alone. She bought it so that she might keep it for the day of my burial. You always have the poor with you, but you do not always have me. (John 12:7-8)

"She has done what she could: she has anointed my body beforehand for its burial. In truth I tell you, wherever throughout all the world the gospel is proclaimed, what she has done will be told as well, in remembrance of her." (Mark 14:8-9)

A 36 year old father of three came home from work, walked off the commuter train, crossed the tracks, and deliberately placed himself in the path of the oncoming train. He was killed instantly. Later it was learned that he feared he was going to be "downsized."

My family lived through the Great Depression of the late twenties and early thirties, the four of us barely getting by. Similar stories then were not all that uncommon. Today's subprime market's collapse leading to severe unemployment and foreclosures is seen by many financial gurus as a confirmation of an impending financial disaster not unlike the one my family lived through. Many of these experts are deeply concerned about widespread unemployment and the crippling indignity which always comes in its wake. This young father's suicide may be a tragic parable of our times.

We are a day into Holy Week. The gospel of Jesus and the great saga culminating in Easter at heart tell another parable, a parable of hope and abundance, a parable of peace and of justice. There is every reason to believe that our congregations will swell in these immediate days and that more than the usual number may be in search of these very gifts, those realities of which our invitation to the Passion and encouragement of its redemptive healing assures them.

The church is called to be, and the church must be, especially in these times, an embodiment of this gospel parable rather than merely one more religious institution bewitched and bollixed with the fear for its own survival. Instead, the church must turn to its commission to be both pastor and prophet in these times. For this parable is one not only of compassion and nourishment, but, as well, one of prophetic indictment of the very divisive forces in our society that bring about these current conditions that humiliate and denigrate ourselves and our neighbors.

I cannot recall when in recent time have the commitments in our Baptismal Covenant been more central to our ministries. We have embraced those and must and can be ourselves refreshed by our fellowship and by our liturgies, by our resistance to evil, by our repentance, by our proclamation of the Good News of God in Christ, but above all in these days by a Christ-seeking and Christ-serving leadership that strives for justice and peace and most importantly the respect and dignity of all.

The church is the family where these things can and do happen, indeed, the church is the family where they must happen. The church is the family where women and men can be loved until they can come to love and respect themselves and then come to love and respect others. It is this we must offer and this to which we must find the winsomeness for it to become irresistible.

Richard Wheatcroft, a good friend and colleague, has put this ministry, this parable for dignity, like this: "In the Liturgy of the Eucharist we come to kneel before the Altar to receive the body and blood of the crucified and risen Jesus. Kneeling on the same level, side by side, we are all equal. The clergy are servers distributing of bread and wine equally to all. All receive the same amount of bread and wine. When the priest says, The Body of Christ, the bread of heaven, I hear The Body of Christ, the bread of justice. When a chalice bearer says, The Blood of Christ, the cup of salvation, I hear The Blood of Christ, the cup of compassion." Jack Nelson-Pallmeyer writes, "It is in food and drink offered equally to everyone that the presence of God and

Jesus is found. But food and drink are the material basis of life, so the Lord's Supper is political criticism and economic challenge as well."

By the grace of God and with Jesus's presence, we must make that happen.

Tuesday in Holy Week *ABC

Fools

Consider your own call, brothers and sisters; not many of you were wise by human standards, not many were powerful, not many were of noble birth. But God chose what is foolish in the world to shame the wise; God chose what is weak in the world to shame the strong... (1 Corinthians 1:26-27)

It's Tuesday, so it must be Jerusalem. According to Mark, it's the "busiest" day in Jesus's Last Week. We call it holy as if somehow, the other fifty-one are not. I wonder if Jesus ever thought like that. But it is of the way we have come to have with words. "Holy Orders" and "reverend" for us parsons as if somehow we are more-so than the others, as if baptism is not holy enough to cover all the bases (and the baseness) — then, now, and when. It is one of the ways we turn church into Let's Pretend... Chalice in Wonderland.

A Franciscan prayer that is a favorite of mine strikes an agenda calling us to service of a kind that demands our absolute most. It's final call after that exhaustive list is for God to bless us with enough foolishness to believe that we can make a difference in this world, so that we can do what others claim cannot be done. It ends well, for sometimes foolishness alone provides the energy to drive us into that servant leadership for which the blessing prays and to which God calls us.

Isn't it just like God to do that sort of thing. A perceptive theologian once said that to know the will of God is for us to trust our hunches. Hunches are not usually thought all that trustworthy by us humans. On the other hand, a techie friend tells me that intuition is indispensable to understanding the mysterious ways of computers. I suspect there's an awful lot of science that would yet lie hidden without there having been a few intuitive hunches here and there. Furthermore, curiosity is a prime sign of human maturity and hunches may be one its implements. Maybe it's what gets cats into a lot of trouble, but it is also what makes them so charming and obviously so much smarter than we. So foolish?

By our standards, the Samaritan was foolish and so was the lady pouring Chanel Number Five all over Jesus. Whether they were consciously following Paul's counsel to be a fool for Christ or whether they'd ever even heard such is problematic, but they did prove that one doesn't have to be a Christian to act like one. Trouble is, just be a fool now and then, like vote for universal health care, and some passers by will get so fearfully worked up, they might spit on you. Then God will probably give you some of her own foolishness to compensate and keep blessing you with more, cause there's lots of spit out there, maybe even more than there are fools. Just ask Jesus.

Wednesday in Holy Week *ABC

Driven

Therefore since we are surrounded by so great a cloud of witnesses, let us also lay aside every weight and the sin that clings so closely, and let us run with perseverance the race that is set before us, looking to Jesus the pioneer and perfecter of our faith… (Hebrews 12:1-2a)

Ted Weddell, onetime warden of the College of Preachers, told of his being a visiting fireman on a college campus celebrating Religious Emphasis Week. In an evening fireside chat, a coed asked him to talk about the Holy Spirit. He answered, "Well, first of all, let's get it straight that it wasn't that blessed pigeon."

He obviously had reference to the baptism of Jesus when the dove came down and landed on Jesus. The doves in our yard are anything but that friendly. They fight a lot, and to associate them with peace is, as Weddell implied, to stretch the image.

Perhaps not so when Jesus was baptized in the Jordan River. Imagine that picture. As Jesus comes up out of the water at the hands of his cousin John, the bird lands, and the voice speaks — "Thou art my beloved son; with thee I am well pleased." (Think James Earl Jones or maybe the great film director John Huston.) Then the Spirit drove Jesus — not led him, but drove him — into the wilderness for forty days to savage not only with his vocation, but with old Screwtape itself. And ultimately to bring him to this, this Last Week in his life. But that's another story.

It's God's pleasuring with Jesus that attracts me. "Beloved son." "Well pleased." Whatever, but that God's Spirit drove Jesus away to find himself, he was surely, in God's eyes, still a work in progress. Son, beloved, pleased — but not finished. Incomplete, not yet ready for the task ahead.

On the other hand, and perhaps this is where we come in, God has modeled here for all to see what he means by human being. This is the image of God we hear about, that we, indeed, are, ourselves. This is the Christ-in-us touted in the Baptismal Covenant. It's almost as if God is a sculptor of sorts and stands back from his creation, admiring, pleased, smiling, laying down his mallet and chisel, walking around to get different, perhaps better perspectives. Yet, not completely finished with Jesus — nor neither now with us. Our tradition confirms that to be human, to be imagined by God, is to be free to choose… to be free to choose to love, to create, to reason, to live in harmony with all of creation — the atmosphere, the spotted owl, the great redwoods, the wetlands, the wretched neighbors next door and the ingrates over in the middle east, the works — and with God. Lord, how many times have I beat this horse (metaphorically, of course!)? But I suspect I shall never tire, for it is so true. And then, to take it another step, there's this:

There's church. Church is not the Smithsonian Institute for the preservation of the Lambeth Quadrilateral which can take care of its ever-loving self. Church is not parchments vacuumed under glass. Church is not a place just for the warm and fuzzy confirmation of Aunty Sizzle's nostalgia.

No. Church is a gathering of worldlings with all our warts and languages and biases and ethical stumblings, holy and spiritual to the core precisely because that's the way God makes us. Church is all this humanity cobbled together with one mighty calling — to grab this spirit God gave us by the tail and, with God's always inclusive grace, shape it, inform it, and build it into the human being God imagines.

The church's vocation is to make us human. God creates us and says, "These are my beloved children in whom I am well pleased," and then stands back and smiles. Our vocation is to get on with becoming these loving, reasoning, creative, harmonious stumblers, these canonized Slobs that God has in mind, but maybe most of all to keep God smiling, maybe even laughing in surprise whenever — on our way to the wilderness — we get it right.

That's all.

Maundy Thursday *ABC

Remember

Having loved his own who were in the world, he loved them to the end...[and he said to them] I give you a new commandment, that you love one another. Just as I have loved you, you also should love one another. By this everyone will know that you are my disciples, if you have love for one another." (John 13:1b, 34-35)

Memory may well be the only way we know who we are.

When we lose it, as Alzheimer's devastation can attest, our world disintegrates. Every morn when we awaken, we must reinvent our "wheel." We are known, but we do not know. We forget, but we are not forgotten, for so much of us exists now only in the memory of another.

So it is with those who follow the Way from Jesus to the Christ. Come back to this moment. Through scripture and our family history, remember that we are the children of Abraham and Sarah, Isaac and Rebekah, Jacob and Rachel and Leah, as many as the stars, as many as the grains of sand.

Come back to this moment. Through symbol and story. Through the cross, through color and chorale, through holy community and Holy Communion. See it, hear it, be it. Do this — in remembrance. Not like a class reunion to celebrate nostalgia, as sweetly painful as is the sound of it. Not to rehearse our anecdotage, as boringly painful as is the drone of it.

For we're here not merely to share a memory, but to answer a mandate to remember — and not by some lowest common denominator of passive aggression, but by lifting high the cross of aggressive passion. "Do this," our Lord commanded on the very eve of his crucifixion, "in remembrance of me."

Do this in remembrance that we — and the world to which we are called in service — may know and never forget.

Good Friday *ABC

Truth

Pilate asked him, "So you are a king?" Jesus answered, "You say that I am a king. For this I was born, and for this I came into the world, to testify to the truth. Everyone who belongs to the truth listens to my voice." Pilate asked him, "What is truth?" (John 18:37-38a)

Archbishop Desmond Tutu spoke to a packed audience at Vanderbilt University during Holy Week a few years ago. Instantly, as he walked on stage and before saying a word, a spontaneous and vigorous standing ovation burst forth, seemingly almost without end. His hour-long address was punctuated often with such praise.

It came my good fortune to be invited to celebrate Eucharist with Bishop Tutu and his family the next morning (Maundy Thursday) in their hotel suite. The "Archbishop of the World" sat at coffee table in tee shirt, walking shorts and knee-length black sox and presided over the Church of South Africa liturgy.

Afterwards, I asked him how he felt about his Vanderbilt engagement. He said he was surprised and quite moved by his reception, that he had not expected such warmth and approval in the south. Then, he asked me why I thought he got such response. I was stunned to have my opinion sought by such a man, but I could hear myself say, "Because you and all you say and stand for are symbols of hope and of truth. Because you together with others have shown that peaceful revolution is possible not only in South Africa but everywhere else, even here in this tortured country." He smiled, nodded his head, and touched my arm with gentle firmness.

When we read about Pilate's question to Jesus "What is truth?" might we realize once again that Jesus's silent presence was the answer, an answer that can only be understood by faith. Thomas, the disciple, asked similarly, "Show us the way." He was told, "I am the way, the truth, and the life."

The question What is truth? is as old as the ages, and there's no sign that it has lost any of its vitality. Philosophers, theologians, now, even quantum physicists strive to codify it. Some even claim to succeed.

Any thoughtful person asks that question sooner or later. Why am I here? What does life and my life in particular mean? Jesus came to Gethsemane, that garden in the shadow of his cross, looking for meaning and asking the same questions. What he found is essential in our trying to understand how there can possibly be anything "good" about Good Friday. Paul put it like this in his letter to the Philippians:

"Have this mind among yourselves which is yours in Christ Jesus, who, though he was in the form of God, did not count equality with

God a thing to be grasped, but emptied himself, taking the form of a servant… obedient unto death, even death on a cross" *(Phil 2:5-11)*.

In his search, Jesus seemed always to embody the tension between religion and faith. That tension may be nowhere more evident than in the events that we commemorate during this week now passing. For in his commitment, Jesus emptied himself of all pretense in order to become a servant. Thus committed, he made Good Friday an in-your-face confrontation with both religion and the state. It was his "Yes" to God and to the cross that turned the world around.

A colleague who is a priest was asked where she sees that same Christ today. Noticeably, she did not mention the church. Rather, she said, "I look for someone who has told me the truth so clearly [that] I want to kill him."

Holy Saturday /Easter Vigil *ABC

Stories

My trust is in you, Yahweh; I say, "You are my God." Every moment of my life is in your hands. Rescue me from the clutches of my foes who pursue me; let your face shine on your servant, save me in your faithful love. (Psalm 31:14-16)

Our family tradition as the children of Abraham is told through stories. All these stories, however old they are, however embroidered they are, are our stories.

The Easter Vigil liturgy gathers these stories of our heritage, our genealogy, together in one celebration that consecrates our beginning into that heritage through our baptism and again renews it through our family reunion in thanksgiving around the Holy Table.

Over and over, we come together to tell these stories. Some actually happened at a place in time. Some probably did not. All of them may not be factual, but all of them are true. For myths and stories and family remembrances and no telling how much of our anecdotage are always true. We cannot live well without them. We dare never to try.

These stories are true because they seek meaning rather than fact. These stories are true because they seek understanding rather than explanation. And these stories are true because they, like the carillons in bell towers, ring changes on the three great themes of our biblical tradition.

We are created in God's image, we are as God imagines us to be. God's gracious love for us is completely, totally unconditional. Our lives in faith have no other purpose save simply to be all that we can be. The humorist Erma Bombeck had a most appropriate word for us in this season. She said, "When I stand before God at the end of my life, I would hope that I have not a single bit of talent left and can say, 'I used everything You gave me.' "

Jesus offered his life like that all the way from the Wilderness to the Garden to the Cross and said, "It is finished." He had used it all. He had made Good Friday good.

That we can strive through faith and God's grace in our own lives in our own ways in our own stories is enabled in the Easter Eucharist and in this community together with all the others who have gone before. This is where we consume such love that we may in turn be consumed by it.

Easter Morning *C

Women

Then [the women] remembered [Jesus's] words, and returning from the tomb, they told all this to the eleven [apostles] and to all the rest. Now it was Mary Magdalene, Joanna, Mary the mother of James, and the other women with them who told this to the apostles. But these words seemed to them an idle tale, and they did not believe them. (Luke 24:8-11)

Becca Stevens is the very creative and imaginative chaplain for our ministry at Vanderbilt University and wherever. She has three sons. When the oldest was crowding ten years or so, she asked him what he wanted to be when he grew up. Did he want to be a musician-composer like his dad? No, he said. Well, did he want to be a priest like his mom? No, he said emphatically, that's woman's work.

Opinions vary.

One of our former bishops called the ordination of women "apostolic suicide." His successor said it was the greatest thing the Episcopal church did in the 20th century. Women make up an increasingly large enrollment of students and faculty in our seminaries. One need pay not a lot of attention to discover how impressive is this new leadership, how rich are these new ministries, and how consistent they often are with the gospel's pastoral and prophetic commissions.

This Easter's gospel story of how the Good News was first told by women and how the limply men responded to it and how it spread anyway makes one wonder why did it take so long. Karl Barth, the great Swiss theologian, affirms his belief in the Virgin Birth simply because it is God's way of saying the wait had been long enough for the men to get with it and that Mary was chosen to make it altogether clear that if necessary God could get along quite well without them.

Mary Magdalene and her cohorts became the apostles to the apostles. They set the model for all us churchers to show and tell our experience of the risen Christ by the way we live our lives, and as one worthy once said, even to use words if necessary. "Apostolic succession" is merely a claim to an authority that is meaningless without our incarnating it. Our Baptismal Covenant reminds us of that succession as we are asked to "continue in the apostle's teaching and fellowship..."

Its presence can be in effect quite apart from who bears it to the world. Even children, as Jesus once said, for of such is the kingdom of God.

Then [the women] remembered [Jesus's] words, and returning from the tomb, they told all this to the eleven [apostles] and to all the rest... But these words seemed to them an idle tale, and they did not believe them *(Luke 24:8-11)*.

Isn't it remarkable how small families of the people of God in faraway places so often enjoy such witness by women leaders who remember Jesus's words and tell them by their deeds to all the rest of the world. Easter brings us together once again so that when all of us leave here we can say, "Been there and done that," go and tell it on the mountain, and turn the world upside down.

That's woman's work. The Lord is risen. He is risen indeed.

Easter Evening *C

Once

Then [Jesus] said to them, "Oh, how foolish you are, and how slow of heart to believe all that the prophets have declared!" (Luke 24:25)

Easter Morning ended the calendar time, at least, of a remembering of what was one helluva week for Jesus. John Evangelist says of him at that last supper with his friends that he was "troubled in spirit." One should think so. Says that he knew that one of them was to betray him. Says that he knew who it was to be. Says that he told him to get on with it. And the plot is set in motion. Jesus is the plot. There's a constancy about this week we call holy. It's built around the deliberate and intuitive will of Jesus. What would Jesus do? some ask in their decision-making. What would Jesus be? is the better question. How could Jesus be what and who he was midst the storm and chaos? How can we?

Jesus was surely running on empty when it came to the energies one needs to cope with the anxiety alone, not to mention that certain uncertainty that had been building in him all along from those first forty days consorting with Itself in the wilderness all the way to Gethsemane's wrenching and final choice.

A couple of millennia later, we rather take Easter Day as the end of it, the settlement of it, the final — and successful — resolution of the whole theological melange. Low Sunday symbolizes something like that with its kind of Wholly Whew. In anticipation, our preacher yesterday, when welcoming the usual larger-than-usual congregation, reminded us that we do this every Sunday here. He was greeted with what might be called a mild murmur.

Easter Day may be the end of all the Lenten and Holy Week hoopla, but it's only the annually renewed beginning for us of what Jesus was all about. Maybe it was his Last Week last week, but it is ever again our first. Another shot at it. Maybe we might find some semblance of holy continuity or again merely gird ourselves with diversions that allow the so-called lifestyles of others once again to impede the style of life to which we are called. After all, Easter came only once for Jesus, and that was plenty. How many times does it take for us churchers to get it right?

Second Sunday of Easter *C

In deed

[Thomas] said to them, "Unless I see the mark of the nails in his hands, and put my finger in the mark of the nails and my hand in his side, I will not believe." (John 20:25b)

Many of us probably remember the Apostle Thomas more for his doubt than for his faith. We forget his courage and his enterprise. That we overlook this probably gives him a lot more grief than he deserves.

While the rest of the disciples were cowering up in the loft for fear of the Romans and probably full of resentment that they'd bet their lives together with what fortunes they may have had on a loser, Thomas was out pounding the pavement, risking arrest, renewing old contacts, checking the want-ads, and looking for work.

He didn't believe the talk about Jesus. He wanted better evidence than the cringing behavior of his old pals. But when he got it, he signed on for good or ill, accepted his commission as an apostle, wrote a gospel, and, some say, started a new church over in India.

Obviously, Jesus believed Thomas's commitment, and actually, Thomas could hardly have done otherwise. John's gospel stresses that Jesus specially blessed those who had not seen and yet believed. Likewise, those for whom John wrote in the first place — that's us, that's you and me — that "believing, may have life in his name" *(Jn 20:31b)*.

We don't have the hard evidence Thomas got. John knew that, but maybe he knew something else, as well. Faith is not only always surrounded by doubt and without evidence, but that faith also creates both doubt and evidence.

Faith is risk, and risk, by definition, contains doubt. But faith that comes only after evidence is no faith at all. It is merely a kind of trust one way or another. Trust has anchors for good or ill. Faith is that daring commitment that walks life's planks and then leaps. That's all the evidence we get.

Faith creates evidence. Your faith is evidence for me. My faith is evidence for you. Our faith as a community is what makes church church and is the best kind of evangelism. The groveling disciples in the upper room would probably never have convinced Thomas until he personally experienced the vision of the risen Lord. So it is that were fear our only motivation, we'd probably never convince any who pass by.

For not until we show the world by the way we walk the talk, by the faith by which we risk our love for one another can our witness ever become the winsome and compelling evangel of the Lord, himself. That's church — not just the place, but the community where the Lord is risen. That's where the Lord is risen indeed. In deeds of your faith. In deeds of your love and mine, indeed. Like Jesus said, you can tell they are my followers by the way they love one another. Ultimately, Thomas knew that by faith. In deed.

Third Sunday of Easter *A

Pulse

And [Jesus] said to them, "What are you discussing with each other while you walk along?" (Luke 24:17)

Luke uses an interesting literary device in recounting the walk down the road to Emmaus. He writes a story within a story. (Shakespeare did it in "Hamlet" and maybe got the idea from Luke.)

History already knows about Good Friday and Easter for more than 2000 times. Luke's early readers knew. We know. But these two men walking along the nine miles from Jerusalem to Emmaus did not know. There they were, right on the front line of the news that we call the Good News, and they didn't know. Maybe better it is to say, they didn't know that they knew. And then begins the story within the story.

Jesus, as he has a way of doing, suddenly shows up from nowhere. Finding an audience for their fear, their anxiety, the men excitedly and sadly tell him about how the crucifixion had crushed their hopes. But then, they say, yet startled beyond belief, that some women claimed they'd been there and done that and seen the empty tomb and had a vision of angels who told them Jesus was alive. The men didn't believe them, so they went to look for themselves, and all they found was an empty tomb. I like to think that's all they saw because of the way they looked, they saw only what they expected to see.

"O foolish men," says Jesus, "and slow of heart to believe..." (And there's the tip off — slow of heart, slow of perception, slow of faith.) Then Jesus offers for them his own private accounting — Moses, the prophets, all with the whole sweep of scripture up to and including himself. They still do not know who he is, but they're obviously intrigued, invite him for dinner, and in the breaking of bread together, their capacity is opened finally to know that they knew.

Life is a story within stories. It is a collection of stories, my story, your story, our family's stories, the world's story as the geologists tell it from the Big Bang to the fractal changes our own saga makes on the cosmos. We are a part of the pulse of a kind of cosmic, interstellar cardiovascular system. Here we are pumping along and, it seems until we learn otherwise, giving it heart and voice and mind. Our own histories are made as we tell of them, as they unfold, as we walk them and come ever so often to our own forks in the road, and, like Yogi Berra said, take them.

The ever-present Jesus is always on the road with us, but, as Luke's story tells it, our eyes are kept from recognizing him. As I've read this story so many times before, I've always presumed it was Jesus who kept his identity to himself. But no, I suddenly realize that whatever, it is I who keep his identity from myself. I keep my eyes from recognizing him, from seeking and serving Christ in all persons, from loving my neighbor as myself.

For he is there in every act of kindness, in every gift of freedom and justice, in every act of compassion, in every risk of faithfulness, in every warmth and inclusion and reception, in every act of love and commitment and justice. And, of course, he is there confronting when just the opposite of these things takes place. Faith opens our eyes to see him wherever he joins us on our road and especially as we come to Table with him in the breaking of bread. He is the Story within the story, the story within our story, the story within the church's story.

Fourth Sunday of Easter *C

Plainly

It was winter, and Jesus was walking in the temple, in the portico of Solomon. So the Jews gathered around him and said to him, "How long will you keep us in suspense? If you are the Messiah, tell us plainly." Jesus answered, "I have told you, and you do not believe." (John 10:22-25a)

John tells the story that the Jews were standing around there in the Temple marveling at this Jesus, and that they said to him, maybe even with a tinge of disdain, "If you are the Christ, tell us plainly."

What I'd like to suggest is that this may be and probably is the question being asked of the church today by anyone who cares enough to ask it, consciously or unconsciously or both. It may not always be asked this way, but it seems it is always asked with that intent. Tell us plainly, and tell us without all the exclusive, judgmental religious gingerbread and internecine squabble.

Occasionally, the Fourth Sunday after Easter falls on April 29th, a personally important day for me. April 29th gives me the pleasant opportunity of remembering and being grateful for two birthdays. One is for my son Scott, the other, for Duke Ellington. I think of the Duke whom I admire so deeply not only because he taught us all so much about creativity and jazz, but because I like to recall his famous parting greeting. It was almost a kind of blessing. He would say to all within earshot, briefly and plainly, "Love you madly. Love you madly." And I think of one my fondest memories of my son. He was barely five or so, and when coming in from play, he would stand in the doorway, look about, and seeing no one, he would shout, "Hey, somebody, I love you."

Plain words. Indiscriminate, unconditional, inclusive, no-strings-attached words. "I love you, madly..." whoever you are. "Hey, somebody, I love you..." wherever you are. The kind of plain words that not only communicate, but also nourish, especially in our time, those of us who starve for them.

The Jews were marveling at this Jesus, and they really wanted to know for whatever reason who he was. "If you are the Christ, tell us plainly."

The trouble, their trouble and perhaps ours, was that they could not or would not see and hear the answer which was as plain as could be. It was too plain, too simple. Jesus's answer to the Jews in John's accounting was simply to point to the evidence that bore witness to him. It was in his stories and in his acts.

He suggested neither creed nor catechism. He told stories. "My sheep hear my voice..." he said, and the sheep and I are instantly in business. It's like this. "I give them eternal life, and they shall never perish, and no one shall snatch them out of my hand."

Listen and watch, pay attention, he said. Out of this pour the blessings. Unconditionally. Inclusively. How dearly does the world and the church need to be so assured in this way in these times. By the stories we tell. By the acts we do. By the attention we pay to the simple, the obvious, by how stewardly we are, for example, not only with our spiritual goods, but with our material goods, as well.

Perhaps it's too simple. Like God's living conditions for our forebears in the Garden of Eden, perhaps they just seemed too obvious to be taken seriously. Then, as now, for our human relations, for our own environmental stewardship, we just have to make things more complicated ever than necessary.

I remember the irony of a war hero like General Dwight Eisenhower, when he became president, naming his presidential airplane not with a militaristic aphorism like the current "Air Force One," but instead, as "Columbine." The word means "dove," the worldwide symbol for peace. And I remember how when he left office warned us to be wary of the so-called military-industrial complex and its lust for power and control. And I remember today how we've never learned that lesson and are paying today with our money, our environment, our health, and our lives as a consequence.

If there is any answer to this agony run wild, any peace, any justice, it is here, in sheepfolds like the church is called to be, where all of us and our children can know how deeply we are cared for and what treasures we are, where Jesus is the doorway in which we all can stand, both looking in and looking out, and simply say, "Hey, somebody, I love you."

Simplicity is always simple, simply too simple, too plain to be true, to be respected. And besides, it just doesn't look much like you're doing anything. When people come to 12-step programs with any intention and enthusiasm at all, any will to confess and to recover from their addictions, the first thing they want to know is What to do. What must I do to recover from this malady? They want a formula, a mantra, a routine. And they want it immediately… a quick fix. Like the Jews confronting Jesus, they want to be, indeed, often demand to be told plainly.

Not altogether coincidentally, "Keep it simple" is the first and most frequent counsel for the newly-recovering addict, and "Keep it simple" is the second hardest thing to do after the initial abstinence, the last drink or whatever. It's apparently so much easier to complicate life. And we addicts, like many of us who speak for the church, can complicate life — and even the simple 12-step program — with the very best of them.

A nun who was a recovering alcoholic spoke in a meeting about how difficult it was for her to take the Third Step. You know the one. It's when we are asked to turn our will and our life over to the care of God as we understand God. But this Sister, with all her vows and her theological skills, her disciplined prayer life, her commitment, and her truly exemplary ministry, even with her currently successful abstinence, she simply could not do it, she could not "take" that Third Step. Until one day, as she told her story, she realized that out of all the complicated creeds and catechisms, devotions and liturgies of her religious life which had served her so well to be where she was, she was letting them get in her way to taking the Third Step.

Naturally, she was trying to turn her will and her life over, like the step said, to God, to God as she understood God. What else? Who wouldn't? One might say, in her case, that she had a pretty impressive understanding of God in anybody's league. But the Step had never quite "worked" for her. And to hear her tell it, it sure wasn't working now.

Then, in a very simple, but maybe not all that obvious turn of phrase, she realized why. She was pounding at the gates of her understanding of God, at her definitions, at her descriptions of God as they had come down to her through her long and devoted training, but all limited to how she understood them.

Yet, all the while, the gates of the God who transcended her understanding, but was not limited by it, the God who gave her and all else in her life meaning, who made all her skills and her freedom possible, these gates of this God were swung wide open. It was very simple and oh, so very profound. God, you might say, was standing there, waiting to say to her plainly and without condition…

"Hey, Somebody. I love you." Or maybe, like the Duke, "Love you madly."

Fifth Sunday of Easter *A

Place

[Jesus said,] "In my Father's house are many rooms; if it were not so, would I have told you that I go to prepare a place for you?" (John 14:2)

Wendell Berry lives in Kentucky, but he is everybody's neighbor. He wrote that if we don't know where we are, we don't know who we are. He is not talking about the kind of location that can be determined by looking at a map or a street sign.

He is talking about the kind of knowing that involves the senses, the memory, the history of a family or a tribe. He is talking about the knowledge and sense of place that comes from working it in all weathers, making a living from it, suffering from its catastrophes, loving its mornings or evenings or hot noons, valuing it for the profound investment of labor and feeling that you, your parents and grandparents, your all-but-unknown ancestors have put into it.

He is talking about a sense of place. Fewer and fewer of us enjoy a sense of place in that sense in this day and time. Not because we are not farmers, although awareness of the land is essential for our good health, but because we are so mobile, so restless, so displaced. Berry is talking not only about the sense of place that land gives us, but even more so, the sense of place in which our poets specialize.

It takes not much stretch for me to imagine that this is the kind of knowing, the kind of sense of oneself that the poet Jesus specialized in. He said, "In my Father's house are many rooms; if it were not so, would I have told you that I go to prepare a place for you?" It is not only there, in that house of many rooms, where Jesus prepares a place for us that one day we may occupy, but it is also from that house that Jesus reaches out to us and prepares a place for us that we can now in this day and this time occupy. Perhaps one of the major causes of our social malaise is that we have become indifferent to, even contemptuous of, or afraid to commit ourselves to, our physical and social surroundings, always hopeful of something better. We seem as hooked on change as we are afraid of change. A lot of us have never stayed in one place long enough to learn it, or have learned it only to leave it.

In our displaced condition we are not unlike the mythless person that Carl Jung wrote about, who lives "like one uprooted, having no true link either with the past, or with the ancestral life which continues within him, or yet with contemporary human society. He... lives a life of his own, sunk in a subjective mania of his own devising, which he believes to be the newly discovered truth."

It is only a step from this to another: that no place is a place until it has had a myth, until it has a story, a spiritual genealogy. No place, not even a wild place, not even a place where all of Maurice Sendak's wild things are, is a place for us until it has had that human attention that at its highest reach we can call poetry.

What Frost did for New Hampshire and Vermont, what Faulkner did for Mississippi and Steinbeck for the Salinas Valley, Wendell Berry is doing for his family corner of Kentucky, and hundreds of other place-loving people, gifted or not, are doing for places they were born in, or reared in, or have adopted and made their own.

I doubt that we will ever get the motion out of us, for everything in our culture of opportunity and abundance has, up to now, urged motion on us as a form of virtue. The way we drive our roads makes it seem that even vengeance has become a virtue. Our tradition of restlessness will not be outgrown in a generation or two, even if the motives for restlessness are withdrawn.

Our frontiers have been explored and crossed, at least in geographic terms. It is probably time we settled down. It is probably time we looked around us instead of looking ahead. We have no business any longer in being impatient with history. We need to know our history in much greater depth, we even need to know our geology, for our geology is only our history projected a little ways back from our founding fathers and mothers.

History was part of the baggage we threw overboard when we launched ourselves into the New World. We threw it away because it recalled old tyrannies, old limitations, galling obligations, bloody memories. Why else would our present administration speak of "old Europe" with such disregard and disdain? Plunging into the future through a landscape that had no history for us and defiling the natives who were here already and had their own history, we did not only them, but both the country and ourselves considerable harm. Neither the country nor the society we built out of it can be healthy until we stop raiding and running, and learn to be quiet part of the time, and acquire the sense not of ownership but of belonging.

"The land was ours before we were the land's," says Robert Frost's poem. Only in the act of submission is the sense of place realized and a sustainable relationship between people and earth established. The place Jesus makes for us is uniquely ours, a gift of grace from which we can grow and become the human beings he intends for us to become. It is our story. It is our myth. He is our vanguard, but as well, he is our shepherd in the here and now. With him, as T S Eliot reminds us, "We shall not cease from exploration / And the end of all our exploring / Will be to arrive where we started / And know the place for the first time."

Sixth Sunday of Easter *B

Friends

"You are my friends if you do what I command you." (John 15:9-17)

"What a friend we have in Jesus."

I never did like either that hymn or the one about Jesus wanting me for a sunbeam. Let alone the hokey tune, the friendly lyric itself sounded like that if Jesus was looking for a friend in me, he had gone wanting. Later on, as maturity began to creep up on my blind side, I didn't like the way it challenged me to get serious about what it means to be a friend. It's like Jesus has never stopped challenging me. Maybe that's what it means to be a friend. Somebody who never stops caring, pushing, tough-loving like Francis Thompson's Hound of Heaven.

Did the disciples, do we, truly realize what Jesus offers when he offers his friendship — "[All] that I have heard from my Father I have made known to you," he told them *(Jn 15:15b)*. The very intimacy he had with God, his Father, he was passing down? And then there's Moses. It says over in Exodus that "The Lord used to speak to Moses face to face, as a man speaks to his friend" *(Ex 33:11)*. And God says the same thing about Abraham, "Abraham, my friend" *(Is 41:8)*. It is a staggering thought to be included in such company. But that is where we are if we are even halfway faithful to the apostles' fellowship and teaching as we claim in the Baptismal Covenant of a Sunday morning. The love of God. The mercy of God. The judgment of God. You take your shoes off when you think about that. But the friendship of God? *(cf Frederick Buechner)*

Nobody can be a friend alone, apparently not even God. Further, friendship is something far more about what we are than what we do. I can love you. I can even make you my beloved, but I do that altogether on my own, single-hearted. If my love is not returned, I'm in for some big withdrawal pain, a lousy hangover, and a longing for thou, for "I-Thou" as old Martin Buber put it. But on the other hand, I suspect it's not possible to befriend someone, and do it all alone and stand there slack-jawed, wondering at the incompletion of it, the where-did-it-all-go of it. I wonder if friendship is not the original tango that it takes two to do?

George Fox, the founder of the 17th century so-called Quaker Movement, actually preferred to think of his followers as friends of Jesus. They called themselves The Religious Society of Friends and they took their name from this same story in John's today's gospel. The Quaker name came from Fox's constant stirring up the status quo and frequently ending up in court. He told a judge once that he ought to be trembling before the Lord. The judge was not impressed, but just called Fox a trembler, a quaker, instead. But "Friends" is still the name that stuck.

I suppose one does not "earn" friendship or be "worthy" of it any more than one earns love. There are certain things in life that one wills, one chooses if possible to be, that nothing of any consequence can stem. At least two of these are to be loving and to be a friend, both sort of a part with each. Both imply profound risk. Jesus knew that. Even though he took up carpentering, he knew from his wilderness testing by Satan that there was more to it, that he may be driving nails and sawing boards, but that he'd also been born to risk. Not to put down carpentering, it was once a great pleasure to me, but to be more than a carpenter. To remember that life is not an exact science.

We churchers are, I believe, to be about friendship, about friendship like that with Jesus and his friends. I have friends. They have me. Like you, I've had many friends over the years, some, with only that pale, at best cool translucency, others of impenetrable substance. Friends, the way Jesus used it, is not an "instead" word, some casual synonym for servants. Friends is an inclusive word. Servants maybe cannot be friends, but friends for sure must be servants.

There's something about the verb "to be" that makes love and friend become beloved and befriend and to change their meaning, sort of to make them verbs. Beloved, befriend.

One of my colleagues signs off his email with "Be blessed." It is a gentle command, an attention-getter, a question — it says to me, "Why don't you allow yourself to be blessed, to let Jesus call you his friend? For Jesus to call us friends is a blessing in itself. The old hymn "What a friend we have in Jesus" doesn't sound even half so bad now as it once did.

If there's nothing much else here, I'll leave you with a tired old story.

Sister Mary Ecumenica's assignment in her Order was to stay in touch with the "Others," the other denominations. It came upon her in the keeping of this work to visit a Quaker Meeting. She arrived at the appointed hour, took her seat, and waited. Silence. Later, more silence. Later, still more silence.

Finally, thinking she'd made some indiscreet mistake, Sister discretely asked the person sitting next to her, "When does the service begin?" Only to hear the even more discrete answer, "As soon as the Meeting is over."

And if that doesn't charm you, don't forget Cole Porter, who said these words that may have helped out old George Fox when he got too friendly with Jesus: "If you're ever in a jam, here I am / If you ever need a pal, I'm your gal / If you ever feel so happy you land in jail; I'm your bail / It's friendship, friendship / Just a perfect blendship / When other friendships have been forgot / Ours will still be hot."

Ascensiontide *ABC

Up

Then he led them out as far as Bethany, and, lifting up his hands, he blessed them. While he was blessing them, he withdrew from them and was carried up into heaven. And they worshipped him, and returned to Jerusalem with great joy... (Luke 24:50-52)

I am told that the astrophysicists have begun to talk about their science less with theories and formulas and more with metaphors. I am glad for that. We churchers have been into metaphors all along and continue to be, so we might at least give our colleagues an ear. Some of them have begun to write about the universe, for example, as "elegant," even made up of strings. In Genesis, when God admired her creation and thought it was good, I don't remember her stringing us along, but I know that elegant would have been as fine a word as any.

Ascensiontide is as good a tide as the next if not better to talk about astrophysics. It is so mostly because I don't really understand either of them all that well. But I can attempt to confuse both us and them.

I cannot think of Jesus's Ascension without thinking about "up." Back when he was in the flesh, heaven was always "up," and it's pretty much stayed there ever since. That's, of course, when we only had the three dimensions — up, down, and around. We call it space. We also had time, but not all that long ago, we've begun to think of time as a fourth dimension. Add them all together, and for lack of a better name, we call them space-time. This leaves us not only with up, down, and around, but with up, down, around, and on-the-go. That's about as much as anybody could even think about, let alone understand. But now, those in the know believe we could really have not only four dimensions, but as many as eleven to fret over and maybe even another universe alongside this one. If all that's a fact, that puts a whole new perspective on the Ascension, like, which way did Jesus really go?

The problem with getting preoccupied with that is to risk missing what really might after all be the point. For to hear Jesus tell it, it is that he went that is important, not so much the way he went. We know that he couldn't stay around in the flesh forever. Further, he said that his leaving was the condition for our receiving his Spirit, his Holy Spirit, and that there wasn't room here for the both of them.

We need this Holy Spirit, he said, because that is the way he can best remain with us and give us enough chutzpah to become a church. And also this could give us something special, like another riddle to puzzle over and call the Doctrine of the Trinity. The answer to that mystery is really God's business and the way God chooses to be. Even if along with astrophysics we don't understand that, either, and if that's God's option, it is surely elegant enough for me.

What if there'd been eleven dimensions back in the space-time of Jesus instead of only three? Maybe it would have been more to the point. For like Jesus said, it wasn't so important where he went, that we couldn't go there, anyway. But what was important and remains important is that he went. For now, with the profound help of Holy Spirit, the only up that really matters, is the up that's up to us.

Seventh Sunday of Easter *C

Answer

I ask not only on behalf of these, but also on behalf of those who will believe in me through their word, that they may all be one. (John 17:20-21a)

John's Gospel on this eve of Pentecost offers a part of Jesus's so-called "high-priestly prayer." He asks that the work which he is about to leave be continued in the world. He asks that we be given the same authority that is given to him, the authority of truth, the authority of love, and he asks that we might become one as he and his Father are one in order that through us — as once through him — the world might then know indeed who is among them.

This, of course, is the language of grace. The religious always recognize it, even claim it as their own, but only the faithful understand it and know from Whom it comes and how it might be implemented.

Most prayer is not only directed to God, but expected to be answered by God. But not this time. To be sure, this great high-priestly prayer is offered to God... but the startling reality is that answer depends not on God, but on us.

The question is asked often — Is prayer ever answered? Talk about irony.

That God would leave so much in our hands, would be so willing to commission us, should not now at this late date surprise us. After all, if she understands herself as a shepherd who would abandon ninety-nine nearsighted sheep to go after one or as a vintner who would pay a full day's wages to a picker who worked only half an hour at sundown or if her son could drop off for a nap on the fantail of a boat at sea during a hurricane or if she'd commission an internal revenue agent named Matthew to take more interest in our salvation than in our taxes. Looking at all that, then we become merely the latest installment on that splendid wild and crazy ride down the kingdom Way of irony and grace.

An apocryphal story recounts some angels talking with Jesus. They ask what are his post-Ascension plans for commissioning someone to carry on his work, just who are to be his heirs, the ones to tell the story. He answers that he's called out a small community, one we might imagine and hope maybe like the one up at Lake Wobegon where the women are strong, the men are good-looking, and all the children are above average.

The angels fall into a respectful silence. Then one blurts out, "Is that all? What if they fail?" "Yes," Jesus answers, "that's all. That's my only plan."

No other plan. Only the grandest plan of all. A loving community of reasonably foolish people imagined into free being by God to be respectful of God and all creation, and, of course, imagined equally as free not so to be. A plan in which God waits... waits for us to say "Yes." Waits for us to become a community bound by love, not agreement, by covenant, not by canon law, by hope and faith, not by race and neighborhood, by compassion and service and mission, not by budgets and resolutions, by humility and even when in conflict nourished by mutual respect, not by the simple merit of circumstance, and certainly not by orthodoxy, but simply by the grace of God for those who let go and let God.

Such is the language of grace. So let us not merely become proficient in that language, but let us come to understand and walk such talk. Let us not be satisfied merely to be a religious people, but let us become a faithful people, and let us dare to risk ourselves as Jesus's only plan and, ironically, as the only answer to his prayer. Is prayer answered?

Pentecost *A

Breath

Jesus said to them again, "Peace be with you. As the Father has sent me, so I send you." When he had said this, he breathed on them and said to them, "Receive the Holy Spirit. If you forgive the sins of any, they are forgiven them; if you retain the sins of any, they are retained." (John 20:21-23)

The Earth's atmosphere is a relatively thin envelope of gases composed of 78% nitrogen, 21% oxygen, and a smidgen of others. Perhaps our most vital activity in return for our lives, together with all the rest of creation, the animals, the plants, is constantly to be at the process of recycling this envelope. For it connects us in an essential and almost intangible ambiance. Philosopher-scientist Lewis Thomas, it was, who likened our atmosphere and its function most to the walls of a living cell.

In a remarkably similar way does God's Holy Spirit wholly envelop us. It sustains our lives, creates our communities and connects us in them, and most importantly, enables our reconciliation with one another. No wonder that in so many languages spirit is translated as "breath." And further, we well remember how it exists quite apart from us and like Jesus more or less told Nicodemus, this Holy Spirit lives and moves, comes and goes as it damn well pleases.

Unlike the Earth's atmosphere, God's Spirit seems limitless. We, by God's grace, become the occasions, the stewards to receive and recycle its energy in service to God's will. We are created by God as those spiritual beings whose vocation is to give human shape to the Spirit as we mature into the way God imagines us to be. Indeed, a case can be made, can it not, that this life begins with our first breath just as it ends with our last. That is a reality with which both pro-life and pro-choice advocates must contend.

Have you ever imagined how a symphony orchestra or a chorus or a pipe organ and a church choir or a big jazz band could function if there were no air, no breath? There is no sound, indeed, no life in a vacuum. The wind instruments, the strings, the percussion, all depend on there being an atmosphere if there is to be music, an atmosphere which they can move and sculpt if there is to be music.

So is our mission as churchers to shape Spirit. In the way a musician shapes the air into sound, so must we take our lives, the instruments God gives us and use them to play God's melodies, to shape God's Spirit uniquely in service to God and to our fellow human beings, as well as to be sparing in our observations of how they uniquely shape their own.

Perhaps one of the most grievous examples of the way we cripple this stewardship is our continuing effort to transfix Holy Spirit in our own interests and not in God's. Of course, the mere thought of such a thing is ludicrous. But not a day passes that we churchers do not strive to fashion and refashion that Spirit in some way so as to warp the gift, and, of course, seem to forget what Jesus told Nicodemus.

Just as we contaminate the Earth's atmosphere by our carelessness so do we defile God's Holy Spirit by forcing our or some other religious identity and constriction upon it. Global warming pales beside the toxicity of any religion's selfish obsession with its manners, morals, and means at the expense of its mission. We must remember that we are not only the community created at the bonfire of the first such gathering, but we are, as well, the community commissioned for Pentecost. We are Spirit-enabled to become nothing less than Spirit enablers.

Scripture overwhelms us with this good news. Acts' accounting of the fire, wind, and apostolic headiness that birthed God's church (*Acts 2:1-11*). Paul's catalogue of the gifts of the Spirit to fulfill the church's purpose with shape and substance (*1 Cor 12:4-13*). Jesus's granting of apostolic ministry by the power of his own breath, a portend of the Spirit to come (*Jn 20:19-23*). We are called and called again to such ministry. "Breathe on us breath of God," we sing and pray to brace and refresh us, to call us back to and enlist us in the Way, the Truth, and the Life revealed in the Upper Room. This Pentecost blessing comes to drag us kicking and screaming away from our fascination with ourselves and our need for ecclesiastic security. It comes to license us as God's agents as Mary's Magnificat sang to show the strength of God's arm, to scatter the proud in their conceit, to cast down the mighty from their thrones, to lift up the lowly, to fill the hungry with good things, to send the rich away empty, and to champion God's peace and justice and love for all.

First Sunday after Pentecost / Trinity Sunday *A

(Warning: Early on when I thought I knew the answers and was only searching for the questions, a sage mentor advised me that no self-respecting Anglican cleric ever preaches on Trinity Sunday, but schedules Sunday School graduation instead. No longer having a Sunday School handy to graduate, here's some evidence to support his counsel. — LD)

Riddle

"Go therefore and make disciples of all nations, baptizing them in the name of the Father and of the Son and of the Holy Spirit, and teaching them to obey everything that I have commanded you. And remember, I am with you always, to the end of the age." (Matthew 28:19-20)

In the olden days of a few decades ago, there was a Trinity season, now preëmpted by Pentecost. Maybe it's a good choice. The linguistic ribaldry of the Feast of Pentecost and its interminable half-year following is maybe easier to take than the Trinity's puzzling incoherence.

So here are some Trinitarian sermon fillers for the more brazenly secure among us:

On the Doctrine of the Trinity: They took poetry and made it into a rule. — Anon

The Word became flesh, and theologians made it words again. — Karl Barth

On the other hand and for those less theologically inclined among us, this brief homily recently came down the wireless: "The Father Incomprehensible. / The Son Incomprehensible. / The Spirit Incomprehensible. / The Whole Damn Thing Incomprehensible. Amen." — Anon, of course, for who would claim it?

Or if you prefer longer, more narrative preachments:

Jesus asked his disciples, Who do people say that I am? And his disciples answered and said, "Some say you are John the Baptist returned from the dead; others say Elias, or other of the old prophets." And Jesus answered and said, "But who do you say that I am?"

Peter answered and said, "You are the Logos, existing in the Father as His rationality and then, by an act of His will, being generated, in consideration of the various functions by which God is related to his creation, but only on the fact that Scripture speaks of a Father, and a Son, and a Holy Spirit, each member of the Trinity being coequal with every other member, and each acting inseparably with and interpenetrating every other member, with only an economic subordination within God, but causing no division which would make the substance no longer simple."

And Jesus, answering, said, "What?"

Then there's this one: "It takes a mighty big stigma to beat a dogma."

Dorothy Sayers said it. She was British. She was also a theologian, a mystery novelist, a poet, and a Dante scholar. So she knew, it's safe to say, what she was talking about, whether I do or not.

She could have been talking about Trinity Sunday, the only place in the entire liturgical keeping of time that a dogma assumes front stage center, can leave a stigma all over one's preaching, and elbows all those majestic events like Christmas and Easter and Pentecost to the wings.

Preaching on Trinity Sunday can make one feel like the heart attack victim that called for a priest who, on arriving, moved the gathering crowd aside, knelt beside her, and asked, "Do you believe in the Father, the Son, and the Holy Ghost?" With great effort, the stricken woman addressed those surrounding her, "Here I lay dying, and the Father is asking me riddles."

Dogma, that's doctrine with legs, seems always to be faith's more or less futile attempt to make sense out of nonsense. Whereas faith, not unlike love (and they're not all that different), is about as exposed a position as a person can take and with very little reason to support it. It's like getting caught with your hand in life's cookie jar. It makes you feel like you need some kind of excuse. Dogma, on the other hand, gets you out of hock and, as well, with an alibi. It somehow makes me mindful of that grand and eloquent creation story from Genesis that wraps a security blanket around the whole idea *(Gen 1:1-2:3)*. It reminds us that we are put here to tend God's creation by giving the universe something to talk with, giving God someone to talk to, and giving us somebody to talk about *(cf Frederick Buechner)*.

And further, Genesis says that whatever we do about it, even to the making of enigmatic riddles, God thinks that it is good and makes us unconditionally in God's image. Which is to say that we and all the rest of us — and them and it — are gently and lovingly shaped and brought forth with cause out of the unfathomable riches and depths of God's ingeniously fecund imagination.

And not as mere clones. But as beloved sharecroppers in whatever may be our capacity in all this exercise in fertility. And that, beloved, is very scary stuff. So scary, and yet, so enticing, that right off, we blew it out of the garden and have needed the safety belts and air bags of doctrine and dogma ever since.

But dare not overlook that doctrine, dogma, and all their theological progeny serve us well. We want everybody to buckle up. But be aware, as well, we are reminded — and warned — too much of this good thing can be at the expense of our imagination and worship. Such insight as that is perhaps no more obvious than in the turn of phrase at the very heart of the collect for Trinity Sunday, as we pray, "Almighty and everlasting God, you have given to us your servants grace, by the confession of a true faith, to acknowledge the glory of the eternal Trinity, and in the power of your divine Majesty to worship the Unity…" *(BCP p 228)*

We acknowledge doctrine. We worship God. We're not to confuse these. For it is in the imagination of our worship that we are most godlike, most as God creates us to be, imagining and incarnating our spirit into human being — and what is more leading us forth to walk the talk.

Second Sunday after Pentecost *A

Welcome

"Whoever welcomes you welcomes me, and whoever welcomes me welcomes the one who sent me." (Matthew 10:40)

So far as Jesus is concerned, the last thing card-carrying Christians need is a card to carry. If, indeed, there are any credentials required at all, love and justice will do jes' fine. And according to Matthew's take on the Good News, Welcoming.

Welcoming one another is not only what makes us disciples, it's what makes being a disciple about. It's what makes us who we are. No amount of grandstanding, breast-beating, ecclesiastic gerrymandering, confessions, or decades of evangelism can take its place. Wellcome (sic) and welcome all and thass all.

So what does it mean for us to love one another in this welcoming way? And how on earth will anybody, presuming they should much care one way or the other, ever know whether we do or don't? How can you tell a disciple from a devil without a program?

Our founders were mighty smart to separate out the religious and the secular institutions in our nation, to make them — and to insist that they remain — unbeholden to one another. Church is not state and vice versa. It was probably the best thing that ever happened to the both of us.

And they were smart, as well, not to talk a lot about love. What they were after for a welcome change was a just and open and fair society and a government that could pull it all off and keep it that way. Even a welcoming church was welcome to help out, but all the same, was also welcome to stay out. We churchers would look a long way before we'd ever find a political system more conducive to or nourishing of our own self-understanding. We'd also look a long way before we could embrace such an experiment with the full empowerment of our stewardship, both to enable and coax it along whenever it wavered and to indict and admonish it with something like the Isaiah two-step whenever it erred and strayed.

But the best way and, indeed, the only way to embrace this herculean ministry, of course, is to be such a society ourselves, then to do it, to model it, to make it so attractive folks simply have to have a piece of the action for themselves. It is to take this ministry far more seriously than we take ourselves. It is to realize that loving and welcoming one another in any kind of institutional or even communal way is to practice justice and fairness and civility and respect in our own common allegiance and worship.

So all the while this grand experiment in justice our founders imagined and birthed has come upon what may be the worst of times in its two centuries, where's the church? Championing justice? Loving one another? Modeling fairness and acceptance and inclusiveness? Calling the hands of our nation's leaders back to the premises of our founders, but tending to our own, as well? Welcoming?

Where are these disciples when we need them the most? How can one tell a disciple from a devil?

Third Sunday after Pentecost *B

Puzzles

In his gospel, Mark recounts that, *"With many such parables he spoke the word to them, as they were able to hear it; he did not speak to them except in parables, but he explained everything in private to his disciples"* (Mark 4:33f).

There is a parallel story in Luke's gospel in which the disciples are puzzled about parables, and they ask what a certain parable meant. And Jesus answers, *"To you it has been given to know the secrets of the kingdom of God; but for others they are in parables, so that seeing they may not see, and hearing they may not understand"* (Luke 8:4-10).

And then Paul in 2d Corinthians, who is not always so obscure as we might think and as if to answer Jesus's puzzling comment, reminds us, *"for we walk by faith, not by sight"* (2 Corinthians 5:7).

There is often a certain ironic humor at the heart of the parables. And I shall try to say why I think so. At the least is Jesus implying that he uses them because he doesn't want anybody to catch on to this radical Christ Movement.

Let us first take notice, then, that humor is not comedy. The difference between humor and comedy is the difference between the one that endures as a part with us and the one that evaporates almost on contact. Humor gives, comedy takes. Humor has character, comedy, mere personality. Paul was talking about humor when he said we must be fools for Christ, not just to fool around. Humor doesn't fool around, and that is the ironic paradox. When Father Emil of the Church of Perpetual Reponsibility up in Lake Wobegon had to tell his parishioners that the Bishop required them to use the Peace in the Liturgy, he said, Though you must do so, you don't have to make eye contact.

This mystery in which we live and which we call life draws on irony to reveal its story. That's why life, like irony, often seems to mean the opposite of what it seems to mean and requires that we give it special audience for understanding, audience that takes the risk of understanding, which means the risk of finding meaning. A life in faith is a splendid name for that audience, that risk. Like Paul told the Corinthians, "for we walk by faith, not by sight." *(2 Cor 5:7)* Humor, especially at its most caustic as satire, reminds us that everybody sooner or later and maybe more often than not is sometime exhausted, wicked, afraid, frustrated, and desperately alone. That is humor's perspective and its restorative power, its healing energy over life's menaces. By identifying us and identifying with us, that is as is said, by knowing our number, humor can be redemptive.

Humor does not wish us ill, but always wishes us well, and there is much to say for that. At times, it may condemn us and make us livid, often embarrass us, but always it instructs us, informs us, not simply pedantically, but by shaping us and giving us form, preparing us to receive it, by the tough love of breathing spirit into our clay. Humor unites us with ourselves, our neighbor, and with the roots of life, the awesome mystery of beginnings and endings, purpose and destiny, love and fear. Take not light the startling similarity of humus and human and humor.

And humor works best through story. Such story takes a mythic form that creates our worlds for us, that reveals to us our role in the drama, and that prepares us for it, as well. This mythic form takes shape in the parables.

Again Jesus says, "With what can we compare the kingdom of God, or what parable will we use for it? It is like a mustard seed, which, when sown upon the ground, is the smallest of all the seeds on earth; yet when it is sown it grows up and becomes the greatest of all shrubs, and puts forth large branches, so that the birds of the air can make nests in its shade." Everybody knows that mustard plants never get that big except in our imagination or myths which are no less true perhaps even truer.

With many such parables Jesus spoke the word to them, as they were able to hear it; he did not speak to them except in parables, but he explained everything in private to his disciples" (Mk 4:31-34). The kingdom of God is a parable, it is ironic. Another way to speak of it is that wherever the brokenness of the world is healed, wherever healing takes place, there is present the kingdom of God.

Listen to the parables of Jesus. But listen to them by envisioning and imagining them, putting them on, wearing them. Be the lost sheep. Be the mustard seed. Be the importunate woman banging on the judge's chambers. Be that guy on the other side of the road beat within an inch of his life. Be the prodigal son. Be the son who kept the rules.

This is what faith is about. We do an injustice to the parables to expect them to create faith. Like scripture as a whole, they do not create faith. For in a real sense, faith creates them. One comes to them with the ears of faith, the risk of faith, the key of faith which unlocks the parables to us and which so often reveals the subtle humor and wit in their core. We enter the parables that way, the way that in a real sense we "put on" Jesus. A lot about this marvelous gospel of ours is ludicrous, is it not? Especially that God would care for us so sincerely and so gently as to have his beloved son to tell us stories, stories about ourselves.

But there can never be enough of that kind of humor. For God is a God of irony. It is in that mystery and at that level in us that God moves. Maybe one of the greatest impediments in our national life in this time and for sure among us churchers is that we just don't get it because we're just too darn serious, because we lack a sense of humor, a sense of our humor.

And so remember what Jesus said to his disciples, he also says to us present-day disciples, "To you it has been given to know the secrets of the kingdom of God; but for others they are in parables, so that seeing they may not see, and hearing they may not understand"

And Paul also saying to us, "for we walk by faith, not by sight."

Fourth Sunday after Pentecost *C

Tension

"But now that faith has come …all of you are the children of God, through faith, in Christ Jesus, since every one of you that has been baptized has been clothed in Christ. There can be neither Jew nor Greek, there can be neither slave nor free, there can be neither male nor female — for you are all one in Christ Jesus." (Galatians 3:25-28)

Major league baseball (like organized religion with beer) is a mass mechanism for the experience of hope and the deep contemplation of humility. *(R D Rosen, "New York Times," 21.8.01, p A19)*

Anybody knows, of course, that Anglicanism is hardly an organized religion. Also that it is arguable just how well it offers a venue for either hope or humility. (And that some preachers will use almost anything for a lead.)

Whatever, somebody seems always itching to tidy up our ongoing American experiment in British piety — also known as the Episcopal Church — so that it at least seems bespoke. Think Nigeria, Anglican Mission in America, the Network and any number of other gatherings of bewildered bishops and congregations here and there who might be expected to know better. Some of whom might even try to hook a rheostat to the sunset.

In the face of all this, it is good that Paul reminded the Galatians of some things that we, ourselves, might be better off being reminded of — and practicing — today. He said, "Now before faith came, we were confined under the law... our custodian until Christ came, that we might be justified by faith... But now... through faith [we] are all [children] of God. For as many... as were baptized into Christ have put on Christ. There is neither Jew nor Greek... slave nor free... male nor female; [but] all are one in Christ Jesus... heirs according to promise" *(Gal 3:23-29 more or less)*.

Faith and law. The problem now is that we seem to forget Paul's gently firm and comforting admonition from two thousand years ago. For we are in the same old bind between religion and faith that so troubled the Galatians.

The Anglican tradition has managed this tension rather well over the years, if somewhat loose handedly. But there are those of late who can't seem to tolerate this way of following the Way. They just don't seem to want let go and let God. They don't seem to understand that the more they tighten their grip, the faster they lose it.

A crisis now and then is inevitable, maybe even necessary or welcome, but it doesn't have to resort to ecclesiastic genocide. Anybody knows that religion in whatever form is always the more powerful and well-organized and lethal than is faith. It will continue its often desperate endeavor to control faith (ie, collapse the tension between the two) by rendering faith not only memorable, but, more importantly, manageable. It will use and attempt to justify almost any means at hand with which to do so — if not canon law, then canon lawlessness, whichever seems most convenient. On the other hand, faith is usually too naive and indifferent for its own good up to the point of not even recognizing when it's being used and patronized. Faith, like love, communicates by spiritual osmosis, not by systems. This reality frustrates and beguiles some of the Anglican satrapy and leads them into their present ridiculous behavior.

The security of church as institution and the uneasy wishful thinking of church as sacramental community is always caught in this impasse and has been at least since the 4th century Council of Nicaea.

What was created at Pentecost to be a theater of expectation has often become at any cost a theater of the absurd. And we wonder why folks lose interest and why the established (aka organized) religions wane.

Like any other healthy, decision-making tension, the one between religion and faith is anything, of course, but soothing. The current lust after orthodoxy arises out of a climate of fear as it attempts to assuage and even appease such discomfort. During the middle ages, similar crises and their inevitable subsequent religiosity led precisely into the arms of the Inquisition. Today, that same intolerance for anything but "doctrinal purity" ironically creates a crippling and paralyzing climate in the very community whose true vocation is rather to love and to champion justice.

TEC's often clumsy and sometimes maladroit search for grace through its collegial system of doctrine, discipline, and worship obviously irritates the purple socks off some prelates. Especially those who prefer organized religion over love and justice and inclusion and who have precious little patience for apostolic lip. Heretics aren't often burned at the stake these days. But ignorance ("any 'C' student can become president of the United States"), together with threat, intimidation, indifference, exclusion, and enough dissimulation to cover some episcopal backsides, have effectively replaced the bonfires.

So what is one to do when an 800-pound primate knocks on the narthex door? Grab a valid baptism certificate, of course, and run to beat hell. Who knows when we may even need passports at the altar rail? And be sure and keep a copy of Paul's letter to the Galatians at hand because beating hell is what it's all about.

Fifth Sunday after Pentecost *C

Shelter

For freedom Christ has set us free. Stand firm, therefore, and do not submit again to the yoke of slavery. (Galatians 5:1)

Angus Dun, onetime bishop of the Diocese of Washington, was often invited together with other prominent prelates to attend high-level state dinners in the capital city. As he sipped a glass of wine at one of these gatherings, a colleague of a more fundamentalist persuasion observed, "I'd sooner commit adultery than drink that wine." Politely, the bishop responded, "And indeed, who wouldn't?"

If you're not shocked or even startled by Paul's catalogue of fleshly malfeasance and warnings thereabout to the Galatians, you've been making the rounds too much. If you are, perhaps you need to get out and circulate. Nevertheless, it is well to take note that Paul puts all these options — both the works of the flesh and the fruit of the Spirit — under the umbrella of freedom with the gospel's characteristic redundancy, "For freedom Christ has set us free…"

It has been said that the only person who is truly free is the one who can turn down an invitation to dinner without giving an excuse. Such freedom is what grace is all about. Indeed, without freedom, we could hardly even entertain taking on any of Paul's list of errancies, let alone practicing them. Without such freedom we cannot finally accept grace in all its nourishing grandeur.

If we are not free to choose between wine and adultery or none of the above, we are not free at all. But with such freedom, a wise person once said, the possibility of making complete fools of ourselves appears to be limitless.

The old prayer speaks of God "in whose service is perfect freedom," a paradox that is not so hard to understand as it sounds. For it is Love incarnate who calls us into service. To obey such a master who above all else wishes us well, is an obedience that leaves us the freedom to be the best and the brightest that we have it in us to become, to be fulfilled as the human being whom God imagines us to be. For the only freedom totally contrary to such Love is the freedom not to love and thus quite possibly to destroy ourselves, as well as others. A dear mentor of mine once said that if I love my neighbor and hate myself, God help my neighbor.

The gospel for this Sunday tells of this very thing. When the Samaritans rejected the disciples' plea for hospitality, they chose not to love, they rejected wholeness in favor of boundaries. They rejected God's freedom in favor of indenture. This is how religiosity always stifles faith… and, indeed, love.

The Samaritans disapproved of where Jesus was heading, so they spurned his need for shelter. They put their dogma ahead of another's humanity, a practice that continues, that has apparently never been out of vogue, and remains quite firmly planted there today. The Samaritans were not alone in forcing Jesus to say that even though all else has its place, "the Son of Man has nowhere to lay his head."

Saint Theresa of Lisieux surely meant something like this when she wrote with such great spiritual insight that, "If you are willing to serenely bear the trial of being displeasing to yourself, then you will be for Jesus a pleasant place of shelter."

For when those times come that we cannot accept ourselves for some self-imposed reason that rejects God's forgiving grace and prevents our own wholeness, then we have turned against this "freedom [for which] Christ has set us free."

But if we can love ourselves in spite of all we know to be unlovable about us, if we can will to bear serenely that trial of being displeasing to ourselves, then we will be for Jesus a pleasant place of shelter where the Son of Man can lay his head, indeed.

Sixth Sunday after Pentecost *A

Parables

[Jesus] put before them another parable: "The kingdom of heaven is like…" (Matthew 13:31a)

Patience has been called a minor form of despair disguised as a virtue. God is usually very generous with it. If you ask for it, you'll more than likely get it. And you'll probably be sorry.

I don't know about you, but Matthew has been testing my patience these past few Sundays. He's been in what might be called "parable-of-the-kingdom overload," reporting Jesus telling one parable after another. There's been the parable of the sower, the parable of the wheat and the tares, the parable of the mustard seed, the parable of the leaven, the parable of the pearl of great price, and finally, the parable of the indiscriminate net, the one that that catches all sorts and conditions of fish. Finally, the twelve who'd been his upfront audience all along, sound a bit like they've run out of patience. They ask, in effect, What's with all these parables?

Jesus takes a breath, maybe somewhat out of patience, himself, and answers with this: "To you has been given the secret of the kingdom of God, but for those outside, everything is in parables; so that they may indeed see but not perceive, and may indeed hear but not understand; lest they should turn again, and be forgiven" *(Mk 4:10-12)*. I hear that, and I wonder, Does that include us? Does that include his church? These wall-to-wall parables and all the others here and there sound like a mystery wrapped in an enigma. When we don't get them, does that mean we've not been given the secret of the kingdom? Is it not the kingdom we are supposed to savvy and to tell others about?

What are we to think? The disciples get the password to the kingdom, and all the rest of us churchers are handed the parables to do with the best we can lest we figure it all out and get saved? What can we say, then, about the parables and about the kingdom of God? We can say this: A parable is a small story with a large point, not with a lot of points all over the ballpark like an allegory. You can easily miss the point altogether if you start assigning people and things to the parts like a stage production. A parable is not an allegory.

Many of the ones Jesus told reveal the intriguing irony so common to and so revealing of the ways of God. They make a statement of facts readily enough, but in a mystifying way that tends to an exclusiveness intended only for an inner circle, just as Jesus says. Some of them illustrate that a foolish question deserves a foolish answer. The disciples' question reminds me of one put to Louis Armstrong when a fan asked him, "Pops, what is jazz?" only to hear him answer, "Man, if you gotta ask, you'll never know."

Parables are ripe with metaphor and are indeed often metaphors in themselves. There's a lesson herein for any who would need to make Scripture into some infallible verbal inerrancy only to render it altogether impotent, to rob it of its poetic beauty and power, and indeed of its parables, of their truth.

At any rate, like jokes and jazz, if you've got to have parables explained, don't bother. Parables are not to be explained, they are to be understood, and like most of the important things in life, they are understood only by our opening ourselves to them and listening with wonder and imagination and the faith that undergirds these presents, participating in them in a way, accepting this freedom as the gift from God it is intended to be.

Parables, Jesus seems to be saying, are not stories that cause or intend us to be faithful, but stories that open themselves to us through the eyes and ears of whatever faithfulness we can bring to them. We are to find the meaning in them. In other words, these parables of the kingdom do not exist in and of and for themselves, but for to give God a place, a room with a view to maneuver in our lives.

In one of his delightful theological *ABC* books, Frederick Buechner says things like this... The parables of Jesus are not historical allegories telling us how God acts with us, neither are they moral example-stories telling us how to act before God and towards one another. They are stories that shatter the deep structure of our taken-for-granted world. In the parable of the Laborers in the Vineyard, the legalists are outraged when Johnny-Come-Lately gets as big a slice of the worm as the Early Bird *(Mt 20:1-16)*. The point of the Unjust Steward is that it's better to be a resourceful rascal than a saintly schlemiel *(Lk 16:1-8)*. In the parable of the Talents, spiritually speaking, playing the market will get you further than playing it safe *(Mt 25:14-30)*. *("Wishful Thinking," pp 66f)*

Parables remove our defenses and make us vulnerable to God. It is only in such experiences that God can touch us, and only in such moments does the kingdom of God arrive. At such times we best realize the startling irony that true security is the serenity that comes from accepting insecurity as our mortal lot. The thoughts and stories in the Bible do not furnish easy assurance, but awaken and challenge us with their contradiction even of each other.

And so what of the kingdom of God, the freight these parables are designed to collect and to move and to deliver? What would these stories have meant to Jesus's audience? First, their primary and essential reference is to the sovereignty of God conceived in the most concrete possible manner, that is, to God's activity in ruling. The kingdom of God is the authority of God expressed in deeds. It is that which God does that reveals to us that God is king. It is not a place or even a community ruled by God nor even an abstract idea of these things. The kingdom of God is the activity of God as king and places the major emphasis on those acts wherein and whereby God's sovereignty is made manifest. Once again, the parables and their devastating challenges to the status quo provide room for God to reveal these acts in our lives. W H Auden put it like this, "You cannot tell people what to do, you can only tell them parables; and that is what art really is, particular stories of particular people and experiences... "

Perhaps their most important relevance in these times is to remind us that biblical morality is not about sex and abortion and gay marriage. Biblical morality is about caring for the poor and dispossessed, about our stewardship of the environment, about our life together in communities where justice and peace are as welcome and tangible as when the sun also rises. The Lutheran bishop and scholar Krister Stendahl spoke most winningly, I think, of the message of the parables when he said, Wherever and whenever the brokenness of the world and our life in it is being mended, there is present the kingdom of God. Jesus reminds us as he did the disciples, parables are not told to convince or convert us to God, but to enable us through our faith to understand God's presence and to make room for God, for us to find meaning in our lives, to realize that all along Jesus is God's parable, and that we by our own faith-filled imaginations can become parables ourselves. That is at least one of the secrets of the kingdom that has been given to us.

Seventh Sunday after Pentecost *C

Flat

(My good friend and fellow country preacher Joel Keys over on St Simon's Island, GA, once told a slightly longer version of this tale at his church's Saturday night Golfer's Mass. I'm preëmpting it here and now [without permission and with hope of forgiveness]. — LD)

But wanting to justify himself, [the lawyer] asked Jesus, "And who is my neighbor?" (Luke 10:29)

Once upon a time, Joel said, when a friend of mine was a student at Yale, he and another guy were on the road in a "college student" car (the kind students had before everybody got rich). It was in the middle of the night in the south Bronx, Tom Wolfe's *Bonfire of the Vanities* territory. They had a flat.

Before they could open the trunk to see if they even had a spare, an ancient, rusty car squealed to a halt in front of them in the breakdown lane. Out climbed two large men speaking Spanish. The students figured, "This is it." They were frozen in fear. But before they had a chance to decide whether to scream for help or run for their lives, the two Bronx types started changing the tire. They were done in minutes.

As they started to leave, Joel said, my friends tried to pay them. The helpers ignored them, walked away, got into their car, and left. If my friends had followed their fear, they wouldn't have got the tire changed, and they'd have had to go and get help in the middle of the night.

That's what our inner attitude can do. That's what xenophobia, our fear of strangers can do, that's what dismissing people by stereotype can do, that's what demonizing people and calling them trash can do. And as well, that's how our corporate anxiety drives our confusion and dismay over how or even whether to be neighbors across our national boundaries. It often means how those who immigrate here — legally or illegally — don't even have a chance for anything, let alone a good deed. What is even worse, it means we may never learn from them either about their selfless giving or any other of the manifestations of their culture and language if we won't even let them help us out.

The lawyer asked Jesus "Who is my neighbor?" Jesus began his answer as he did so often, with a story. "But a Samaritan, as he journeyed…" Imagine the lawyer saying, "Aw, cool it. I'm not listening to any stories about those Samaritan trash. I thought I was going to learn something from you. So long, Mister Savior of the World."

If he had, he never would have learned about neighbors, and he never would have learned that sometimes our neighbors aren't necessarily our friends, but, nonetheless, in our neighbors we might see the reflection of the face of God, and in our neighbors, we might learn how to let our own faces reflect God to someone else. The lawyer wouldn't have learned that and more than likely, neither would we. For it's only when we allow God to let us look through the barriers we erect to separate ourselves that we can see God's examples.

And then, as Jesus said, we might get one more blessed chance to "Go and do likewise."

Eighth Sunday after Pentecost *A

Walking

When the disciples saw [Jesus] walking on the sea they were terrified. "It is a ghost," they said, and cried out in fear. But at once Jesus called out to them saying "Courage! It's me! Don't be afraid." (Matthew 14:26-27)

Once again, having fed all those thousands on such a slim budget, Jesus is needing some privacy. So he has the disciples shove off and go back across the sea. Of course, and as in every dime novel since, "it was a dark and stormy night." When it got good and late and the waves were up and the wind was stiff and the boat was half way to the other shore, along comes Jesus. As if feeding all those folk didn't seem enough grandstanding for one day, he chooses not to rent a boat or to swim in the water, but to walk on it. Peter may be terrified by all this like the story says, but seeming never at a loss for an inappropriate idea, tests Jesus. "Lord, if it is you (test # 1), bid me come to you on the water (test # 2)." "Come," Jesus says. And sink, Peter does.

That winsome novelist and essayist Madeleine L'Engle once said that if we believe as we surely do that Jesus was fully human and could walk on water, then so can we walk on water. It's only that we forget how.

I don't like to think of us that way. I like to think of us as a remembering, not a forgetting people. We remember every time we gather around this Table and celebrate Eucharist. We remember the Christ and we reaffirm the Christ in each of us and in all of us as a worshiping community. But I suppose maybe we are, as well, a forgetting people, and we forget a lot more than just how to walk on water. Of course, we should not overlook that we can be deeply grateful that when Jesus said "do this in remembrance of me," he was at supper and not at sea.

Maybe L'Engle is right. But if she is, our forgetting how to walk on water, as exciting as such a skill may be, is but a symptom of something far greater. It means, in effect, that we've also forgot how to be human. After all, if Jesus is God's prototype of what it means to be human, and he could do all these logic- and science- and gravity-defying things, then we've forgot a tolerable lot.

But then there's not much sense in our anguishing over that when there's something else that we've apparently forgot, and is much nearer at hand and altogether more doable in God's human scheme of things. And the church's spiritual rehab program is the place to go about doing it.

"Spiritual rehab" is probably a misnomer. "Human rehab" may be better. For with God's imaginative creation of us, we are already spiritually rehabilitated enough. But given that kind of moxie by God, becoming human beings in the manner of God's great, sometimes shaky, plan of incarnation may well be more doable.

But how? By choosing to be, that's how. Here we are, charged with spiritual energies beyond our most fanciful conception. And here we are, suited out in all this human hardware whose very first gift as God imagines us is the freedom to choose. Our tradition tells us that to be created in the image of God means we are free to choose to be loving, to be reasonable, to be creative, and to live in harmony with God and all God's creation. And God, in the giving, tells us also that we are also free to dump the whole gift down the trash chute. That we end up making a mix of all these favors and privileges is what makes the party so exciting.

But there it is and no less. Not a one of us who has ever tried these freedoms could ever claim that such an owner's manual and job description doesn't turn out altogether quite well. On the other hand, the evidence not only suggests, but proves on the whole how unstewardly we are at all levels of our society.

We're making a mess of the environment and giving everybody asthma. Millions live below the poverty level while millions more benefit on their backs from irresponsible taxation and corporate welfare. We restrict morality to the bedroom and exempt it from the Pentagon's war room and the White House's oval office.

All this freedom to choose started out and was quickly thwarted in Eden. It was redeemed in Gethsemane, once again reinvigorated at Pentecost, and set forth on the Way which is coming our way. When we get it all straight and get our humanity more or less up to speed, then maybe we can take a shot at that water again and show old Peter a thing or two.

Ninth Sunday after Pentecost *C

Cocktails

And forgive us our sins, for we ourselves forgive everyone indebted to us. (Luke 11:4)

Once upon a time, there was a cocktail party. Heaven only knows why, but I was there. Along with whatever else I had in my hand, there was this small paper napkin. As small paper cocktail napkins seem to go, this one displayed a message. It said, "To err is human. To forgive is out of the question."

Luke's accounting of things this morning starts off with Jesus at prayer and the disciples standing around waiting for him to finish. When he finally does, one of them asks, Why don't you teach us how to do that? Now one would think that the disciples of all people would by now already know how to do that, but not so, not the way Luke tells it.

So Jesus gives them a quick answer, like maybe he's given it some thought more than once, and like any good Jew would teach, that is, by not answering questions before they're asked. It's a lesson any parent or, for that matter, any parson should learn early on but rarely does.

Jesus tells them to use the prayer we've come to call after him, the Lord's Prayer. We might almost expect him to add, "found on page 364 in the *Book of Common Prayer* — and a lot of other places including the heads of pins and that it is rather an anchor in all our liturgies and that it is a prayer which if we're not careful can go in one ear and out the other," He might have, but he didn't.

There is a lot to say about the Lord's Prayer, but since I'm more or less stuck with my cocktail napkin story, it's that phrase in the Lord's Prayer about forgiveness that I'd like to talk about. By the time it got to us, that phrase became "forgive us our trespasses, as we forgive those who trespass against us." Some others use "debts" and "debtors," instead, and we've got a newer translation about sins and sinners, all of which I suppose is because "trespassing" is hardly common parlance except maybe largely to show up on barbed wire fences out in the country and yard signs that say "No" along with "Beware of the Dog."

"To err is human, to forgive is out of the question."

Like many good one-liners, that saying's of a truth. Forgiving a wrong — even especially one of our own mistakes — may be one of the most difficult choices we human beings ever face, and that, for some of us, we *never* face. Not the least of the reasons for this reluctance, I suspect, is not only the pain of bringing it up and fretting over it, but that the meaning of forgiving and forgiveness is pretty confusing stuff anyway and like Scarlett O'Hara said for those who can remember, often best thought about tomorrow.

First off, let's get rid of the notion that to forgive means also to forget. Hardly. Neither does forgiving mean that wrongs have no consequences nor any need for punishment nor that these things can be dismissed altogether.

"Further, Jesus is *not* saying that God's forgiveness is conditional upon our forgiving others. In the first place, forgiveness that's conditional isn't really forgiveness at all, just Fair Warning, and in the second place our unforgivingness is among those things about us which we need to have God forgive us most. What Jesus apparently *is* saying is that the pride which keeps us from forgiving is the same pride which keeps us from accepting forgiveness, and will God please help us do something about it." *(after Frederick Buechner, in "Wishful Thinking," on page 29)*

To forgive — and the meaning is always close with to reconcile — means at least that if at all possible, we're keeping the channels open, the relationship intact. Forgiveness allows us to reexamine our roles in family and in church and in society. For even hostile communication is better than none. And this applies to all levels and kinds of relationships from the intimately personal to the radically public international and geopolitical. Like the Baptismal Covenant says, Christ is in our neighbor whatever the size, whether next door, or across town, or on the other side of the planet.

But there is still another take on forgiveness, and it may be the most important of all. We should forgive simply because it is of the essence of good mental health and sanity. For those unable to forgive are indeed unable to accept forgiveness, let alone their own and that of others, but also unable to accept the forgiveness of God's Holy Spirit who is the very agent and source of forgiveness and reconciliation. The refusal to accept God's forgiveness is ultimately and precisely what the gospel calls the "unforgivable sin," the blasphemy against the Holy Spirit. Because *we* will not allow ourselves to be forgiven, God's freely given grace respects even our faulty judgment. In the last analysis and perhaps most important of all, those of us unable to forgive will ultimately be consumed by our own pain and anger. Those of us dining at the table of smug self-righteousness will find that we are dining on ourselves.

Personalities aside, take the terrible wrong committed against us and against all humankind that we've come to call 9/11. We seem to justify almost anything, any kind of behavior in response to that, even to jeopardizing our own blessed system of governing ourselves and sacrificing thousands of lives more, to compensate for it. *But rarely if ever do we hear about forgiving it.* May we never lose sight that as difficult and unreasonable as it might be and though 9/11 is something we will never forget, *it is something we must inevitably forgive.* Otherwise, so much for the Lord's Prayer and so much for this notion of our being a Christian nation.

It's up to us, of course, and to God's grace, whether we ever forgive anything, personal or public, individual or international. Yet, it is still ours to give, not only for our own spiritual well being, but for that of our people, our nation, and ultimately for that of the entire world. We must remember. We must never forget. But we must, as well, forgive. We are not exempt from that apparent burden and neither then are we denied that obvious blessing.

So we're not talking only about individuals in a family or a congregation where love and forgiveness might be more readily accessible, where the steps outlined in the gospel just might more likely be followed. We're talking about a whole country. But just as countries or nations make clumsy at loving their neighbors, just so are they altogether maladroit at forgiving. But there is a reason, and there is a way.

We are a nation already proven vulnerable precisely because of our commitment to liberty and justice that has been used as a terrifying and devastating weapon against us. But the irony is that it is these very principles, themselves, at national and international levels, that are the stuff of forgiveness and reconciliation. Loving never has cured its own vulnerability, and it never will. It only makes it more so.

We must ask, then, How does a nation enter into reconciliation? What are the instruments of justice and liberty? How are they manifest? By vengeance? By isolation and withdrawal and unilateral action? By denial and arrogance? By breaking promises? By dissimulation? It should be obvious from our own personal experience that these not only prolong, but as well, intensify hostility and resentment and the postponement of any possible resolution into a peaceful community, whatever the size — be it only two people or two trillion.

The clue is in our Declaration of Independence where our founders made a startling offer. Their offer had as much to do with our nature and with what we wanted to become as a nation as almost any other of those great documents that signaled our founding. In the prologue to the Declaration, we express that "a decent respect to the opinions of [humankind] requires that [we] should declare the causes which impel [us] to the separation [from Great Britain]."

And then we said, as we outlined our grievances, "let [these] facts be submitted to a candid world." And then, near the end, we appealed to the "Supreme Judge of the world for the rectitude of our intentions…" It is clear that the Declaration of Independence is in fact a declaration of *inter*dependence. For this nation to enter into a multilateral mode of forgiving and a desire for true reconciliation, we must first keep our own founding commitments clearly in mind and what is more, we must practice them among ourselves. How profound it might be to begin by asking forgiveness for ourselves both from this country's Native Americans and from our fellow African Americans for the many wrongs we have committed against them. And we can use our political inheritance to that end. One of the most important steps we can take in that direction is not to let our fear and its ensuing anxiety and anger, resentment and guilt, no matter how justified, distort our system of government, hamper our capacities to use it fully and honorably, and blind our vision to be and to become who and what we are.

This American political experiment begun by our founders is currently on precarious times. Not only is it in jeopardy from without, but, as well, in peril from within by an all too casual, passive, and permissive manipulation of its impressively and uniquely balanced systems of justice.

So let us take this heritage and this commitment once again to ourselves. Let us start with our churches. Let us ever more renew our Baptismal Covenant and the posture of forgiveness and justice at its heart. Let us reach out to one another in all the ways we can find appropriate for us and our system. Let us choose and call on our leaders in church and state to enlighten the minds and stir the consciences of all. We've spent untold amounts of our wealth on war over the ages and millions have died, so often in vain. Might that wealth have better been spent on preventing poverty and genocide and on adequate health care and clean air?

Justice is always compromised precisely as forgiveness and reconciliation diminishes. War never has winners, it has only losers. The message on the cocktail napkin was uncomfortably close to accurate, but for us, it must say, instead, that to err may be human, but to forgive must never be out of the question or, as is often said these days, "off the table."

God's criteria are always love and justice and peace for all, including our enemies. St Paul put it a bit differently when he said forgiving our enemies is a good thing because it heaps coals of fire on their heads. Oscar Wilde had a similar idea. "Always forgive your enemies," said. "Nothing annoys them so much."

And then, if these criteria don't move you. Do it anyway — because Jesus said so.

Tenth Sunday after Pentecost *C

Stuff

All I have toiled for under the sun and now bequeath to my successor I have come to hate; who knows whether he will be wise or a fool? Yet he will be master of all the work into which I have put my efforts and wisdom under the sun. That is futile, too. (Ecclesiastes 2:18-19)

But God said to him, "You fool! This very night your life is being demanded of you. And the things you have prepared, whose will they be?" (Luke 12:20)

A few years ago when we remodeled a major part of our home, one of the things that had to go was the garage. When it came to cars, it never was much of a garage anyway, but when it came to stuff and getting things out of sight and out of mind, it was a splendid example of ingenious irresponsibility

It's now a handsome kitchen and library of which we're also irresponsibly proud. But then, without the old garage, there was still all that stuff which it had previously contained quite handsomely.

The rich man in the parable this morning brings all this to mind. Certainly not because of his wealth, but mainly because he got rid of his stuff by building a barn, and we got rid of ours by building a shed.

He stored his plentiful crops. We stored our plentiful stuff. You know — the mower, the backhoe, the old paint cans and plant food, the Christmas tree stand, assorted old tools and license plates, and, of course, the left overs of my once upon a time career as a geologist, ie, the box of my favorite rocks. It's the one the movers always ask, "do they go?"

The propers this morning are altogether discomforting for pack rats. That old cynic who wrote Ecclesiastes thought everything is just blowing in the wind. But still, he's accumulated a lot that's very valuable to him, and he's anguishing over whether it will be inherited by a wise person or a fool. He knows surely that it'll be a fool and will be got by somebody who didn't work for it at all, let alone work as hard as he did. I worry like that. But I figure that most of our stuff will just be thrown out.

It's not all that easy to get rid of stuff and even harder to think that somebody else might not appreciate it at all and might not want it around as much as we do. We churchers can learn a lot from that, not just about our own personal rat-packing, but about the incessant need some of us have to live in the past and to turn the church into a kind of religious and institutional warehouse with a St Whosit Storage Pod on every corner complete with a Museum Mission Statement.

All this is not to belittle the past. Far from it. John Steinbeck in *The Grapes of Wrath* has a character ask an important question, "How will we know it's us without our past?" We need to remember and to be reminded always that we are the spiritual children of Abraham and Sarah and Hagar, of Isaac and Rebekah, and of Jacob and Leah, and someone added Hazel once, but I never knew why. There is no way to live into, appreciate, and understand our Christian heritage without that past, no way to keep track of who we are. But neither is there any healthy way merely to live only in the past, for to do so is to lose track not only of who we are but of who we can become. Paradoxically, if all we do is live in the past, of course, there will be no past for us. It will merely turn in on itself in a kind of moebius strip of being, one of those two-dimensional bands with no beginning and no end — and no depth. We'll not be creating our past. Our past will be creating us.

Our faith tradition says of human being that we are imagined by God to be free to choose: to love, to create, to reason, to live in harmony with all of creation and with God. Such imaginative choosing creates the past. But such imagination, as well, opens us to the future. That perceptive Roman Catholic nun Sister Joan Chittister put it this way, "Nothing we do changes the past. Everything we do changes the future."

The church will only die if, like the cynic in Ecclesiastes, it doesn't honor the past, it doesn't live in the present, and it doesn't trust the future. Like the rich man storing up his past, it will simply commit suicide from overdosing on itself and suffocation. We do well to see in these stories today the truth also seen by the Zen poet who wrote: "I do not seek to follow in the footsteps of those of old. I seek the things they sought."

Eleventh Sunday after Pentecost *A

Gardens

From then onwards Jesus began to make it clear to his disciples that he was destined to go to Jerusalem and suffer grievously at the hands of the elders and chief priests and scribes and to be put to death and to be raised up on the third day. (Matthew 16:21)

"I never promised you a rose garden."

That's the often familiar copout when the chore we took on for somebody doesn't turn out as comfy as we thought it might. I don't know why roses. Rose gardens are lovely, but anybody who ever planted one knows they're no snap to nurse, and that their thorns last a lot longer than their blooms.

Being faithful to the call of God is like that. Do it, and life right away is likely to get complex and tumultuous as well as simple and peaceful. The stories from Jeremiah and Paul and Jesus that make up today's lections can all testify to this. The common theme? Faithfulness will either get you nowhere or maybe somewhere you'd rather not be.

Jeremiah tangles with God's dynamic and swings between faith and doubt, peace and turmoil, certainty and confusion *(Jer 15:15-21)*. Paul's commitment to the Gentiles only drives a deeper wedge between himself and the Jews *(Rms 12:1-21)*. Jesus's certain awareness of the perils ahead challenges the loyalties of his disciples and puts their relationship on very shaky ground *(Mt 16:21-26)*.

Any church worth its salt lives in this kind of tension all the way from leaving its doors open 24/7 and risking theft and vandalism to exposing — even "wasting" — its program and budget in the interest of the sick and the poor and dispossessed. Too many of us never get that far being preoccupied with orthodox niceties like we so often are. Faith is always risky and even clumsy, especially when we try to use canon law and discipline as instruments for grace and love.

Today's church is too often busy setting standards for membership in pew and pulpit and requiring of its clergy to withhold its blessing for love wherever and in whatever form we may find it. When Jesus sets his demand for discipleship — Take up your cross and follow me — it's not in terms of rules to be followed or specific tasks to be accomplished. He talks about the need for us to get out of the way of ourselves with an open invitation to follow him when we have not the vaguest notion where his Way will lead and are not all that sure that he does, either. In short, to let go and let God. As well with Paul's counsel to the Romans. "Do not be conformed to this world... " but be "transformed by the renewal of your mind" Do not be conformed to the world's obsession with the symbols of power and prestige, but be transformed in Christ. Do not be conformed by and to the exploitation of others, but be transformed by letting your love be genuine. Do not be conformed to the way of vengeance and hatred, but bless them that persecute you and, as Jesus urged, even love them and offer them justice.

acing the world's current traumas, how is such a ministry informed and shaped? What might the world's families be like now had our response to 9/11 been to set out to conquer poverty and genocide by pouring our billions into such a mission rather than into the explosive and interminable violence of Iraq? How might the victims of 9/11 and their families feel about our giving love and generosity and justice in their name and the memory of their loved ones? How might our armies of death now function and what might they have accomplished had we enlisted them rather as legions of peace? What if we had truly risked modeling our constitutional democracy as a palpable community of justice more consistent with our founding rather than trying to transplant it into a cultural soil not all that fecund and receptive?

I don't remember any rose gardens ever figuring in the gospel scheme of things. But I do remember a couple of memorable gardens that did. Eden and Gethsemane stand prominent in our tradition. One, a garden of irresistible temptation, another, a garden of redemptive commitment.

Twelfth Sunday after Pentecost *A

Presence

Luke said that Jesus said, *"Do you think that I have come to give peace on earth?"* *(Luke 12:51a)* and Matthew added, as if for good measure, *"I have not come to bring peace, but a sword."* *(Matthew 10:34)*

From the way these two figured it, the Prince of Peace had had it. "You want peace? I'll show you peace." Anybody who'd thought it was all rock and roll from there on out had to have got another think coming. It reminds me of the critic whose ire was also up when she reviewed a complete dramatic production in only one sentence. "The scenery in the play was beautiful, but the actors got in front of it."

Peace and justice and love make for splendid scenery, indeed. And there've been moments of late when we can almost sense their breaking through into action. But then we Christians can't handle it and get in front of it to make our point. Like Gandhi said, "I've no brief with Christianity. It's the Christians I cannot abide."

If Jesus doesn't just plain zap us soon, then it makes one wonder if he's even paying attention. No, I take that back. It's just that maybe you can, but I simply cannot understand grace and love. I know it couldn't be the sweeping paternalism and mindless offers of tranquility that masquerade for so much of the Christian religion in our day and time. It's certainly not the schmarmy patronage and goody-two-shoes father-knows-best-ism of the Anglican Network panderers. But I trust and I'm confident the scenery of the Good News is back there somewhere if these pretenders would just clear the stage.

Dorothy Sayers lamented how this Jesus is so often made into a "household pet for little old ladies and pale curates," reminding us of those bucolic portraits that line the walls and counters of so many so-called "Christian" bookstores. I can't imagine Jesus would have a lot of patience with his peace being conjectured as such a serene, chicken-soup caprice of the gospel.

Peace on earth and good will to all? Were the angels smoking dope? Prince of Peace? Is this simply a misnomer? "The peace of the Lord be with you…" Is it all mere liturgical fakery?

Well, yes. Until we realize, as Frederick Buechner put so well, "the contradiction is resolved when you realize that for Jesus peace seems to have meant not the absence of struggle but the presence of love." Our new Presiding Bishop hails us so often with the ancient Judaeo-Christian salutation "Shalom" which means the fullness and strength of having everything you need to be wholly and happily yourself. Maybe Jesus is suggesting that if not a sword, then at least a scalpel and some major spiritual surgery to bring that to pass.

The church can be such a presence and simply and devastatingly recall us to the beautiful scenery of loving God and neighbor and self, then firmly remind us to let God… let go, and then get out of the way, singing the old hymn that got it so right. "The peace of God, it is no peace, but strife closed in the sod. Yet let us pray for but one thing — the marvelous peace of God" *(1982 Hymnal # 661).*

Thirteenth Sunday after Pentecost *C

Timing

"The ruler of the synagogue, indignant because Jesus had healed on the Sabbath, said to the people, 'There are six days on which work ought to be done; come on those days and be healed, and not on the sabbath day.'" (Luke 13:14)

Jesus's breaking of the sabbath seems pointless and unnecessary. He is not performing a good deed that, if delayed, would become unperformable. This is not a person who needs immediate rescue, not a person lying unconscious in a burning house. This woman has been ill for 18 years. Why in God's good name can't Jesus wait out the afternoon and cure her without flying in the face of the Torah? Why can't he sit with her till sunset and use the time to center her mind on the graciousness of God? Why can't they search the Scriptures together and set the stage so that the healing will be seen in all its unquestionable rightness? What is the point of this unnecessary muddying of the water?

Whenever someone attempts to introduce a radically different insight to people whose minds have been formed by an old and well-worked-out way of thinking, he is up against an obstacle. The new insight is always at odds with the old way of looking at things. The only intellectual devices we have to pick it up with are the categories of the old system with which it conflicts. We will go to those devices rather than to the point being made and, having done that, we will understand the new only insofar as it can be made to agree with the old — which is not at all.

Jesus constantly announces the coming kingdom in words and deeds that run counter to the people's expectations for the kingdom. He comes from Galilee, from where no prophet comes. He talks with a Samaritan — and a woman, which no decent male Jew would do. He eats with tax collectors and sinners. He is accused of being a glutton and a drunkard. He directly confronts their understanding of the Sabbath Laws. Eventually he will die as an accursed criminal on a cross.

We want to "see" Jesus through the lens of our own understanding of what a savior should be like. As long as we "see" in this way, we cannot see.

Jesus instructs them with a constant awareness that the one thing they must not do is see, because they would see wrong, nor understand, because they would only misunderstand. For he knows that the only thing that can save them — himself, in the mystery of his death and resurrection — is the one thing they cannot accept on their present view of salvation. One way of dealing with an unappetizing message, is to kill the messenger.

Accordingly, he gives them not one thing to confirm their present view — or, more accurately, he always includes one solidly unacceptable thing on which their minds will gag.

Generally, if we are stuck in a system or a particular way of understanding, it helps to be startled out of the old and into the new. Logic and reason usually doesn't work. Just try to convince people about making changes in the church. Jesus could have spent all day arguing with the synagogue leader about whether or not it was legal to heal this woman on the sabbath all the while she remained ill. How many of our meetings are discussions about what should be done, rather than actually getting things done? This healing of the woman took place before the discussion about whether or not it was the right thing to do. When should we just do things that we believe are right, and then deal with the repercussions afterwards? When do we need to discuss and come to an agreement before taking action?

Systems theory indicates that any time someone upsets the balance — the comfortable way we are used to, someone is likely to sabotage the plans and attack the one making them. Being pushed out of balance causes anxiety. Anxiety provokes anger. Anger threatens our good health both individually and as a community.

It is always astounding the way Jesus's actions millennia ago remain so relevant.

Fourteenth Sunday after Pentecost *A

About

"Have I no right to do what I like with my own? Why should you be envious because I am generous? Thus the last will be first, and the first, last." (Matthew 20:15-16)

There must surely be better times than these for to tell a Bible economics story, especially the parable of the Workers in the Vineyard. But come to think more about it, in our work-ethic, merit-rewarding society, there's never been a good time for this story. It has always been an absolute plague either for labor or management. Those caught up in both 21st century America and its miasma of biblical literalism must wish to skip the whole matter. But it's a parable about the kingdom of God, not the economy of western culture, and we churchers can't just stand here with our fingers crossed behind our backs.

Thus and so, if it's a parable about the kingdom, it's a parable about grace. We've an economy based on merit, some think it's full of voodoo. And the two — grace and merit — have never mixed all that well. Grace. Will we ever hear the end of it? Grace is inevitably, sooner or later, always a pain in our pride, right where God plants his foot. Until we find out what grace is about, what the kingdom of heaven is about, nothing about this Gospel will ever make much sense, for even so, it'll never make sense anyway because making sense is not the way of Jesus's good news.

"About" is a good word to start with. With that word, Irma Rombauer in her *Joy of Cooking* gives us a clue to understanding Jesus. With each new food entry, Irma writes a short piece concerning what it's about. About meat. About sweet potatoes. About berries. Even if you're not a cook, you know the drill. If you don't cook, look at the book, anyway. It's a charming little thing she does, always what it's about, not what it is. Well, so does Jesus. The kingdom of God is about, he says, not the kingdom of God is, but what it is about, what it is like. It's about a careless shepherd, it's about a widow's small change, and on and on.

The whole Bible is an about book, not an is book. So with life, so with us, each of us and all of us are parables. We are parables emulating Jesus who is the Parable of God. Jesus is not God. He himself said he wasn't God. Jesus is about God. So, with grace, so with the payroll for the laborers in the vineyard. It is precisely where we turn all these analogies upside down and take then literally, that we emasculate the Good News.

One of the big troubles with religion is how difficult it is to get this straight. Religion wants to be an is way of handling grace instead of an about way. On the other hand faith is an about way. Religion needs faith to keep it honest. Faith needs religion — or a reasonable facsimile — and pretty near any religion's as good as the next — like we need our bodies, to keep us between the curbs. But the two are never the same.

So, the kingdom of heaven is never a place, but a relationship with God nourished by grace and implemented by faith. It is a story, a parable, and, like all good stories, it leaves much to the imagination. It is for this relationship that we are imagined by God and freed to sign on in the vineyard at the beckon of the landowner and at whatever time we choose. Or, we can just stand around shuffling back and forth outside the unemployment office.

Fifteenth Sunday after Pentecost / Holy Cross Day *C

Cross

"Whoever does not bear his own cross and come after me, cannot be my disciple." (Luke 14:25-33)

Our time is consumed by war. We're in one war that's finally wandering down the path to closure and another that seems casually aimless to wherever. We were told at the outset of all this eight years ago not to worry, just to go shopping, that evil's not going to be all that hard to whip. Then we were told just to go relax, it was over. And you know the rest. The rest is tens of thousands of deaths, a trillion dollars spent, and an economy in ruins.

Historian Barbara Tuchman once defined war as the unfolding of such miscalculations. It's a definition that's not lost much if any of its purchase. It is likely that she had in mind the kind of war that had nations at each other's throats hoping that the winner will be better off. Or maybe, at least, that the other fellow will be worse off, or maybe then settling for the satisfaction that he's certainly not any better off, and finally, surrendering to the great surprise that whaddya know? Everybody's worse off.

Ms Tuchman was right. We've kept on keeping on, one miscalculation after another. Looking back over human history, war seems hopelessly inevitable. Some sociologists have argued that warring is in our very nature, even going so far as to suggest that we somehow delight in it.

Theologian Jack Gessell spoke of war as an inappropriate adolescent response to enormous frustration. He wrote that war is a failure of intelligence, imagination, and politics. That it is the failure of the human spirit. That justice requires that we do better than this to secure peace in today's world.

"Whoever does not bear his own cross and come after me, cannot be my disciple."

Is it not possible that war may well be our cross? Was Jesus warning us about something like this when he talked about discipleship and taking up one's cross? He had some very hard words for this vocation of cross-bearing, about it somehow meaning we must surrender things that are very dear to us. Maybe in and for our time it means refusing to choose war as any kind of solution. Maybe Gessell is right. "War is a failure of the human spirit. Justice requires that we do better than this to secure peace in today's world." When Jesus's cross of peace and justice becomes our cross, perhaps it will show us the way and remind us that justice is Jesus's way.

Bearing a cross finally has less to do with the way we engage hardships that come our way than what we do as a consequence of commitment to Jesus… not to a creed or a catechism, but to a person and to his way, his truth, and his life. It's not the popular and faddish "What would Jesus do." It is rather the totally commanding commitment "What would Jesus be…" a being that determines and defines a doing far more than the other way around.

The church nowadays talks a lot about discipleship, about "planting" churches to "make disciples" as if we're taking on some sort of celestial gardening project. The church doesn't talk much about taking up a cross, unless it's one of those designer models in the parish book store or that we hold on high to lead processions. There's actually an adult education program afoot to "take Christ to the Muslims." Maybe taking up our cross can mean to become a disciple rather to enable Muslims to worship with justice and peace and in their own way. Surely that would surpass taking the risk of steadily being into one miscalculation after another.

Jesus's hard words in this gospel do not say that one cannot become a disciple, but that one cannot be a disciple apart from complete commitment to following him. It's not a part-time job. The call to be a disciple is all-consuming. It's no wonder to me there seem to be so few of us. But the irony is the continuing joy and wonder time and again to find that there are any at all.

Sixteenth Sunday after Pentecost *C

Excess

"Just so, I tell you, there is joy in the presence of the angels of God over one sinner who repents." (Luke 15:10)

There's a certain sort of excess in Jesus that I used to find outrageous, but increasingly now find absolutely joyful.

He zaps helpless fig trees. He sleeps on the fantail of a boat in a hurricane. He feeds thousands with next to nothing. He praises a shepherd who'd ignore ninety-nine beetleheaded sheep just to go after one that's lost. He heals. He admonishes. He predicts, and he indicts. He commends a poor widow who finds a lost coin and spends whatever others she has left just to celebrate. He makes one wonder whether the gospel's not only about change, but also about small change.

And this is the son in whom God is proud and to whom God also wants us to listen? This is the one for whom we should seek in our neighbor? This is what happens when the Word becomes flesh? This is the Way? The Truth? The Life? The Christ?

Well… Yes.

It's no wonder the tax collectors and sinners were curious. The prophets may have been easily enough ignored, but not this. They could identify with Jesus even for no other reason than his apparent profligacy, a certain kind of recklessness that in a way rather confirmed their own. And it's no wonder the religious leaders and lesser satraps got even stiffer in their necks than usual. One audience with him, and all their careful religion school curriculum was either ready for rewrite or else down the drain.

Is there any conceivable message for us, his church, his disciples, those of us gathering together Sunday in and Sunday out in his name? Maybe. Perhaps the tithe is more like ninety percent than ten. It's all finders-keepers with the rest.

But then... When God imaged us, was it not to be free to choose, to love, to create, to reason, to live in harmony with God and all creation? That's not so difficult to imagine, now, is it? Except maybe the harmony part. No, but it's often a total pain to make a go of it. Rather does it seem if we're going to be "religious" at all, we'd prefer to make religion into a mold out of which we could make faithful people, a corporate endeavor to make faith both memorable and manageable.

What Jesus wants is faith, that one sheep, that one lost coin, not the religion that would control it. For faith is always risk, not certainty. Jesus had no place to lay his head. He had no altar, not even a pew. Why should that be so important to us? We are so often asking what Jesus would *do*, when what Jesus would *be* seems the more central, the more daring thing. The church and we its members are about healing and mending. This is our ministry. If our religion and its liturgies do not support that, do not point us that way, if Jesus's excesses do not excite and inspire us, then maybe we might consider attending again the way we have chosen.

Seventeenth Sunday after Pentecost *A

Few

For many are called, but few are chosen." (Matthew 22:14)

The Japanese name for Korea is "Chosen." The U S Marine veterans who fought there in that mid-twentieth century misunderstanding rightly call themselves, "The Chosen Few."

Now that I've got that homiletic spin out of the way, what on earth was Matthew talking about that Jesus was talking about? How has the Chosen Few, an aphorism that has stood so well and so perplexingly down through the ages, attached to the story of a desperate and fickle king like that told in today's gospel?

Maybe it was because Matthew was a bit fickle, himself, and was throwing his evangelical weight around. Maybe it was a hint to is neighbor Luke not to take himself so seriously. Frankly, one may wonder, as some authorities do, whether Jesus ever said it at all. But there it is as plain as mud in the scriptural canon for all time. One reason I believe it has is that the Holy Spirit has a lot to do with what is said there, including what Jesus says there, and with how the church interprets what is said there and, unlike Luke, we'd best take it more seriously than not what is said there.

"For many are called, but few are chosen." One dare not overlook that what we do with our lives and the choices that demands are at the very core of our Baptismal Covenant. Surely there are no more important concepts about the life in Christ than vocation and choice. The Greek word for church is ekklesia. It means something like "those who are called out." The very characteristic of what it means to be a human being is not only to be called, to have a vocation, but also and perhaps even more distinctively, the capacity, the freedom to choose that calling — or to refuse it. This is what it means to be created in the image of God. This is what God means by imagining us into being.

Jesus realized that God had a special calling for him when he confronted Satan out there in those early forty devastating days in the wilderness. He was still wrestling with that calling as late as Gethsemane where he sweated blood trying to get it straight about God's will for him. We must never overlook that he said Yes, and that that Yes may be the saving act, itself, part with the cross. Vocation and choice.

"For many are called, but few are chosen."

Maybe that means that God calls a lot of us, maybe all of us, to be his church. Maybe it means not that God chooses only a few, for, after all, he's called us all, but that only a few of us exercise the freedom to choose or not to choose his calling, which probably means whether or not we choose to be human as God has imagined human to be. Let us understand the church, the called, to be where we work out that vocation and perfect it, where we follow through on it and become not only the chosen few, but, as well, the few who choose.

Eighteenth Sunday after Pentecost *B

Deed

John said to him, "Teacher, we saw someone casting out demons in your name, and we tried to stop him, because he was not following us." But Jesus said, "Do not stop him; for no one who does a deed of power in my name will be able soon afterward to speak evil of me. Whoever is not against us is for us." (Mark 9:38-39)

I suppose there's a certain comfort in having an "exclusive," in being the only one to know about something and to break the news and to claim the rewards. News media and especially their reporters understandably get a lot of mileage out of such exclusive stories.

Apparently, it was no different with the disciples of Jesus. They were the "in" group, the ones who'd been commissioned not just with a message, but with a unique authority to heal and even with a power greater than daemons. They were discovering grace, but embracing that novelty had a steep learning curve and was still not without a residual touch of merit — as, indeed, it is yet for us. They may well have been remembering painfully what it had cost them and what risks they'd taken and continued to take by throwing in their lot with this Jesus. So when they discovered they weren't the only ones with this new mastery, that there were others in on the Jesus trail and who had apparently not made such sacrifices, one can understand how their noses got altogether out of joint.

Strangely, things are not a lot different now. We Anglican/ Episcopal Christians tend to get a little smug ourselves from time to time. I'm speaking, of course, from my own bias, but not, I think, without reason. The early 20th century evangelist Billy Sunday called us the "sleeping giant of Christendom," implying that we really didn't know what we had in our tradition or even worse that if we did, we were not much about using it. Billy Graham once told a group of us clergy that his pattern and plan for mission was simply that defined in the Archbishop of Canterbury's Commission on Evangelism. He also wondered out loud why we never used it ourselves.

The present discomforts in our Communion which rend our hearts as well as our fabric seem not all that dissimilar from those that provoked Jesus's disciples. Some insist that we are not an inclusive church. That strikes me as but another way of saying that we are an exclusive church.

"Whoever is not against us is for us." This new gospel of God's love is about God loving and including all, not just those who follow some strict doctrinal line or who stand in what we've made and called in these latter years an "apostolic succession," what the disciples could easily have meant when they said the man casting out daemons was "not following us."

I believe that as clumsy and messy as it is, the collegial polity in the American and perhaps the Canadian church is surely a way of achieving the healing justice and love that continues to be altogether consistent with "Jesus's name." It is an albeit ponderous way for seeking and serving "Christ in all persons, [and] loving [our] neighbors as [ourselves]" as we have committed to do in our Baptismal Covenant. Just so does this story of the distraught and subsequently admonished disciples reinforce the very inclusiveness of grace and justice, healing and well-being that are of the gospel's substance and that now rise to the nub of the church's present malaise. The disciples wanted a corner on this ministry they'd risked their lives for. Who can blame them? Many of their latter-day successors — risk or no — today seem to think they should have one, too.

Perhaps it is another story at another time, but this is also a story about witnessing. Witnessing, not simply as telling our own faith, our own stories, but witnessing as pointing to wherever we see these same gospel signs by whatever name and "performed" by whomever, commissioned and ordained or no. Jesus was quite clear about that.

The New Testament scholar and Lutheran bishop Krister Stendahl once put it like this: Wherever we witness the brokenness of the world being mended, there is present the Kingdom of God.

Nineteenth Sunday after Pentecost *B

Human

"What God has joined together…" (Mark 10:9)

One of my more interesting and sometimes more intriguing heresies (to me, at least) suggests that if Jesus was as fully human as God intended and as we believe and he could, for example, walk on water, then if we were as fully human as God intends us to be, so could we. I am not alone in this opinion, for no less a narrative theologian than Madeleine L'Engle makes this point in her book, *Walking On Water.*

Since we apparently don't seem to be able to walk on water (and I don't know of any evidence of anybody else being able to, maybe with the exception of Peter who took a few steps and sank, and of a few others who imagine they could if challenged), then we've either forgot how or don't hold our mouths right or just don't concentrate or maybe just don't care one way or the other. It also occurs to me that being human, fully or otherwise, also includes being a creature of one's own time, era, history, environment, ambiance, whatever. Whether our unique characteristics are determined only by DNA or by environment or by both, it's pretty hard to avoid the effect of the times and, of course, of the integral human beings that we are, connecting with one another in all the ways which this insists upon. The me is we and unavoidably so. So, then, with Jesus, himself. Indeed, he was so fully himself, the self God intends — "this is my beloved son in whom I am well pleased… " etcetera — and we take such a dim view of what being human means that we're razzle-dazzled into imagining that he simply must be divine if for no other reason than that we cannot come up with a better description or definition of what we see and hear. "To err is human," we hear so often, "to forgive is divine." Such a statement as, "I am only human," is, of course, an insult to God. *(cf BCP p 845, entry: Human nature)*

We dare not, however, let that divinity, which is far more than we can ever imagine, distract from or diminish Jesus's humanity — as we are often wont to do. Like the question, "Did Jesus know about television and jet engines." Of course not. There's plenty of evidence for all this contained in the Passion Narrative if you're too busy to read or reread the gospels.

Maybe none of this "floats your boat" as they say, but it does, I suspect, help understand Jesus's comments about marriage in today's gospel. There's this about it, at least.

If Jesus's way of life is any indicator, marriage is obviously not essential to being human. Though one might argue that it certainly helps, perhaps even enhances. Nevertheless, the New Testament's picture of Jesus, the da Vinci Code to the contrary, is that it's not all that necessary. Second, though Jesus's affirmation about marriage is unequivocal, the church's subsequent tradition and reason is clearly more ambiguous than otherwise. The practice of multiple marriages may be said to be commonplace and, if reluctantly, no less accepted by the church, even among its bishops and other clergy.

This account of Jesus's words about marriage in Mark's gospel, "What therefore God has joined together, let not man put asunder," though it's obviously about marriage, seems even more importantly to be about authority, specifically biblical authority. It raises the continuing question of how Anglicanism views authority as threefold, the scriptures being the normative tradition of the Christian faith essential as parameter and guideline for all subsequent decisions and moral action. The remaining balance pertaining to tradition, that is, how the church as understood biblical morality as affected by the times and mores down through the centuries, and to reason, how that understanding has been formulated.

The Lambeth conferences beginning in 1867 and meeting every decade have served to interpret scripture and tradition and have illustrated well for the Communion how temporal environment affects opinion. They are descriptive and reflective, not definitive and are only a part of the total authoritative fabric of the church as we understand it.

Such sayings of Jesus as this in today's gospel are perhaps easier to accept by those who view scripture as verbally inerrant. For Anglicans, they are received with profound respect and attention, but not as absolute. They are interpreted through the tradition of the times and through reason. It is altogether possible that we — and I — are especially wrong. God's grace tells us, however, not only that it may be right to be wrong, and that forgiveness is far more accessible than permission.

Twentieth Sunday after Pentecost *C

Bond

Then one of [the ten lepers], when he saw that he was healed, turned back, praising God with a loud voice. He prostrated himself at Jesus' feet and thanked him. And he was a Samaritan. Then Jesus asked, "Were not ten made clean? But the other nine, where are they?" (Luke 17:15-17)

In a *Doonesbury* comic strip, Mike is on a jet to New York, nervous, praying to "get a grip on himself." A part of his uneasiness comes from the fact that his seat mate is dark, wears a turban, has a mustache, needs a shave, and is talking on the phone about cash, a rental car, and a motel. Overhearing all this, Mike panics, confronts the man, and says in uncontrolled frustration, "Okay, look! I'm trying not to profile here." The man, interrupted, says into the phone, "Hold on a moment, will ya, mom?"

As different as we think we are (and we can come up with some doozies), we have a lot more in common with one another than we have in uncommon. Everybody has a mom and, of course, a dad, too, but somehow, the moms are more often better reminders of how close we are. Surely you've noticed that when the camera pans the crowd at the ball games and some people hold up a sign of greeting, it hardly ever says, "Hi, dad."

The story about Ruth and Naomi in the book of Ruth is a story that our lectionary architects omitted today. It is also a story about families, families not all that unlike our own. It is one of the better known and more heartwarming stories of all those in the biblical saga of our spiritual genealogy. Naomi, though a mother-in-law, mothers her sons' wives no less, actually all the more. This poignant tale of tragedy, love, and loyalty can, if we'll let it, be a pleasant comfort in our own time of fear and anxiety, anger and vengeance. *(Ruth 1:8-19a)*

The confusing and tormenting events of these times drive deep down within us and test the spiritual bedrock common to all human beings, regardless of how this manifests itself. They challenge us to be present to and to listen to others. Many of us yet need to share our continuing consciousness about 9/11 and our reactions to the war's recurring escalation. Our lives are being changed in dozens of ways, not to mention the ongoing changes that come in every cycle of life. In this season of terror, all this can get lost in the noise or downplayed as unimportant.

The gospel story tells of lepers, people to whom nobody listened, people cast out of society and made almost totally inaccessible. Their very presence created fear. They were accustomed to being rejected. Perhaps they'd heard of this Jesus and rightly suspected that he'd treat them differently. So they cried out to him, moving in closer than the safe distance required by the law. The story says that Jesus heard them and responded with healing words and with his usual compassion *(Lk 17:11-19)*.

In our times, we consider well Jesus's and Naomi's examples of warmth and reception, listening and healing. This is not a time for keeping a safe distance from other people. It is a time to draw close, to listen, to touch, to offer an embrace.

This spiritual genealogy we all share makes of us a common family, however it may reveal or not reveal itself. It calls forth from us our imaginations and the knowledge of our own occasions of loneliness, pain, grief, and joy. It can enrich our faith and open doors into new and unheard of experiences. Such faith-in-common is the key to discovering and appreciating the grace that today's collect reminds us "precedes and follows, making us continually given to all good works" *(Proper 23, BCP p 183)*.

Imagination, after all, is one of the most important ways that our faith is implemented and made incarnate. Can we not imagine, then, the healing bond that faith complimented when Ruth said to Naomi, "Where you go I will go, and where you lodge I will lodge; your people shall be my people, and your God my God..." *(Ruth 1:16b)*, and when Jesus said to the leper, "Rise and go your way; your faith has made you well" *(Lk 17:19b)*.

Twenty-first Sunday after Pentecost *B

Rank

"You do not know what you are asking." (Mark 10:38)

Bishop Daniel Corrigan was one of this church's remarkable servant leaders in the decades from the 1950s to the 1970s. His distinction combined both prophet and pastor in the very finest sense of those words. But among other skills, he was not above devilishly teasing and testing the old 1928 *Book of Common Prayer* around its somewhat rigid edges.

In the 1928 liturgy for Holy Communion, there was no form for a Dismissal following the Blessing as there is now. So perhaps you can imagine the shocked surprise of the hundreds assembled at a college work conference one time when Bishop Corrigan, presiding at the celebration, stood at the completion, pronounced the customary benediction, paused for that solemnly silent moment, then boldly dismissed the congregation in full voice, "Get up! Get out! And get lost!"

Mark's gospel reminds us that however we read our vocation as Christians, its center is always God's call to servant leadership. On this particular occasion along the way, we find those slow learners James and John continuing to do some insider trading on how Jesus plans to set up his hierarchy. "Grant us," they plead, "to sit one at your right hand and one at your left" *(Mk 10:35-45)*.

Perhaps they'd be pleased to know that their question is still alive. Beyond their fondest dreams and by some not altogether clear technicality, we Anglicans claim a continuity of clerical authority down through the ages that indeed also has a lot to do with where people sit. We call it "apostolic succession." Actually, it is a concept well-intended to conserve order, and sometimes it works quite well. Had Jesus thought of such a thing at all, however, it seems clear from his response to James and John, that he would never have intended apostolic succession merely for the purpose of "apostolic success." It recalls old journalistic curmudgeon H L Mencken's definition of an archbishop as a Christian ecclesiastic of a rank superior to that never attained by Jesus.

I'm not promising you any rose garden, Jesus says to the aspiring leaders. The others overhear this conversation and are instantly indignant. Then Jesus reminds them that this is not a Trinity Network production — no majestic thrones, no fancy threads, and no big hair — and that "it shall not be so among you; but whoever would be great among you must be slave of all. For the Son of man also came not to be served but to serve, and to give his life as a ransom for many."

Our Baptismal Covenant (BCP p 304f) is as neat a sum-up of what it means to be a Christian as one might ever imagine. It actually begins with a reminder of this scene with Jesus and his followers by asking us after all these centuries to "continue in the apostles' teaching and fellowship."

It rightly construes that fellowship as a collegial assembly through all the orders grounded in Holy Baptism and given appropriate shape as bishops serving priests, priests serving laity, and laity serving the world. Further, it understands apostolic teaching as that which honors equally and with no distinction the integrity of all people in a world rather like Garrison Keillor's up in Lake Wobegon where "all the women are strong, the men are good looking, and the children are all above average."

Even a casual look at church history reminds us that within hardly a century after Jesus's time, this revolutionary understanding of community disappeared into an ecclesial fog that had largely sold out to a secular/imperial model of rank and privilege and sexist discrimination that replaces respect with intimidation, awe with indifference, and grace with merit.

Is it any wonder, then, that we must be reminded by hearing the good news over and over as Mark recounts it that we — all of us — are called to lead in each of our respective capacities by serving?

Bennett Sims, one time bishop of Atlanta and founding president of the Institute for Servant Leadership, speaks to the church's viable realization of a New Testament integrity of servant leadership in this way:

"What is needed for hope's encouragement is to see that evolution is not first a matter of humanity improving morally, but of humanity rising to a higher level of consciousness — a new awareness that awakens to the fundamental relatedness of all life and finds its fullest joy in relationships that honor the integrity of all others. This, I believe," he continues, "is the meaning of peace. And it is the true source of any higher morality — not in admonitions or promises to do better, but in the emergence of a finer sensitivity to the dearness of the earth and the beauty of the souls of others." *("Servanthood," Cowley, 1997, p 174)*

The goal of our servanthood in whatever order from lay to bishop is to enable such things to happen. The church's ministry is not to admonish us or even to teach us to "be good," but to stir and awaken us to ourselves and our vocation. That vocation is to be a place where people can explore and share their awe over their deepest mysteries and commitments without intimidation and where a just peace reigns, a community whose posture, like God's, is one of persuasion through attraction.

As old Bishop Corrigan often charged us, may we "Get up, get out, and get lost" to engage our servanthood in the world, listening for our neighbors at work or home or ballpark or saloon or, indeed, even church, who are challenged by life's mysteries groping not only for answers but for ways to cope and be better stewards.

And may we show and tell them about a place — this place — that could aptly be called "searchers anonymous," where to sacrifice something is to make it sacred by giving it away for love and where they can be loved until they can discover how to love themselves and others. Such a place surely is at the "right hand" of Jesus.

Twenty-second Sunday after Pentecost *B

Reach

"Jesus, son of David, have mercy on me!" (Mark 10:47)

God is not established in our lives with the help of a dictionary or even by a course in systematic theology, but through a relationship. Whether it is a relationship of hostility or of hospitality, or of indifference, it is yet a relationship. For that is what matters.

It takes faith to have and to hold and to manage a relationship: God's faith in us, our faith in God, in ourselves, and in our neighbor. Such faith can and does open in us an imaginative consciousness and a willingness to risk laying our lives on the line. We simply cannot assume that God is any more accessible to us than we make ourselves accessible to God. Isaiah said it: "Seek the Lord while he wills to be found…" *(Is 55:6)*. God's creatively imagining us is built on that kind of freedom.

The story of old Blind Bartimaeus that Mark tells about in today's gospel is a case in point *(Mk 10:46-52)*. Bartimaeus cried out to Jesus for mercy. We cannot be absolutely sure how he wanted that mercy to take form and shape, but simply that it was overdue. He knew that this Jesus was a prime source, and that he was handing it out all over the place. Heaven knew he could use some simple mercy in his life in very much the same way as can we.

But mercy turned out to be more. It was not a laying on of hands or even a handout or even a handshake. Jesus never even touched Bartimaeus. It was simply Jesus stopping to listen. It was Jesus paying attention. Jesus said, "Call him." Jesus told his disciples to put aside their sense of urgency, to stop and to listen, to enable the beggar's cause, to encourage and to respect him as a fellow human being in need. That's the miracle, that kind of listening, that kind of attending is a reaching out that's always within reach for every one of us.

Healing moved between them in the vital and palpable conduit of the faith that connected them, that enabled them to share in the willful meeting of anguish and with a willful nourishment of compassion and concern. It was this that made them whole in relationship.

We have a similar exchange whenever we celebrate together a baptism in our churches. Obviously, we must never discount our faith as sponsors (whatever happened to that lovely word "godparents"?) and as parents, but also as the community surrounding the sacrament and giving our support and commitment and, indeed, for our faith. We can take with us that exchange, that moment of grace, along our own Jericho roadsides when we pray for others and even in those challenging moments when others are not all that enthusiastic about our praying for them. "Go your way," Jesus said to Bartimaeus, — and to us — "your faith has made you well." And immediately he received his sight and followed him on the way" *(Mk 10:52)*.

With that renewed sight — and with our renewed insight — we can also remember that Bartimaeus, even though offered the option to go once again on his own, chose Jesus's way, instead. That kind of miracle is readily within reach to us with the same prayer — "Jesus, have mercy."

Twenty-third Sunday after Pentecost *B

Justice

Jesus answered, "The first [commandment] is, 'Hear, O Israel: the Lord our God, the Lord is one; you shall love the Lord your God with all your heart, and with all your soul, and with all you mind, and with all your strength.' The second is this, 'You shall love your neighbor as yourself.' There is no other commandment greater than these." (Mark 12: 29-31)

It strikes me that the Great Commandment to love God and to love neighbor as oneself must surely have been easier to keep track of back during Jesus's time. Even if there was only one God then as there is now, surely there were a lot fewer neighbors.

On the other hand, justice and fairness were no less important. So, as Matthew tells us, the early church devised its own system of appeals to find it all the way from one-on-one — to only a few — to the whole community. If all that process failed, then it was down the chute along with all the other sinners. Although something tells me that not Jesus, but some of his confused followers came up with that "chute" idea.

This Great Commandment, this summary of the law and the prophets, talks about love, but it is also about justice. Justice is the way societies and institutions and governments best love one another. Justice is the way our nation began and once again has the opportunity to embrace the stricken Gulf Coast remembering how deeply connected are we all. Justice has always been the very heart of the gospel. A just peace for all continues as the thrust of the church's ministry and the message we proclaim in the name of God. Be it not only for the way we treat one another in our congregations, but be it also the way a diocese learns to live together and to use its energies in

God's name and not its own. And be it that way on and up to the highest courts in our land.

Hearing Jesus's counsel about a just society once again well serves to remind us and to recall us to that charge. We surely now don't want for enough neighbors on whom to practice.

But justice is on hard times. We are so distracted, it's difficult to do anything about it. Not long ago, in a church right here in our community and with a lot better media connections than we have, the religious right got considerable press claiming — actually judging, if the truth be known — that our courts are as bad and as dangerous as, if not worse, than the terrorists. A short time later, one of their patrons closed his case by recommending assassination be added to the simple and somewhat gentler appellate system just now suggested in Matthew's gospel. Lets hear it for terrorism.

This nation at its founding declared its interdependence with all nations and affirmed the notion that we are created equal... and endowed by our Creator with certain unalienable Rights, that among these are Life, Liberty and the pursuit of Happiness. — That to secure these rights, Governments are instituted among us, deriving their just powers from the consent of the governed. Further, our founders struck an international chord consistent with and resonant to the gospel understanding of human being when they wisely devised a system of justice by balancing authority in our judicial, legislative, and executive branches. They left us this legacy surely that we might be its beneficiaries, but even more importantly, its stewards. They certainly did not have in mind that it be hijacked by some or any religion and thus thrown into imbalance with total disregard for their wise counsel and, I might add, their understanding of the gospel and its Judaeo-Christian tradition.

But if Justice is the grammar of things, Mercy is the poetry. The Cross says something like the same thing on a scale so cosmic and so full of mystery that it is next to impossible to grasp. As it represents what in one way or another we are always doing to each other, the death of that innocent man hanging up there convicts us as the whole of humanity, and so it would seem that we deserve the grim world that over the centuries we have made for ourselves. As it also represents what one or another thing we are always doing not so much to God above us somewhere as to God within us everywhere. That is the justice of things.

But the Cross also represents the fact that the good is also present in the grim, and God is present even in the godless. That is why the Cross has become the symbol not of our darkest hopelessness, but of our brightest hope. That is the mercy of things. Granted who we are, perhaps we could have understood it no other way.

So long as the religious right remains wrong about justice, it will never be right about mercy. If the hurricanes are punishment about anything — as some say they are — they are surely the consequence of our continuing lack of stewardship, not only of our environment, but, as well, of our system of checks and balances, of our social responsibilities, and of our economic inequities. A carelessness that gradually bulldozes our relationships into what could ultimately become a class warfare beyond our wildest imagination.

Jesus fulfilled the law and the prophets and what they portended. He fulfilled it by consummating it with justice and peace and love. We are commanded to go and do likewise, for that is our stewardship. That is the way out of Gethsemane through the Cross, back to Eden, and into the kingdom of God.

All Saints Day *B

St Isaiah

On this mountain the LORD of hosts will make for all peoples a feast of rich food, a feast of well-aged wines, of rich food filled with marrow, of well-aged wines strained clear. And he will destroy on this mountain the shroud that is cast over all peoples, the sheet that is spread over all nations; he will swallow up death forever. Then the Lord GOD will wipe away the tears from all faces, and the disgrace of his people he will take away from all the earth, for the LORD has spoken. It will be said on that day, Lo, this is our God; we have waited for him, so that he might save us. This is the LORD for whom we have waited; let us be glad and rejoice in his salvation. (Isaiah 25:6-9)

Somehow, come All Saints Day and its ambiance (we once kept it as an octave, remember?), I feel a sort of twinge for the Old Testament prophets. I wish they got more attention any time, but especially this time of the liturgical year.

I know God-in-Her-heaven easily includes them among the calendar of saints, but somehow, I never hear of the church following suit. There're lots of St Whosits and St Whatsits and the like, but whoever heard of the Church of St Isaiah?

There's a kind of imposed holiness we ladle all over the common calendar saints that is somehow always missing from the prophets. I don't want to be misunderstood, and I know the saints probably make better dinner companions, but I think we should include more prophets in our celebrations, especially during these days. Indeed, the New Covenant says we're all saints. I'd just like to hear us show a bit more appreciation for the prophets.

It's not fair to the saints, of course, that we tend to stereotype them like Dorothy Sayers said we stereotype Jesus as household pets for little old ladies and pale curates. For my money, the saints are all spiritual major hitters in their own way, some, borderline if not downright pungently prophetic. But it's those brass plate prophets that jerked Old Testament satraps around that I miss. Where are they when we need them most?

There's plenty of work for them to do. Take civil disobedience, for example. Methodist theologian Walter Wink suggests that present-day civil disobedience when true to its form is a modern form of exorcising daemons. And he has a special name for them. Instead of St Paul's "principalities and powers" and the "mighty" the Virgin Mary would have cast from their thrones, he calls them "domination systems."

You'll recognize the type. The war-makers. We know them as the military-industrial complex that President Eisenhower warned us against. The desert-makers, those whose greed disregards our stewardship for the earth. The hunger-makers who disdain the poor and in doing so forget that it is God's grace not our merit that redeems us. And of course, the sexists who put down women at every turn. All these, according to Wink, are functioning and devastating systems of domination that literally force us to cry out.

Jesus took that famous text from Isaiah when he preached about these systems: "The Spirit of the Lord God is upon me," he said, "because the Lord has anointed me to bring good tidings to the afflicted; he has sent me to bind up the brokenhearted, to proclaim liberty to the captives, and the opening of the prison to those who are bound; to proclaim the year of the Lord's favor, and the day of vengeance of our God; to comfort all who mourn…" *(Is 61:1f)*.

Maybe we don't recall such indictments so readily when we celebrate the season of All Saints. Maybe it would help if every once in a while we might add an Old Testament prophet to the roster of the calendar saints. Somehow, it's always filled with Christians and never with any Jeremiahs or Micahs or Hoseas. And then, come this time of year, we add that beat up ragtag list Jesus blessed in his Beatitudes, however much they needed it and whatever they professed or were at the time. Then, trouble is, we tend to make "the saints" into pale, household pets just to be around as dashboard bobble heads at the worst or to bless this and that as our "patrons" at the most. We even name our churches for them in the apostrophic possession (aka St Mark's et al). You ever hear of a church named for a prophet? Sons of the Prophets, the country western band, maybe, but the Church of Isaiah?

Trouble further is that most of them were hardly anybody you'd ever build a shrine to or invite home to dinner more than once or want your daughter to go out with. Even John who lost his head over Jesus more or less and whom many think was the last of them, still gets confused as a founder of the Baptist Church.

It's of a pity, because it's been too long since we've had one and they are just the kind of people we need around so badly these days. I doubt if you'd find one taking faith-based government money or saying the blessing at presidential prayer breakfasts or looking the other way when prisoners were being tortured. Rather would they be telling Enron like they told old King David to stop stealing sheep and taking tax cut subsidies from the federal till and running off with corporate welfare.

They for sure wouldn't be all that preoccupied with our sex lives or with whether creation was by fiat or evolution or whether there was much intelligent design showing up in fiddler crabs. They'd be out and about for justice and mercy and beating AK-47s into plowshares.

If we can't pick up the ministry of the prophets and stop hiding behind the saints — if that's what we seem to be doing — there's not much to say for us. The prophets were also pretty durable customers. They suffered and accomplished a lot and they all had built-in you-know-what detectors, a service we might offer to our society more often than we do.

And you know, they didn't have Jesus like the saints did and like we do. All they could do was to point to him or a reasonable facsimile of whom they never were all that sure. Now, however it seems, I haven't got anything against the saints. They sure lived a better and more productive life than either I or most of my friends and colleagues have. No offense.

On the other hand, a lot of offense. Come to think about it, I hope that later on, Jesus added the skeptical to his blessed list. These are not comfortable times, and we skeptics need all the help we can get.

All Saints Sunday *C

Consciousness

I say to you that listen, Love your enemies, do good to those who hate you, bless those who curse you, pray for those who abuse you. (Luke 6:20-31; The Beatitudes)

So if All Saints Day misses a Sunday, we snag the nearest one and call it All Saints Sunday, instead. Like today. It is good. Chances are more people will hear about it, and that's for the better. Maybe in the discovery, we'll rediscover that saints are not saints after all, but human beings at large.

When animal life moved out of consciousness into self-consciousness, human life got underway. When human life moved into God-consciousness, we called it sainthood because it seemed so holy, we couldn't think of a better word. All Saints Sunday, here we are.

Self-consciousness makes us aware that our individual and fragile lives are part of the very source of life that transcends all limits and shares in that which is eternal. (I'd tell you that this notion comes from John Spong's new book *Eternal Life: A New Vision Beyond Religion, Beyond Theism, Beyond Heaven and Hell*, p 223, but you wouldn't believe me and if you did, you'd be surprised.) But I suspect it's true, anyhow, and it's what the so-called saints somehow discovered for themselves probably without calling it that.

I suspect the saints never much thought of themselves that way then or now, one or all. Like the two-beat Dixieland jazz aficionados say, they just go marching in. All Saints Day and its Sunday afterthought are the times that remind us of that. It's what fools us about Jesus. I suspect he never thought of himself as a saint. Don't call me good, he said. We call our churches "Christ Church," not St Jesus Church. Jesus is what God means by human, by fulfilled consciousness. It's so startling; we can't help but call it divine. For, you know, that just might be what it is.

Properly for today, the Propers are the Beatitudes, all those whom Jesus blessed — the poor and hungry, the sad, those whom we hate and exclude and revile and call evil — and all those whom Jesus cast woes upon — the rich, the satisfied, the scoffers, the praised. It's not all that difficult to look around and, unaware, find them here and now. Appropriate rewards await.

But that's not all. Like when the old country preacher ends his sermon, Jesus tacks a "rousement" on it. He concludes, "But I say to you that hear, Love your enemies, do good to those who hate you, bless those who curse you, pray for those who abuse you. Turn your cheek. Give away your coat. Anybody steals from you, don't ask for it back."

"Beat" and "bless" and "beatitude" have a lot in common. The saints are surely of the "Beat Generation." They're fully human, the fully self-conscious entering into the God-conscious.

The trouble with the term "self-conscious" is that we tend, the many of us, to emphasize the self more than the conscious, especially when it's somebody else's self. It's not when we take ourselves more seriously than we take our work, our purpose, who it is God imagined us to be. But it's to rejoice in consciousness, itself, and what God means for us to do with it together with all the other saints.

Twenty-fourth Sunday after Pentecost *C

Fakery

Some Sadducees, those who say there is no resurrection, came to him and asked him a question. (Luke 20:27)

During the Great Depression in the turn of the 1920s into the 1930s, it was not uncommon for people, mostly men, sometimes a whole family, to come to the back door of our house looking for work and as often for food. My mom would never turn a single one away. She would welcome them in, feed them, sometimes clothe them and let them bathe. Once when I asked her why, she said simply that she took Jesus seriously when he said that helping one of these little ones or visiting prisoners or healing the sick was doing the same for him. She never knew when he might be standing there outside the back door. There was no "if" about it for her.

When our Baptismal Covenant reminds us that seeking and serving Christ in all persons, not only the poor at the back door, but the insurgents in Iraq and the illegal immigrants at the border, as well, I often recall those times about my mom's ministry. But then along comes Jesus warning us to "take heed," that there are false Christs and prophets out there who'll lead us down the yellow brick road without a moment's notice. Even the Good Samaritan, he implies, might have been in jeopardy for being a bit overly zealous.

How easily we impose our notions and our experiences framed by this world on what God may have in store for us in a newer age, let alone this one. Perhaps it is truly unavoidable that we do, for we would seem to have no other alternative. Even so, it is best that we not lose sight of how easy it is to risk underestimating the power and authority of God.

Jesus's encounters insist that we be open to the unexpected gifts of grace. Perhaps the key element in the story is how important it is for our time and our time's contention over the question of the authority and meaning of tradition. Jesus reminds the Sadducees in their time and us in ours that we must take care lest our understanding of the past — including our reading of scripture and tradition — makes us unable to see new manifestations of God's will in the present and — more importantly — in the future. That God is constantly making all things new seems so to unnerve us and thus constantly to defy our capacity to embrace it. As well, the story warns us against limiting the range of God's grace as though anything or anyone could be beyond it, the so-called unforgiveable sin that God's Holy Spirit is incapable of forgiving and renewing and reconciling us. If even the dead — and what is more the seeming finality of death — are not beyond that grace, then surely no race or social or economic status or even religion can escape it, but only refuse and reject it.

This refreshing good news of the gospel in Jesus's hands can and must inform the way we live together as a society of law and order. Our systems of government — and especially of the way we church together — are consistent with that news only when they enhance and enable and inform the gospel's message of justice and peace, love and freedom. They are altogether contrary to it when they seek to restrict it by imposing our own limited understandings about who we are and the ways we must live together.

False Christs, Jesus said. An oxymoron of some dimension, I'd say. Perhaps a disguise that even Satan itself could not trump. An evil personified that could easily sandblast our usual naiveté and even our informed faith.

So, blessed Lord Jesus, I pray, how does one know a false Christ, let alone a false prophet, when one sees one? Or perhaps more practically, since there are not nearly so many folk claiming to be you as there are those of us who wear our Christianity on our sleeves apparently without a lot of sincerity, what are the signs and wonders you say these impostors will show? How can we recognize them? What gives with such evil that I might even suspect it, let alone recognize it in life's lineup, when it shows up as You, of all people?

"Well, my son," Jesus might (repeat might plus unlikely) say, "do you remember Scott Peck, the psychiatrist who had some rare moments with fakery and evil and even with exorcisms? He wrote a book about evil and lying and he was right about how inseparable they are. He was a professed Christian, perhaps with a few reservations, but I'd say he knew something about anybody who would masquerade as me. Indeed, since he joined us only recently, I suspect he knows a lot more now."

I'm never sure just how Jesus talks to anybody, let alone me, if ever. But just suddenly remembering Peck's criteria for recognizing evil at a moment like this might mean something, but we don't have to go there.

Well, we ought to keep wide-eyed. On the other hand, I suspect Jesus would not want us all to be paranoid, either. But he did say a lot about watching out for the sudden arrival of something called "the hour." And there's always the possibility of their being good reason for paranoia. We'll just have to take responsibility for that, ourselves, I suspect. Or maybe bring it up with our neighbor when passing the peace instead of the buck.

Twenty-fifth Sunday after Pentecost * C

Hardly

"Make up your minds not to prepare your defense in advance; for I will give you words and a wisdom that none of your opponents will be able to withstand or contradict. You will be betrayed even by parents and brothers, by relatives and friends; and they will put some of you to death. You will be hated by all because of my name. But not a hair of your head will perish. By your endurance you will gain your souls." (Luke 21:14-19

Dorothy Sayers was one of our brightest scholar-theologians. She said that far too often is Jesus made into a household pet for little old ladies and pale curates. On the other hand and long before we started that kind of Jesus makeover, Gospeler Luke, in on the ground floor and closer to the action, could say in response, Hardly.

In his recounting today, Luke picks up midst the shaking of foundations and the coming of false christer-imposters, and he has Jesus list a whole catalogue of personal damages for his followers ending with, "you will be hated by all for my name's sake" *(Lk 21:18)*.

Little comfort. I suspect that if the foundations aren't shaking, we aren't following. It's that simple. I've not noticed anybody much hating us, just puzzled by our behavior. For the real reason why anybody who truly follows God is persecuted and the foundations are shaken is simply because of who they are and because of this Jesus, whose name they call on. I've no idea where the Sunday School book stores ever got that insipid profile pose of the stargazing Jesus that they promote, for there's little suggestion of that in the gospel. Sayers was right. So long as it's Jesus, the household-pet, we claim, there'll never be any foundations shaken, and the church will remain on its duff arguing about sex all the while thinking it's doing the will of God.

We know the followers of Jesus not only by the way they love one another, but by the way they bear witness that true authority lies beyond this world and that the only real power there is in this world is given from beyond, and the powers of this world cannot bear to hear that their power is limited — and that so are they.

Jesus always warned that his followers should be prepared for many things. And it's no different today. Be prepared to suffer for your faith; beware those who, when the foundations are shaking, go around talking about "peace in our time" or offer you a warmed-over Jesus (where on earth came the phrase "luke-warm"?). Rather must we be firm in the midst of it all, continue to follow the way, and continue to witness to the world that Jesus alone is the source of power, a power that lies in a Jerusalem far beyond the corrupting powers of this world.

My friend Louie Crew says it something like this, Have great expectations when you challenge those who disagree with you or punish you because of your commitment to Christ. Be steadfast in the truth. Be even more steadfast in loving your enemies. They may turn out to be your friends sooner than you think.

Twenty-sixth Sunday after Pentecost *C

Remember

Then [the other criminal] said, "Jesus, remember me when you come into your kingdom." He replied, "Truly I tell you, today you will be with in Paradise." (Luke 23:42-43)

A little child, marveling in pleasure at her newborn baby brother, gently whispered in his ear, "Tell me about God and about heaven, while you can still remember."

Though the venue is radically different, the yearning in the story in our gospel this morning is so very much the same when the good thief on the cross asks Jesus, "Remember me when you come into your kingdom."

An essential part of our identity, of our knowing who we are, is anchored in our remembering and in our being remembered. It doesn't have to be much. It doesn't have to be profound. It can be just a card in the mail. It can be a phone call on an anniversary. It can simply be hearing someone call my name when passing me on the street or missing me when I skip church.

All these and many others play a central role in our being who we are. The terror of Alzheimer's is precisely so devastating because it robs us of the capacity to remember and robs those who love us of the assurance of being remembered.

One of the more important reasons for any gathering of people, particularly of religious people is that we come together to remember and to be remembered. Through our scriptures, we keep in touch with all those who, in faith, share our spiritual DNA and have gone before us. For this is our family history. Every gathering for worship is a momentary experience in genealogy.

At the once-upon-a-time so-called "crisis" liturgies — the baptisms and confirmations, the weddings, the funerals, the ordinations — the happy times and the sad times, our emotions and conversations are filled with the common theme of being remembered.

"When you remember me, it means that you have something of who I am with you, that I have left some mark of who I am on who you are.

It means that you can summon me back to your mind even through countless years and miles that may stand between us. It means that if we meet again, you will know me. It means that even after I die, you can still see my face and hear my voice and speak to me in your heart.

"For as long as you remember me, I am never entirely lost. When I'm feeling most ghostlike, it's your remembering me that helps remind me that I actually exist. When I'm feeling sad, it's my consolation. When I'm feeling happy, it's part of why I feel that way.

"If you forget me, one of the ways I remember who I am will be gone. If you forget me, indeed, part of who I am will be gone." *(Frederick Buechner in "Wishful Thinking," p 100)* To be remembered was the plea of the little child and, as well, the plea of the good thief from his cross when he said, "Jesus, remember me…" There are perhaps no more human words we can say, no prayer we can pray so well.

Indeed, our Lord asks the same of us. "Do this," he said, "in remembrance of me."

Thanksgiving Day *B

Yards

"Look at the birds of the air; they neither sow nor reap nor gather into barns, and yet your heavenly Father feeds them." (Matthew 6:26)

It is not all that easy to know God's will. Some folk have less trouble discerning it than others and even seem altogether blasé about their gift. I'm not one of them.

And it's too bad. I suppose it's only natural to expect the clergy to know God's will. We bring it on ourselves. It's tempting for us not to have some handy answer when asked or even when not asked. So, in wrestling off and on with this problem about knowing God's will, it suddenly dawned on me something that is clearly God's will.

God's will is to have yard sales.

They are a good way to celebrate Thanksgiving. Especially if you have them in someone else's yard. They are also a good way to celebrate Rogation Day because it clears out the surroundings for planting should you ever have a garden.

It is God's will to have yard sales if only to remind us of how bountiful is God's creation and how important is our stewardship of it.

For another, to remind us once more of how much more blessed it is to give than to receive. But most of all are yard sales God's will for our children and our neighbors.

Our children might show more gratitude — or any gratitude at all, for that matter — if they realized what a blessing for them is a downright inclusive, widespread, whole-section-of-the-city yard sale. If they'd only think of the attics and closets and garages and sheds and old trunks and mildew and moths and mold (and respiratory systems) that are emptied and cleared and cleansed by yard sales, maybe they'd catch on. Never mind the nostalgia and the tears and the withdrawal pains, just simply forge ahead. Besides all that, it sets good examples for us members of the Greatest Generation to behave this way.

Life as I know it and hear about it from others in these days, with my memory still more or less intact, seems to be a process of accumulation. Not only the accumulation of things, even though most things eventually wear out, and those that remain tend to have value only in the stories they suggest. Not only an accumulation of wealth, as nice as I suspect that that is, because wealth is slippery and, even when clutched, seems scant comfort in the night. Maybe it is good that we accumulate friends, but because some of us live so long, and also thanks to mobility, changes in our lives, and the just plain wearing out of persons, friends become fewer and farther between.

But we do accumulate. What we accumulate seems to be memories. Events, stories, faces, happy memories, sad memories, moments that make us grimace after all these years, and some moments that make us smile. We become more and more — not necessarily more accomplished, or more secure, or more content, just more. We know the words to more songs. We remember more lines from movies. We have seen more dream cars, watched more double plays, held more hands, kissed more babies, cooked more macaroni, shed more tears, lost more dreams, paid more bills, endured more insults, enjoyed more kindnesses, said more prayers.

One of those prayers is for the gift of the Holy Spirit. Some perceive that gift as a prize to be won, perhaps even a sign of accomplishment. Some look for powers, like tongues or prophecy. Some seek the Spirit as proof of worthiness. Some long for energy, enthusiasm, passion. Some want to lose themselves in the great spiritual whoosh of it all and make life into one big mantra.

Jesus talked of remembering. He said the Spirit would come to teach us, specifically to help us remember all that he said and did. What he said suggests to me that life would be to us like layers of paint that turn the portrait from some splashes of color to the shapes of persons or places or things.

Jesus told lots of stories, and he said that life would also be like stories, that life is a story and a pretty good one if we'll listen. Like the story of a wasteful son and a forgiving father. Like the kindness of a Good Shepherd that would find us in our dark nights of the soul. Like the story of the Samaritan woman at the well who became the first commissioned apostle. Stories that we would hear and later tell over and over. Stories that would enrich us and perhaps nourish others.

This accumulation is not all intellectual or susceptible to memory; nor is it all experiential or even noticed. The story of Jesus and the stories he tells just keep shaping us like the tender and understanding love of a spouse. We become more. Not necessarily more happy or more holy. Just more of who God knows us to be and wants us to become.

Not all that the Spirit would teach us is easy or pleasant. Knowing Jesus tends to make people ask more questions, dare more doubts, see more injustice, touch more wounds, risk more choices. Jesus said that the Holy Spirit would be a Counselor who would teach us all things that he has said to us and bring them to our remembrance as they need to be remembered.

And then Jesus said he would leave us peace, his peace, a peace torn out of living, a peace that would leave our hearts neither troubled nor afraid. A peace that is not the absence of conflict but the presence of justice.

He spoke of his leaving. We call that leaving his Ascension. We remember that forty days after Easter like Ash Wednesday was forty days before. And then comes again that explosion we call Pentecost when our apostolic founders seemed smashed with the joy of it all. That day when the Holy Spirit embraced them and inspired them and set them afire just like the Holy Spirit can embrace us and inspire us and turn up our heat.

It is all this and more that we accumulate as we mature in Christ. And it is all this that we must give away to make room for more. And it is all this that is the reason why it is God's will that we have yard sales.

Last Sunday after Pentecost / The Reign of Christ the King *A

King

And the King will answer them, "Truly, I say to you, as you did it to one of the least of these… you did it to me" (Matthew 25:40).

It was a radical idea then. It remains a radical idea through the centuries. Over and over again, Jesus likens the kingdom of God, indeed, the kingliness of God never to the royal purple puffery of pomp and circumstance, but always to the simple cloth and chores of the commonplace. It is a message whose profound clarity obviously deafened the ears of church and state then and continues to deafen those who not only cannot hear, but do not listen. It remains the message of the Old Testament prophets that is of the essence of biblical morality and a message against which the gates of hell will not prevail.

Maybe it is of a truth that the perils of any given era seem to those whose times they are as the greatest perils of all time. Perhaps this is especially true for the children of Abraham, Isaac, and Jacob, and their God, a children whose prophetic sensitivity to justice may have never been matched. And perhaps it is especially tragic that we, those continuing children and heirs, stand now so sorely divided as even to be killing one another. And perhaps it is especially tragic that our united purpose and will may never have been needed more than it is now.

Who are "the least" in our time who are so intimately identified with our Lord in his? To whom do we minister that turn out again and again to be our Lord, himself?

If we believe that poverty in the world and poverty in America, the richest nation in the world, is morally unacceptable, then there is our Lord. If we believe that further tax cuts for the wealthy in exchange for budget cuts for social services for the poor and the working poor is simply wrong, then there is our Lord. If we believe that the "swords-into-plowshares" vision of the prophet Micah for national security is better than that of the president's Department of Defense, then there is our Lord *(Micah 4:3-4)*. And if we believe that social movements with spiritual foundations can truly change history, then there, as well, is our Lord. Then will we know where are "the least" and in whose midst stands our Lord. Then will we know.

One of the reasons for this nation's founding was to rid ourselves from the secretive cabals of a lord-it-over empire and king. And one of the ways we have done that is through a system of balanced powers created for and given to those who would lead us by serving us. It was perhaps the best secular route we could ever take to provide such an authority.

It was not easy then. It has never been all that easy, though it may have worked better in certain times past. It is our calling as servant leaders to make it work better than ever before. Jesus beckons to us through the hungry, the thirsty, the stranger, the political refugee, the naked, the sick, those in prison, and indeed, those who are being tortured. However and whatever we do unto these least, we do unto our servant king.

Bennett Sims, in his splendid book on servanthood, asks us to consider in a contemporary mode the paradoxes that result from the irony of the servant king in the very heart of the gospel, an irony he discovered when he first became bishop of Atlanta. He is convinced that there resides even now in the church the kind of servant leadership essential for a redemptive ministry to take hold and flourish. For Christian faith is ironic, not heroic, as some would make it, and thus makes considerable demands on our imaginations.

Assume a position of leadership, he suggests, and give its powers away. Take authority, but never use the instruments of coercion you possess. Embrace and include the weak and the unappreciated; honor them and allow them to make decisions. Refuse the crown unless all are crowned and do not glory in the trappings of office.

Listen often; pontificate never. Disdain competition and refuse to win if there are losers. When you encounter fear or anger, do not nurture it or use it to your own advantage.

Ask embarrassing questions when in the presence of venerated hierarchies. Insist that those over whom you may have authority claim their freedom and exercise it joyfully and creatively, even permitting them to fail. When confronted with hate and fear, venture love. Bear pain rather than inflict it. Risk everything in the pursuit of your calling.

♪ ♪♪ ♪

PREACHMENTS ON OTHER SCRIPTURES

Advent / Stones

"Do not begin to say to yourselves, 'We have Abraham as our father,' for I tell you, God is able from these stones to raise up children of Abraham." (Luke 3:8)

"Stir up thy power, O Lord, and with great might come among us…" (BCP, Advent 3, p 160)

Saturday Night Live, that durable and pointedly satirical NBC television show, brought me up short one night with its portrayal of one of the continuing heavies in our national drama. They called him "James 'The Episcopalian' Baker."

That startled me for a moment, but it refreshed me, as well. I like to think that we're one denomination that has the uncanny good sense not to take ourselves so seriously as we take our work, one that understands forgiveness as easier to get than permission, one that, if we have not actually cornered the market on grace, at least knows how to recognize it and be amazed by it without going all soupy.

Because these things are probably true, we really need John Baptist. Not just because he gives an Advent voice to the Christmas birth of peace and justice and good will. And not just because he speaks the gospel truth about the way things are and also about the way we are. But perhaps more importantly, because he is simply not "our type," and the James Bakers of the world are.

Thus could John say that if there is to be any flag-waving about who we are and how many of our presidents have been ours let it be a sign of our contrition and reconciliation and not of our pride and our laurels. And thus could he say for us in our time that being an Episcopalian won't get you any more points at the Pearly Gates than being a Holy Roller all the while he's calling us a "snake pit."

John was furious with the religious establishment of his day for claiming descent from Abraham and otherwise living in blithe disregard of God. Bloodline isn't faith. Heritage isn't faith. Tribal identity isn't faith. Political party isn't faith. Denomination certainly isn't faith. It isn't that easy. For faith has to do with deciding, committing, acting, willing. Faith bears fruit not only because of what it is, but because of what it does. But so does sin bear fruit and disbelief bear fruit. Injustice bears fruit. Cruelty bears fruit.

The perceptive poet Maya Angelou tells of a woman in her audience taking offense with her and claiming, "But madam, I am a Christian!" only to hear Angelou answer, "Already?"

Christian identity is an evolving process. We build our faith as we go. We can always give thanks for whoever started shaping us. But if we don't take up the mantle ourselves and make our own fresh approach to the throne of grace in the ways we make daily decisions, we have nothing.

There it is, and there we are, the very mark of our sin is in turning down love and forgiveness as fast as they come because we either don't believe them or don't want them or just plain couldn't care less. But the Gospel Hound of Heaven persists and tells us that extraordinary things happen just as all through the Bible and our tradition extraordinary things happen.

Remember David who got his mistress's husband killed so he could have her all to himself, but was still the "apple of God's eye." And remember Zaccheus who climbed up a sycamore tree a crook and climbed down a saint. And remember Paul who set out as a hatchet man for the Pharisees and came back as a fool for Christ. And remember Peter who denied Jesus three times and walked off with the keys to the kingdom on his belt.

Perhaps whenever we're tempted to take ourselves too seriously, it would be well to recall the audacity of the old Franciscan benediction that speaks of discomfort and anger and tears over the seemingly insurmountable state of things as blessings. And then asks God for enough foolishness to believe that we, in whatever state — poor or rich, smart or not so smart, old or young, sick or well — can make a difference in this world, so that we can do what others claim cannot be done.

If Advent stirs up anything at all like this in us to get us truly ready for Christmas, so be it. Even the stones wake up with this news.

Mary

Mary said, "You see before you the Lord's servant, let it happen to me as you have said." (Luke 1:26-38)

Agnus Day is an on-line comic strip that reports the conversations of a couple of sheep about, of all things, the liturgical lectionary. In their discussion of Mary's exchange with Gabriel, the gospel for Advent 4, they exegete thusly:

One says, What if Mary had said, "You know, this isn't a good time for me…" But, says the other, she didn't! God calls, and his people heed the call. It's pretty straightforward. So, says the first, You're saying that Mary is just a "girl who cain't say no?"

Mary doesn't get much press until Christmas rolls around, and then, she has to share it with John Baptist. Yet, without Mary — and her profound "Yes" to Gabriel — we'd be in a fine kettle of ichthus. For her Yes not only allows the occasion for the greatest redirection of human history as we know it, it also models for us who God imagines us to be and what God calls us to do.

I not only wish Christians as a whole made more of this, but I can't understand why feminists don't. Thank you very much, God says through Mary, but I'll redeem things any way I please and especially without any intervention whatsoever by you arrogant, generally screw-up males. Do what you will with the Virgin Birth, God says, or with any virgin birth at any level of the fauna and flora, believe it or don't believe it, but please never overlook that here's an altogether productive system that does quite well without you.

Christmas has simply got to be a traumatic time for mothers. Not only because they do ninety percent of the work pulling it off at home and hearth and mall, but because, like with their share in Mary's vocation, without them there would be practically nothing to it at all.

Watch women with any baby, not only their own, and you'll witness the richness and radiance of creation in all its glory. Further, how they respond inwardly to the mystery of the Nativity must be one of the greatest ongoing mysteries of all. We men will never know, but the least we can do is get a life and show some appreciation and awe, especially awe, even some shock now and then. This "girl who cain't say no" models for us what the sheep says, "God calls, and his people heed the call."

Don't we wish. One of the popes called Mary, the "Mother of the Church" and by that, I trust, he meant here is what the church is to be. And in Mary's magnificat, when God scatters the proud in their conceit and casts down the mighty from their thrones, lifts up the lowly and fills the hungry, and sends the rich away empty *(Lk 1:46-55)*, I'll bet God means what the church is to be about.

Listen. And we shall hear.

Valentine's Day / Hearts

This is the covenant I shall make with the House of Israel when those days have come, Yahweh declares. Within them I shall plant my Law, writing it on their hearts. Then I shall be their God and they will be my people. (Jeremiah 31:31-34)

God, our God has blessed us. May God continue to bless us, and be revered by the whole wide world. (Psalm 67)

As it is, these remain: faith, hope, and love, the three of them; and the greatest of them is love. (1 Corinthians 13)

Jesus said to him, "You must love the Lord your God with all your heart, with all your soul, and with all your mind. This is the greatest and the first commandment. The second resembles it: You must love your neighbor as yourself." (Matthew 22:34-40)

You may note if you keep careful attention to such things that this Valentine Day is actually the Last of Epiphany with another, more appropriate set of lessons chosen by professional lesson-choosers who know best. As a once-upon-a-time east-Texas country preacher who occasionally wanders in with a dangerous penchant for ignoring rubrics and things, I simply could not resist choosing lessons for today that are about hearts and about love. If I should be taken before an ecclesiastical court, I'd remind the bench that after all Jesus did say the greatest commandment is not about law or even canon law, but about love.

It was probably not because of a shortage of papyrus or that they were handier that Moses first presented the Commandments on tablets of stone. That may be one reason why it is common to say of something that is adamantly immovable that it is written in stone or that it is not written in stone if it is optional. Perhaps to show how urgent was his mission Jesus affirmed in startling metaphor that it was so demanding that even the very stones would cry out for him their welcome and praise.

So to fast-backward into the Old Testament, it was an understandably remarkable turn of events, as our first lesson reports, when Jeremiah transferred God's commandments from tablets of stone to the tablet of the heart. The heart was already thought to be the seat of passion, of knowledge, and, of course, of love. Even the Greek word for heart means the inner-self as in our phrase, the heart of the matter. The law was to become internal and not just in the foyer of the courthouse, ACLU to the contrary.

It is not all that clear why we jump-start from hearts to Valentines, save that St Valentine's feast day was, as was Christmas, chosen to divert attention from a day already devoted to something somewhat less saintly. But February 14th hasn't yet made our liturgical calendar, and we also have a rule that Sundays pretty much preempt most saints' days, especially one that's not even on the books.

(But I cannot resist making an aside that for the life of me, I wonder what the candy people must have been thinking when they went so far as to shape their Valentine boxes like hearts and then fill them full of chocolate-covered cholesterol.)

Nice thing about the day, mayhaps, is to remind us if ever so faintly that love is here to stay, and that the tune by the same name was George Gershwin's last. The chord changes, say the jazz players, lay right in the pocket. The lyric, almost as good as Paul's great paean to the Corinthians, is a mighty fine Valentine all by itself:

Our love is here to stay.

The Eve of Ash Wednesday / Cycles

Blow the trumpet in Zion; sound the alarm on my holy mountain! (Joel 2:1a)

There are crisis liturgies that come only once in a lifetime — baptism, marriage, ordination, burial, and the like. And there are cyclic liturgies that repeat themselves through the years, for some, perhaps, *ad nauseum* — Christmas, Easter, anniversaries. But for others, with renewed meaning and vigor as our own personal and communal histories turn through our lives.

The Eve of Ash Wednesday may be one of these. A sort of ordered mad zaniness makes the substance of it hilarity over anticipating the rigors (for some, anyhow) of the Lenten shroud that covers ever so finely as the ashes to come. We call it Mardi Gras from the French for Fat Tuesday, and Fat Tuesday from using all the lard in the house for festive baking before the meatless Lenten fast. Some call it Shrove Tuesday in honor of the good riddance of old sins and the exciting anticipation of a journey into newer ones.

"New Orleans" is an almost instant thought integral to the image of this day. New Orleans, whose being was savaged almost beyond recognition only a few years ago, now suddenly bursts alive again with the mere thought of it, Mardi Gras. And throughout this planet of storms and quakes and floods and wars and incompetent leaders we all rejoice and let the jazz ring out. We are saints, our gospel tells us, and once more, we've done gone marching in.

Lent / Paradox

It happened sometime later that God put Abraham to the test. (Genesis 22:1-14)

For I am sure that neither death, nor life, nor angels, nor principalities, nor things present, nor things to come, nor powers, nor height, nor depth, nor anything else in all creation, will be able to separate us from the love of God in Christ Jesus our Lord. (Romans 8:31-39)

Anyone who wants to save his life will lose; but anyone who loses his life for my sake, and for the sake of the gospel, will save it. (Mark 8:31-38)

Scott Peck, author of the mega-bestseller, *The Road Less Traveled*, grew up in an unchurched family. Of his first and only trip to Sunday School in all his childhood, he tells of the class being handed a drawing to color. The drawing was of the scene in the story from Genesis when Abraham was preparing to sacrifice his son Isaac. Peck said that he never returned.

It is a daring and frightful story, one not easily calculated to confirm the notion that God is love. Nor is the comparable one in Mark with Jesus's prediction of his impending crucifixion, and his mandate that we, as well, must take up our cross, paradox in hand, that to save one's life is first to lose it.

Not to worry, says Paul to the Roman Christians. "It is God who justifies," he writes, "who is to condemn?... For I am sure that neither death, nor life, nor angels, nor principalities, nor things present, nor things to come, nor powers, nor height, nor depth, nor anything else in all creation, will be able to separate us from the love of God in Christ Jesus our Lord."

We've stepped now through Ash Wednesday's door into Lent. In his letter to his fellow primates across the Anglican Communion, one Archbishop of Canterbury wrote of this time, "Our hearts are still on the way to full conversion, and so the work of the Cross, finished in itself once and for all, is still working itself through the life of every Christian. Lent is our best opportunity to let God move more deeply and permanently into the areas of our lives that still resist his grace."

We do, indeed, resist God's grace. Albeit that grace is a central reality of the gospel, we yet hold back as a meritocracy — both in church and state — an idolized system in which the talented are rewarded and moved ahead on the basis of their achievement, and the vast and growing numbers of the poor are merely left aside to fend for themselves.

Lent is a time to turn from this resistance and to open ourselves to grace. In God's call to Abraham to test his obedience and in God's driving Jesus into the wilderness of temptation to test his, it is not the sacrifice — as devastating a reality as it is — that should command our attention to emulate. It is the choice which both Abraham and Jesus made. It is thus that our faith, if it would be more than mere assent to a creed, must be a willfully open and vulnerable risk to whatever God would have of us. Only that can open the pathways in order that grace may abound.

I was discussing these lessons for this Sunday in Lent with a friend, wondering with her about choice and moral agency. With her usual devoted skill, she suggested some of these insights that follow. When Jesus asks us to take up our cross and to follow him, she said, one of the things he offers is a glimpse into his life, a model of a healthy moral life, not one that's all cut and dried, black and white, but one that's about wrestling with all the moral questions that confront us as they confronted him. He wasn't against the law and the prophets (nor even about a mild meritocracy, I suspect) but he was firmly against a calloused and conventional faith. He wanted scripture and tradition to be real, to be now, to be alive. And the only way for these to be alive for him then and for us today is by engaging in real moral discernment. So Jesus was sent into the wilderness to discover his moral purpose, to realize it, to choose whether he's willing to embrace it. And when he does, he returns a changed man with an unswerving purpose anchored in the cross. Thus choosing, he becomes a singular moral agent commanding the human landscape so that we, as well, can rescind our resistance and surrender ourselves to grace.

The apostle Paul was, himself, a model of one who gave up his life and then received it renewed. Only then could he offer this remarkable paean in his letter to the Romans, an anthem for all who would embrace Lent once again and serve. We can find no better way to greet each of these Lenten days as we live them.

Palm Sunday / Parades

As [Jesus] was now drawing near, at the descent of the Mount of Olives, the whole multitude of the disciples began to rejoice and praise God with a loud voice for all the mighty works that they had seen, saying, "Blessed is the King who comes in the name of the Lord! Peace in heaven and glory in the highest!" And some of the Pharisees in the multitude said to him, "Teacher, rebuke your disciples." He answered, "I tell you, if these were silent, the very stones would cry out" (Luke 19:37-40).

There has been talk, perhaps even suggestion, albeit tangential in my experience, of creating a cabinet-level Department of Peace. If there is a Department of Defense, one might argue, which, of late, has perhaps been more offensive than defensive, why not one of Peace? When one of the more prominent candidates for the presidency heard of this, he was reported to have said, "Peace? We don't want peace, we want victory."

I don't know if he realized how ludicrous was his statement or whether he subsequently backtracked and changed what he said. Strangely, though, I'm rather glad for his remark, for I believe it sums up in brief the truly bellicose, the war-mentality of our time. It seems next to impossible for us to define peace in any other way save in terms of war. And it seems next to impossible for us to define war in any other way save in terms of victory — or the implicit alternative of defeat. The opposite of winning for so many is not losing. It is quitting. Victory — even with Viet Nam continuing so vivid in our minds — is the only acceptable alternative.

Coincidentally, Palm Sunday is about war and about peace, but it is a different peace. It is the peace of Jesus who is the Prince of Peace. It is the peace of the man of paradox, of the one who said, "Do not think that I have come to bring peace on earth; I have not come to bring peace, but a sword" *(Mt 10:34)*. And later, on the very eve of his crucifixion, "Peace I leave with you; my peace I give to you" *(Jn 14:27)*. Perhaps the contradiction fades when we realize that in the overall context for Jesus, peace meant not the absence of violence, but the presence of love and justice.

We celebrate on Palm Sunday, the entrance of Jesus, the King of Peace, into Jerusalem. We even act out his parade in our liturgy. But there was another entry into Jerusalem on that day, an entry of which we rarely take any notice and of which few probably even know, an entry not about peace, but about war and oppression. It was the entry of Pilate, the lesser Roman satrap, not on the foal of a donkey, but with his legions on the armored stallions of cavalry. It was an entrance not to celebrate with the Jews, but to guard against and stamp the Roman boot on the possibility of any colonial insurrection at that time.

A very integral part of our celebration of Palm Sunday must be, then, more than only a reenactment of that exciting and humble scene of Jesus riding on a borrowed jackass, not only of the messianic satire of Jesus's parade. It must also be a choice between defining peace in terms of war and peace in terms of justice, a choice between the servant kingly reign of God and the imperialistic dimensions and temptations of our own worst selves.

On this Palm Sunday and as a whole throughout our own time, we are faced with not only our present international geopolitical reality, but perhaps even more critically with the ongoing theopolitical life of our church. Our nation's leaders are careening unilaterally toward empire and challenging our great political experiment in the balance of powers on their way. And ironically, with so much of our church's manner of governing itself patterned after our nation's, our leaders are wrestling for our lives with those who would turn it once again either toward Rome or some unreasonable and equally imperial facsimile.

As once again we celebrate this great Palm Sunday parade, let us turn to and listen carefully. Across town, there is being led another parade. Will it take the very stones, themselves, to convince us which one to follow?

Eastertide / Something

Simon Peter said, "I'm going fishing." (John 21:3)

Comedian Mort Sahl once observed that fishing is the activity of doing something when you're not doing anything.

As John tells it, he more or less leaves the impression the disciples weren't doing much of anything, just standing around, maybe wondering what on earth they'd got themselves into. But then Peter broke the spell.

"I'm going fishing." At least, I'm going to do something while I'm not doing anything, anyway. (By the by, this story's a good source for some trivia question about the disciples' names over in Jn 21:1-14.) So they all said, in effect, we're not doing anything either, so "we'll go with you."

It's amazing now to remember how simple was this little scene and how simple-minded were these fishers who, John records, couldn't even recognize Jesus who stood there on the beach. It wasn't all that long, remember, since the resurrection, an event, we might imagine that we could expect might just have caught their attention and set them in motion as much, maybe, as a tornado coming across the water.

But no, they'd had to do something when they weren't doing anything. It's easy to miss this turn, blinded by what's probably the mother of all fish stories. And it seems easy enough to miss the big Easter surprise, itself.

I wonder how much of what followed on Easter Day and in the days and years to come could best be understood as a desperate attempt to explain the inexplicable, to get reality back under control? I am trying to understand why the disciples — and we who cherish so our succession with them — respond to the resurrection of Jesus by doing exactly the opposite of what he commanded. Why did they — and we — move quickly to define in precise words a Messiah who spoke in ironically ambiguous (aka imprecise) parables? Why did they — and we — create hierarchies to serve one who clearly rejected hierarchies? Why did they — and we — marginalize women in the name of one who welcomed women to his inner circle and who appeared first to them in such a way that they became the apostles to the apostles?

Why did they — and we — create standards of admission to see and be with a Savior who gladly welcomed and ate with sinners? Why did they — and we — become advocates for war, privilege, wealth, hatred, and pride in the name of one who gave his life to defeat such darkness?

Of course, it was good to catch those fish. Maybe they should just have stayed with it, remained unsurprised, not recognized Jesus, and just let it be. Not try to explain it. Not try to get reality back under control. Not dive under the covers of intellect. Not domesticate surprise. Instead of all that, just savor the moment, allow God to keep on speaking in his surprising ways, and then... start listening.

I wonder if God had more to say on Easter Day, and nobody had the courage to wait and hear what it might be. Me? I'm going fishing. It's a lot safer.

Covenant

"They devoted themselves to the apostles' teaching and fellowship, to the breaking of bread and the prayers." (Acts 2:42)

This simple statement about the early church that we repeat two millennia later as part of our Baptismal Covenant says it all. We are asked, "Will you continue in the apostles' teaching and fellowship, in the breaking of bread, and in the prayers?" And we answer, "I will, with God's help."

Then just so there's no mistaking things, we spell out that teaching and that fellowship and what it means. It means to persevere in resisting evil, and failing, to repent and return to the Lord. It means to proclaim by word and by example the Good News of God in Christ. It means to seek and serve Christ in all persons, loving our neighbors as ourselves... And it means finally and maybe most important of all, to strive for justice and peace among all people, and to respect the dignity of every human being. And our answer at each step is the same... "I will, with God's help."

In other words, we are that fellowship. We break that bread. We pray those prayers. The apostles are us. And we are the apostles. We are the ones who have the commission to be and to do these things.

I don't know if Pastor Jeremiah Wright ever took those vows or a reasonable facsimile, but he sure sounds like he might have. Oddly (and tragically) his one remark that has proven most controversial seems to me fairly basic, as our Covenant attests, to a responsible understanding of the Christian faith.

Actually, when you think about it, even in a casual reading of the *Prayer Book* Daily Evening Office when one comes upon the Blessed Virgin's startlingly lovely Magnificat, you'll find her saying some remarkably similar things.

"The Almighty has done great things for me," she says, "and holy is his name... he has shown the strength of his arm, he has scattered the proud in their conceit, he has cast down the mighty from their thrones... " *(cf Lk 1:46-55).*

Stripped of the emotion and the phraseology, Pastor Wright — and the Magnificat — are saying that the United States of America stands under God's judgment no differently from the way any other peoples in any other land stand under God's judgment. Surely we don't think that when we sing *God Bless America*, we get a free pass or get to be overlooked on the torture we have inflicted in our current as well as past wars, on the bombings of civilian targets, on resorting to armed combat for economic reasons, on the disenfranchisement of native Americans, on the practice of slavery, and on and on. I am seriously depressed at the depth of the civil religion practiced in this country that would exempt us from being held responsible for our national sins any more than it would hesitate to offer thanksgiving for the blessings we have received and the good judgment we have shown.[1]

Are we reflecting on this? Has our House of Bishops or the church in any of its manifestations responded to this current controversy about which the media reminds us over and over again? Surely nobody even imagines that this is in any way even approaching a partisan issue, so why not?[1]

The flak over the pastor's remarks only serves to distract us from the fact that we live in perilous times. Thousands are in serious economic straits. Millions are without adequate health care. We are in a war immersed in a kind of grandiosity and denial that is killing hundreds and leaving hundreds more homeless daily. I need not rehearse that litany. You know it as well as I and also have probably heard all you want to hear.

When a 36-year-old New Jersey father of three came home recently from work, walked off the commuter train, crossed the tracks, and deliberately placed himself in the path of the oncoming train, he was killed instantly. Later it was learned that he feared he was going to be "downsized."

My family lived through the Great Depression of the late twenties and early thirties, the four of us barely getting by. Similar stories then were not all that uncommon. Today's subprime market's collapse coupled with severe unemployment and home foreclosures is seen by many financial gurus as a confirmation of an impending financial disaster not unlike the one my family and some of you lived through. Many of these experts are deeply concerned about widespread unemployment and the crippling indignity which always comes in its wake. This young father's suicide may be a tragic parable of our times. We are deep now into Easter. The gospel of Jesus and the great saga of this season at heart tell another parable, a parable of hope and abundance, a parable of peace and of justice. There is every reason to believe that more than the usual number may be in search of these very gifts, and that some may search right here where these realities by which our affirmation of the Passion and encouragement of its redemptive healing can assure them.

That many of our churches would welcome them instead with an obsession with sex, with some quick-fix covenant, and with how many bishops can stand on the head of a pin is to our shame. It is surely an embarrassment to God. For the church is called to be, and the church must be, especially in these times, an embodiment of this Easter parable rather than merely one more religious institution bewitched and bollixed with the fear for its own survival.

Lessons about the Good Shepherd and the 23d Psalm and the life of the early church recall our commission to be both pastor and prophet in these times. For this Easter parable is not one only of compassion and nourishment, but, as well, one of prophetic indictment of the very divisive forces in our society that bring about these current conditions that humiliate and denigrate ourselves and our neighbors in utter contrast to the Baptismal Covenant we have made.

I cannot recall when in recent times these commitments in this Covenant have been more central to our ministries. We have embraced these and we must and we can be ourselves refreshed by what they call to us to be and to do — to continue in the apostles' teaching and fellowship and by our liturgies, by our resistance to evil, by our repentance, by our proclamation of the Good News of God in Christ, but above all in these days by a Christ-seeking and Christ-serving leadership that strives for justice and peace and respect for the dignity of all.

The church is the family where these things can and do happen, indeed, the church all over this land is the family where they must happen. The church must be the family where women and men and children can be loved until they can come to love and respect themselves and where they can then come to love and respect others. It is this we must offer and this to which we must live out the kind of winsomeness that makes it irresistible.

This ministry, this Easter parable for dignity, spells it all out in the Liturgy of the Eucharist when we come to stand or kneel before the Altar to receive the body and blood of the crucified and risen Jesus. Side by side, we are all equal. The clergy are our servants distributing bread and wine equally to all. When the words are said, The Body of Christ, the bread of heaven, let us hear The Body of Christ, the bread of justice. When the words are said, The Blood of Christ, the cup of salvation, let us hear The Blood of Christ, the cup of compassion.

For it is in food and drink offered equally to everyone that the presence of God and Jesus is found. But food and drink are the material basis of life, so we cannot avoid the further reality that the Lord's Supper is also political criticism and economic challenge as well.[2]

By the grace of God and with Jesus's presence, we can, we do, we must make these things happen.

(1) Comments about Jeremiah Wright are adapted from remarks by the Revd Thomas B Woodward with his permission. 2) Parts adapted from correspondence with the Revd G Richard Wheatcroft with his permission.

Mother's Day / Tough Love

Jesus said to his disciples, *"If you love me, you will keep my commandments"* (John 14:15).

My mom never quite said it like that. Rather did she say, "Whether you love me or not, you will keep my commandments." Usually with a knowing, but no less firm smile on her face.

Somehow, it sounds like the kind of passive-aggressive codependency that shrinks frown on, but all the while simultaneously thrive on. As for my early family life, I have little trouble connecting up to my mom's interpretation. On the other hand, I can't very well at all associate it with Jesus. Nevertheless, there it is, and right smack dab in the middle of Mothers Day again.

But that's not all that Jesus said. And I'm not all that convinced it's quite the way he said it. So far as Jesus is concerned, the last thing card-carrying Christians need is a card to carry. If, indeed, there are any credentials required at all, love will do jes' fine.

"By this all will know that you are my disciples, if you have love for one another." *(John 13:35)*

Loving one another is not only what makes us disciples, it's what makes being a disciple about. It's what makes us who we are. No amount of grandstanding, breast-beating, ecclesiastic gerrymandering, confessions, or decades of evangelism can take its place. Love. Thass all.

So what does it mean for us to love one another? And how on earth will anybody, presuming they should much care one way or the other, ever know whether we do or don't? How without a program can they tell a disciple from a devil?

Our founders were mighty smart to separate out the religious and the secular institutions in our nation, to make them unbeholden to one another and to insist that they remain that way. Church is not state and state is not church. It was probably the best thing that ever happened to the both of us.

And they were smart, as well, not to talk a lot about love. What they were after for a welcome change was a just and open and fair society and a government that could pull it all off and keep it that way. They knew that institutions cannot love one another, but they also knew that justice is the social counterpart of love. The church was welcome to help out, but the church was also welcome to stay out.

We churchers would look a long way before we'd ever find a political system more conducive to or nourishing of our own self-understanding. We'd also look a long way before we could embrace such an experiment with the full empowerment of our stewardship, both to enable and coax it along whenever it wavered and to indict and admonish it with something like the Isaiah two-step whenever it erred and strayed.

But the best way and, indeed, the only way to embrace this herculean ministry, of course, is to emulate, to be such a society ourselves, then to model it, to make it so attractive folks simply would have to have a piece of the action for themselves. It is to take such a ministry far more seriously than we take ourselves. It is to realize that loving one another in any kind of institutional or even communal way is to practice justice and fairness and civility and respect in our own common allegiance and worship. Well, good luck. We'll get back to you later when we winnow out the "bad guys" to purify the remnant. We've got a serious problem going on here. Some folks are loving one another, but they're not doing it by the Book, not as we read it, anyway.

So all the while this grand experiment in justice our founders imagined and birthed has come upon what may be the worst of times in its two centuries, where's the church? Championing justice? Loving one another? Modeling fairness and acceptance and inclusiveness? Calling the hands of our nation's leaders back to the premises of our founders, but tending to our own, as well? Nope.

Jesus knew already, like many of us take a lifetime to learn, that love is a choice. Love is an act of the will. The vows, the covenants we make as Christians are not "I do" vows. They are "I will" vows. One of the ways, one of the very important ways we love one another is with our wills, our choices, our making and keeping commitments. The reason for this is that "willing" has staying power, continuity. "Doing" just shows up for the occasion and goes its way for another day.

Like this one: "On the third day, there was a marriage at Cana in Galilee, and the mother of Jesus was there; Jesus was also invited to the marriage, with his disciples. When the wine gave out, the mother of Jesus said to him, 'They have no wine.' And Jesus said to her, 'O woman what have you to do with me? My hour has not yet come.' His mother said to the servants, 'Do whatever he tells you.'" *(Jn 2:1-5)*

Mother's Day is the day that celebrates that one person who manages to make you feel that you're special and that you aren't living up to your potential — all in the same sentence.

"Do whatever he tells you."

Mother's Day is also a splendid day to celebrate the church's ministry as a mother. Both Matthew and Luke record Jesus lamenting over Jerusalem's killing the prophets and wishing himself to be a mother hen that would brood over her chicks *(Mt 23:37; Lk 13:34)*. Later, one of Mary's early-on titles was "Mother of the Church." Fifteenth century St Julian of Norwich referred to Jesus as "our mother." And of course, we need the church like a good mother always to make us feel very special, but never quite living up to our potential.

And it was Jesus's mother who gave us, indeed empowered us, with her Magnificat, as profound a combination both of our pastoral and prophetic commissions as we could imagine. It's on page 119 in the *Prayer Book*. It's our marching song for Mother's Day:

The Song of Mary
Magnificat Lk 1:46-55
My soul proclaims the greatness of the Lord,
my spirit rejoices in God my Savior;
for he has looked with favor on his lowly servant.
From this day all generations will call me blessed:
the Almighty has done great things for me,
and holy is his Name.
He has mercy on those who fear him
in every generation.
He has shown the strength of his arm,
he has scattered the proud in their conceit.
He has cast down the mighty from their thrones,
and has lifted up the lowly.
He has filled the hungry with good things,
and the rich he has sent away empty.
He has come to the help of his servant Israel,
for he has remembered his promise of mercy,
The promise he made to our fathers,

to Abraham and his children for ever.

Glory to the Father, and to the Son, and to the Holy Spirit:
as it was in the beginning, is now, and will be for ever. Amen.

In a phrase, we could call this canticle "tough love." Hardly a parent, especially a mother, has not been faced with exercising tough love more than once. It is not only at the heart of a functional family, it is profoundly at the heart of a functional church. The church's servant leadership in society is that kind of mothering leadership. Mary's Magnificat defines for us where we often must stand in calling our nation to be faithful to its founding and demanding a just peace in human rights in all our war-making, hunger-making, and desert-making domination systems.

God has done these things. God's word has been made flesh to lead us as an agency of change into a world to which God has promised mercy together with power and authority to make it so.

"If you love me, you will keep my commandments," Jesus said to his disciples. "Do whatever he tells you," said his mom. You make that commitment now in the immediacy of our relationship, and you choose to keep it for the duration. That's what loving is about. That's what our relation is about.

The parting words are initiating words. Jesus establishes a relationship for his disciples with himself and for us with himself and through them that can be sustained only by the spirit to make us whole and to keep and direct our wills in him. In him we experience a spiritual awakening now — and again to come wholesomely for the church at Pentecost. You might say that committing ourselves to Jesus in our baptism, we begin the recovery of our basic humanity in which God created us.

Keeping Jesus's commandments to love God and neighbor and self sums up the law, completes it, as it were, and opens to us the collegiality of the Holy Spirit. We don't recover alone. We recover in community, for that's where Spirit resides, nourishes, and sustains us.

Jesus's little homily in this morning's gospel is his prelude to Pentecost. What you work out with your mom — and your shrink — is more or less up to you. I hope God smiles on it.

Ascension / Git!

And [Jesus] said to them, "Go out to the whole world; proclaim the gospel to all creation. (Mark 16.15)

When the people in the world of the Bible experienced what they called principalities and powers, they were discerning the actual spirituality at the center of the political, economic, religious, and cultural institutions of their time.

Few today ever consider spirituality that way or as anything other than a vacuous synonym for religion and as a more or less irrelevant matter left to its practitioners. A further phenomenon is to presume that if it's spiritual, it must therefore be good, thus to overlook the daemons that lurk not only in our societies, but also in ourselves, for they, too, are "spiritual." That we allow all this to happen is to our ultimate peril.

But we allow it anyway, even encourage it in our public education systems with their disdain for the libraries and the humanities and the arts and the world's religions. That we do so has perhaps never been more obvious and recklessly careless than it is today. No child left behind? I wonder how many, O Lord, how many.

All this leaves an empty space in the way we live, a space into which rush the daemons of denial and grandiosity, pleasure and distraction, and whatever else is at hand, thus rendering impotent the possibility of any creative stewardship of our lives.

Something of that order is happening now in places like the middle east. Iraq and the whole miasma of that area is imploding, and we seem helpless to know what, if anything, to do about it, save regime-change by violence, all the while in denial of the changes needed in our own regime. This, I suspect, is a result of our misunderstanding, just plain ignorance, and, even worse, indifference of how these spiritual energies, these principalities and powers work in societies, certainly in our own, let alone in others.

The Ascension gospel reminds us how the misery of sudden emptiness and withdrawal challenges the hapless and frightened disciples. Jesus had filled that space in their lives. His energy fed their energy, his charisma gave them enthusiasm, his manifest power gave them courage, his teaching gave them direction, and his confidence gave them hope.

Once Jesus left, the little circle seemed vacant, tattered, needing to be repopulated and reenergized. What had seemed so vibrant with Jesus present now seemed cold and lifeless with Jesus absent then. Doubt and fear rushed in to fill their hearts.

The gospel's inherent irony is perhaps nowhere more poignant than in this scene. They'd already heard that something new and exciting had happened, but they chose not to believe it. Then, Mary Magdalene of all people and whom they knew only too well comes and tells them the good news of Jesus's new life. Of course, neither did they believe her, even though they probably knew she'd been freshly purged of seven heavens-knows-what kind of daemons. But the Magdalene was not your average soccer mom, for she becomes of all things the apostle to the apostles-to-become, and with little tribute to the rest of us males who claim to stand in their succession and who miss the point ever so clearly as did they.

In our liturgical keeping of time, we stand in between Ascension Day last Thursday when we remember Jesus' return to his father and the Pentecost next Sunday when we commemorate the Holy Spirit's ecclesiastical labor pains. Perhaps this, as well, can remind us of our empty spaces and call us to attend to how they will be filled.

Will we, as do so many, surrender to the usual crippled understanding of spirituality as merely another organized and irrelevant religion with which we can easily dispense? Or will we welcome this Pentecost, embracing God's Holy Spirit to renew us again as church, letting that presence fill the space in our lives, feed our energy, spur our enthusiasm, encourage and direct us, give us confidence and hope?

As we observe the eleven disciples in the Ascension story, we know that the "space" that the earth-trodding Jesus filled is now theirs — the work, the ministry, the caring, the healing, the teaching, the conflicts, the suffering, the sacrificing, the storytelling, the recruiting, the dying and more. They could no longer follow Jesus as before. For they themselves had to embrace and ingest Holy Spirit as their own to fill the space he once occupied. And it is to our eternal benefit that they chose to do precisely that, thanks to God's gift to them of the Magdalene's wake-up call and that of others like her.

It was like moving to a new home, into space that is all promise and no warmth. It is like starting a companionship with someone who is largely a stranger, or starting a new job and knowing that all the sudden your resumé means nothing.

We can stand here in our religious puffery or we can take Holy Spirit by the horns and heart. Then go out into the marketplace, into the crowd, into the swirl of pilgrims seeking God. The Spirit did not fashion for the disciples a nest, where they would feel safe and comfortable. The Spirit set them on fire and drove them into the wilderness of the streets of the world.

Dan Corrigan was one of our church's more devoted and exciting bishops. In the old *1928 Prayer Book* days, there was no "dismissal" at the end of the Eucharist. So he would stand at the altar, pronounce the closing Blessing in all solemnity, then pause for a moment… then, then in his great, booming voice, he would literally shout at us:

"Get up! Get out! And get lost!"

Pentecost / The Way

Nicodemus said, "How can anyone who is already old be born? Is it possible to go back into the womb again and be born?" (John 3:1-17)

When Jesus told Nicodemus he must be "born anew," it proved to be what I think unintentionally started a firestorm of evangelical craziness midst a so-called born-again Christianity. Nicodemus didn't get it right at first. Instead, he got all anatomical and GYN about it. But he finally figured it out. I'm not so sure they ever have.

Water and the spirit, Jesus said. The image reminds me of when a football team douses their coach with a barrel full of iced Gatorade after winning a game. Nothing might wake up one's spirit like a heavy dose of iced-down juice to remind us that baptism doesn't birth our spirits, it mostly reminds us that we have one, that we are one, that God creates us as spiritual beings for want of being human and sets us forth on a trek to discover our humanity, a discovery that bears all the striking resemblance to a new birth and then gives us a Covenant to help shape the labor pains. No wonder we're confused and want to make something else of it.

Nicodemus got a quick lesson for his slow learning curve that night visiting Jesus, lurking around to stay out of sight of anybody who might get out of joint about the company he was keeping. He got a lesson that in spite of all the proper religious spin he had on his life, it simply wasn't enough. He set a splendid example for us that in spite of whatever our spin, unless we get our priorities straight, we're wasting our time — and Jesus's time, too. Unless we realize that this new birth is God reaching into our spirits and putting them back on track, spirits that are already there by virtue of God's imaginative creation. But, as Nicodemus discovered, that's not where it stops.

The twelve steps of recovery program fame contain one hurdle after another. But one of the most challenging — if the evidence means anything — is the third. It says, "Made a decision to turn our will and our lives over to the care of God as we understand God."

Like Nicodemus, many folk come seeking in a Step Meeting what they know not. More than likely, if they've tried the church or a parson, they've found something wanting. They've heard over and over again, "If you'll just have faith, all will work itself out," and too often with the implication (read judgment) that faith is what enough of they don't have or they'd either never have the problem or too soon get over it.

When they come up on number three with its "turn over your will and life" challenge and its risk and God talk, they react with, "Here we go again, more religion." Even if they get past the admitting and surrendering of steps one and two, they inevitably balk on three. Maybe Nicodemus had the same problem. One of my most refreshing experiences with the third step came at the hands of a nun in recovery talking about her own problem taking it. She realized, she said, that her problem was that she'd been trying all this time to turn her will and her life over to her understanding of God and not to the God of her understanding. So, perhaps with Nicodemus. So, for sure, with me. Religion, with all its sometime good intention, can so easily get in the way of the Way.

Figs

"Sir," the man replied, "leave it one more year and give me time to dig round it and manure it; it may bear fruit next year; if not, then you can cut it down." (Luke 13:1-9)

I prefer not ever to question whether Jesus knew what he was talking about when he was talking about it. It's too easy to put words in his mouth. My words in his mouth. They never fit. Whatever, we've got another fig tree on our hands in today's gospel. I say "another fig tree" because fig trees show up a lot in the Bible. For example, Eve and

Adam started us off with one, the fig leaves of their imagination, and you know where that got us.

But the fig stories and most other stories are good examples of the trouble with metaphor, the often slippery slope of metaphor. First, some people want to make metaphor into allegory which it isn't. They want to take it apart at the seams and make each of the parts stand for this or that. Trouble with that is this — everybody has different this-and-thats, usually whatever they choose, and they change a lot.

Another problem with metaphor is simply to deny it altogether and just take it literally. This is what happens so often with the Bible. "It says what it means and it means what it says." Trouble there is it too often means whatever I say it means rather than what it means it means which is probably not correct and rarely all that clear.

So I'm not going to fall for the sometimes notion that the fig tree over in Matthew and Mark that failed to produce and got zapped by Jesus is simply an allegory about inadequate churchers and their lot (Mt 21:18-20; Mk 11:12-14). Nor am I making a point that because the fig tree comes off a little better in Luke's version today, it means that we get another chance (well, maybe I will). What I am content to read at least is that Jesus maybe specially liked figs (as do I), and that fig trees may have had some additional literary value for him (as maybe they should but don't for me).

So. Now that all that's perfectly clear and I've pretty well put aside parabolic symbolism, I am reminded that parables — like metaphors and as opposed to allegories — are intended to have only one point toward which all their "parts" move. So I shall try that, myself.

This parable of the fig tree perhaps invites us, simply, to consider the gift of another year of life as an act of God's mercy. Earlier in Luke, John the Baptist declared that the ax lay at the root of the tree, poised to strike (Lk 3:9). Any tree that did not bear fruit would be cut down. In Jesus's parable, however, the gardener pleads for and is granted one more year. The year that Jesus proclaimed, remember, "the year of the Lord's favor" (Lk 4:19), would be a year of forgiveness, restoration, and second chances.

What might we do if we had only a year left to live, or, in the light of today's churchy circumstances, what if the church had only a short time in which to get itself back between the curbs and clean up all the opportunities in God's commandment and commission currently being missed? I suspect it would be an important time.

Luke's lesson of the fig tree could be a challenge to live each day as a gift from God. Live each day in such a way that we will have no fear of giving an account for how we have used God's gift, of whether we even, as they say, give a fig.

Treat

"I am the resurrection and the life." (John 11:25)

When Jesus heard that his good friend Lazarus had died, he treated us to the shortest verse in the Bible: "Jesus wept." It was also, of course, the answer to one of the oldest of the trite trivia questions.

But on this same occasion, Jesus also treated us to the knowledge that in one way, at least, he's not all that different from us. It's called grief. It's universal. It's rock-bottom human stuff. His friend died. It broke his heart. We've been there and done that.

And there's even more. In the gospel story of John's that surrounds this short verse, this mutual, affirming identity, there's enough distancing mystery to last a lifetime, and there's nothing at all trivial about it. Jesus not only weeps when he is saddened, but in short order, he overcomes it. And he doesn't resort to Ms Elizabeth Kübler-Ross's five-step grief recovery process, as grand and nourishing as that is.

He just raises his friend from the dead. And in doing so, he also treats us to the knowledge that in another way, at least, he's so radically different from us as to make us give up altogether. And then, as if all this is not enough, he adds a by-the-way — "I am the resurrection and the life."

And we Christians can take that reality to the bank along with the grief.

I find it well at times like this to remember that our faith is a corporate faith. We affirm a first-person plural creed every time we get together. The God in whom we profess belief is present in the entire gamut of our experiences as well as in the experiences of others with whom we share and from whom we learn. This corporate faith is sustained, informed, and inspired by Holy Spirit, by God's very special agent and presence of community. The God I don't believe in, the God I do believe in, the God filtered through my experience and yours would be unlikely to be identical to or maybe even analogous to the God affirmed by the community. Yet this God is the same God as Jesus's God who, when asked, turns Lazarus out of the tomb and unwraps him to start his new life and give this traumatic story a more or less happy ending.

It seems important to me to remember that when Jesus weeps on this occasion, it may not be so much out of his love for Lazarus, as the Jews presume, but out of his possible sorrow for their indifference to the life that is present in their midst. His life. Himself.

"I am the resurrection and the life," he says. So it is with life, the Life that is Jesus, the Life that Jesus is. This life, as John Evangelist understands it, is eternal life. Whatever else that means, it is never satisfactorily defined quantitatively. It is not a matter of time on end. For it is quality time, not just chronology, calendar time, but special event, turgid-with-meaning kairos fat time. And it is not just one-way time. It is two-way time, give and receive, blessèd time.

For it is time that consists not only of receiving God's love and justice as it is present in Jesus then and there. It also consists in accepting our own role as missioners of love and justice in the world for Jesus in the here and now. And here's the knockout punch — we, too, are resurrection and life as those through whom Jesus confronts and engages this world of neighbors with whom we are made whole and share his redemptive grace.

Grapes

"A man planted a vineyard, and let it out to tenants…" (Luke 20:9-19)

When Jesus was telling this parable, surely he wondered how many times before we get it he must tell, and how many changes he must ring on the story of Adam and Eve in the Garden, the story of accountability.

Such is the way with parables. Whether about apples or fig trees or talents or Noah's ark or good shepherds is really a side issue. Unlike allegories that often lead us around the block to look under every rock for meanings that are nearly always off-the-wall and usually wrong, a parable is a story with only one ax to grind. And further, like Jesus once advised his disciples about parables, they're not told to create faith and understanding, but to require and challenge faith and understanding *(Lk 8:10)*.

The Parable of the Vineyard is not about grapes. At its least it is about accountability. It challenges not only each and every one of us to be accountable, but all of the public and private institutions we inform and shape and think up to serve and govern, as well.

Our church's House of Bishops is no exception. Singled out by some heavy-handed maneuvering among the leaders of the several churches in our Communion and tempted to shift into some pontifical mode, themselves, they have set an example for outstanding collegial accountability not only by resisting that snare, but by affirming the integrity of the church that called them to be servant leaders in their own vineyard in the first place.

As an integral part of this Judaeo-Christian heritage and its stories that we claim as our own, this Parable of the other Vineyard especially challenges the church. We're tenant farmers, the lot of us, and our vocation is to be and to set the model of the very paradigm of accountability. How could there be a greater evangelism than the winsome attraction of an accountable leadership?

One cannot avoid being drawn by the evangelical power of our bishops' action, by their obvious assumption of their rightful pastoral — and prophetic — leadership. There's surely a profound sense of relief for all who've yearned so to hear such affirmative and inclusive words, and for the sudden, if only brief, refreshing transformation of what continues over and over to be a morass of self-serving ineptitude. God speaks to the church in such exchanges. In them, God challenges our faith and understanding that we may see and hear him calling to us. We must not only join our bishops in this witness, we must find in it ourselves.

We've been created by and given a gospel to care for and the vineyard which is also its creation. We live our most faithful stewardship not when we stake claims on it as our criteria by which to judge others right or wrong. No. We live it most faithfully when we embrace its message of peace and justice, love and inclusion, confession and forgiveness, and when we become such a community in ourselves. It is this stewardship for which we are held accountable and to which we can now turn our energies and commitment.

Grass

Then he ordered the crowds to sit down on the grass. Taking the five loaves and the two fish, he looked up to heaven, and blessed and broke the loaves, and gave them to the disciples, and the disciples gave them to the crowds. And all ate and were filled; and they took up what was left over of the broken pieces, twelve baskets full. And those who ate were about five thousand men, besides women and children." (Matthew 14:19-21)

Crowds. Jesus was used to crowds, but not always as welcoming of them as in Matthew's story. They were hungry for whatever he might have, surely in this story mostly for food, but perhaps surprised to find there was more to him than some neighborhood catering service. Crowds were in the news then, as well, but it was the Good News. The fishes and the bread didn't stand in the way.

It's not all that difficult to write off this story as one more incredible miracle. These mysteries in our family history never cease to overcome and baffle us. Mystery doesn't sit well with us moderns. We have a hard time comprehending even metaphor and myth and poetry, let alone a miraculous feeding. We surely want to discount these. With mystery, we'd as soon forget it. But we can't. And that may be the miracle of it.

Healing the sick. Raising the dead. Feeding the thousands. Ascending bodily right through airless space without exploding and into heaven. An altar guild friend of mine said once that when Jesus walked on the water she sure was glad he didn't say Do this in remembrance of me. What a sacristy we'd have to build, she said. Only lifeguards could join the altar guild.

We keep telling these tales and trying to believe them, maybe even in our better moments trying to emulate them, wondering why we don't make at least as much fuss over them as we do over somebody's sexual orientation.

But that is the way with us. Mystery is not tangible. It hasn't got any handles, yet its reality keeps staring us in the face. Over and over again it comes. I suppose it doesn't make a lot of difference what we call it. But maybe it's more down to earth to realize that maybe mystery is a form of grace. Maybe we can get a hold on grace.

Grace. We say it at meals and hope it doesn't go in one ear and out the other. We recognize it on the stage and in the dance and in the ballet of a baseball double play. We'll soon be witnessing it daily in the Olympics.

Grace surrounds us. In the fresh new green after a summer rain. In the blessed smile of baby, even though it may be only a mild touch of colic.

A traveling salesman from New England was having breakfast in a New Orleans hotel coffee shop. When his plate arrived, there was this strange, steaming hodgepodge along its edge near the bacon and eggs. What is this? he asked the waiter. Grits, the waiter answer. But I didn't order it, said the guest. Well you got it anyway, said the waiter. You don't ask for it, you just get it.

Grace is like grits. There's no way you can earn it or deserve it or bring it about any more than, as Frederick Buechner once said, any more than "the taste of raspberries and cream or (anymore than you can) earn good looks or bring about your own birth." "A good sleep is grace," he said. "So are good dreams. Most tears are grace… Somebody loving you is grace. Loving somebody is grace. Have you ever tried to love somebody?"

I suspect that when James wrote that faith without works is dead, maybe what he really meant to say had he been a bit more hip was, Don't let the grace grow under your feet.

Woman's Work

Abraham hurried to the tent and said to Sarah, "Quick, knead three measures of the best flour and make loves." (Genesis 18:1-14)

And a woman named Martha welcomed him into her house. (Luke 10:38-42)

A friend of mine who is a priest was having a "What-do-you-want-to-do-when-you-grow-up?" conversation with her young son. She asked him whether he'd like to be a musician and song writer like his dad. "No," he said. Then she asked whether he might want to be a priest like his mother. "No," he said, indignantly, "that's woman's work."

Coincidentally and by the way, the propers this Sunday are about "woman's work," but they may be too subtle to penetrate some biases very widely. Of course. It's always been that way. We're only now coming to our senses about it. It's been only a few decades that we've finally had the gumption and good judgment to ordain women in this sorely maligned province of the Anglican Communion.

On the face of it, they could be just about visiting — desert nomads visit Sarah and Abraham, Jesus visits Mary and Martha. But they're also full of other themes — caprice and laughter, hospitality and surprise, the work ethic and play, even dark humor about whether Medicare might cover nursery expenses. On the other hand, there are still religious traditions that drag these texts out over and over to make their usual anachronistic and insecure pitch for the "place" of women.

But these are no casual nomadic passersby who drop in on Sarah and Abraham. They're not making a survey or taking a census. They already know who lives there and why. They've not hesitated to make the kind of plans for them that tie them down for the rest of their lives.

Furthermore, Jesus, with that terrible and ominous sense of urgency constantly hovering over him, would hardly be whiling away time at high tea over at Mary's and Martha's without a purpose. Just as Sarah held such a critical and essential place in anything Abraham might be doing for the Lord and could never do without her, so can we assume that Mary and Martha must have held an equally critical and essential place in Jesus's plans for his kingdom.

So let us take these stories a step further for a moment and consider them as being not about Abraham and not even about Jesus, but primarily about women — about Sarah, about Martha, and about Mary, and about all those others, unsung for whatever conscious or unconscious reason. These women were not simply "walk-ons" in the drama of salvation. They have names, purpose, capabilities, needs, children to birth and grief to bear, unique ministries to perform, houses to visit, water to share, wounds to heal, a male social hierarchy to tolerate and endure, and, of course, on occasion, bless the Lord, to manipulate and even laugh about. Lady Bird Johnson's death and all the anecdotes surfacing about her being the power behind Lyndon come to mind.

These are not stories only about vocational values and leadership or the relative importance of running a home, and least of all are they about the priorities of what we rather presumptuously call "holy orders." It took no canon law and no discernment process and no commissions on ministry and no General Conventions to design and confirm the validity of the vocational insights of these women.

Jesus and Abraham's desert visitors were building order into God's strategic itinerary, raising up a faithful genealogy of caregivers, shepherds, bearers of the word. Of course, there's much more here than simply gender issues, but these are stories of a radical breaking open of the established, taken-for-granted scheme of things. Each of the principals in these stories had something that the children of Abraham and ultimately the Jesus movement needed.

Of course, within a century or so after Jesus's times, the church in its increasingly pompous and male-dominated establishment of itself had pretty well sold out to the old secular gender hierarchies. It had successfully removed women from leadership, and swiftly put them where they "belonged." Even twenty centuries later, the seventh bishop of Tennessee still could publicly refer to the imminent and inevitable ordination of women as "apostolic suicide."

Incarnating the good news, it seems, does not mean standing still within the comfortable embrace of the inherited tradition, whatever some of our leaders might claim. Rather does it mean prayerfully and thoughtfully informed amazement at God's making all things new, even things that have held back church and state and culture and, indeed, the family, things that have hitherto had an impressively, if regrettably large following for entirely too long.

Many will remember Katherine Graham of The Washington Post. (Yes, another Katharine!) She was a churchwoman and one of the most powerful figures in American journalism. A comment about her in her obituary seems altogether appropriate as we think about Sarah and Mary and Martha and all those who've stood and now stand in their succession.

A colleague wrote, "Throughout the last half of the twentieth century, (Katherine) used her intelligence, her courage, and her wit to transform the landscape of American journalism." And so it has been and is that our women in orders through their intelligence, their courage, and their wit are transforming the landscape of the Episcopal Church in the USA.

My friend's young son, when he quipped that the priesthood was not for him because it is "woman's work," more than likely did not know how close he was to a truism that was and surely has had its day. In a very few years, I trust, I am confident he will find out.

Crumbs

Just then, a Canaanite woman from that region came out and started shouting, "Have mercy on me, Lord, Son of David; my daughter is tormented by a demon." But he did not answer her at all... But she came and knelt before him saying... "even the dogs eat the crumbs that fall from their masters' table." Then Jesus answered her, Woman, great is your faith! Let it be done for you as you wish." And her daughter was healed instantly. (Mt 15:22-28)

Again and again in this saga of the Way we all strive to follow, it is women who so often provide the major turning points. It began for us with Mary's commitment to God's wish even in her frightfully young life on the very edge of her womanhood. That other and later Mary exemplified for Jesus the contemplative life. The importunate widow set the pattern for spiritual endurance with the unjust judge. The Samaritan woman at the well became the first evangelist. And finally, Mary Magdalene became the apostle who gave the wake-up call to the apostles-to-become.

It has often been a bone of contention whether God — or even Jesus — ever changed his mind. I don't know why, for even a casual reading of Scripture — both Old and New — can demonstrate that reality quite easily.

In today's gospel, this Gentile woman with the possessed daughter should leave us with little doubt. Here she is, pleading with Jesus. She even calls him Lord and Son of David to make it altogether clear she knows to whom she is speaking. And what does she get for her reward? First, she's stonewalled with silence. Next, she's shunned by the disciples. Then twice, she's insulted by Jesus. Only then does he realize there's something new going on in addition to him. Then, accepting it fully, he has only to recognize and affirm her faith for her child instantly to be healed.

"Whatever women do they must do twice as well as men to be thought half as good," said Charlotte Whitton, and then she added, "but luckily, this is not all that difficult."

In this simple and maybe not all that uncommon encounter, there comes a major bend in the history of the gospel and of Jesus's ministry

— and, of course, in ours. His way is not only an ethnic religion's fulfillment as Jesus may once have thought. It is far more, for it is now seen as the redemptive Good News for all people everywhere. Without this moment, one cannot even imagine such a ministry as Paul's to the Gentiles, ironically, the Canaanite woman's kin. And without Paul's ministry, it would be next to impossible even to conceive of the bulk of the New Testament as we know it. But maybe there's at least one more equally important and vital thing especially for us.

As a child growing up in the wilds of west Texas, I remember being fascinated by and not a little confused by the term "melting pot." It seemed somehow to be associated with people, especially with immigrants and always with the Statue of Liberty. As I look back, I had a vision of some humongous cauldron that was surely located in New York City, wherever that was. I suppose I never worried about the unbearable heat implied by such an image, rather only the intense and purposeful mixing and blending of the radically different — especially the radically different peoples that might and could and would take place there.

Now, even if I know better and have a somewhat improved appreciation for metaphor, the image is no less vivid. At its outset, this great land of ours was conceived as a vast and inclusive undertaking. And further, this remarkable political experiment and concept welcomed in its Declaration of Independence not only the audience, but also the judgment of the whole world to this daring venture as a new nation state — under God. "To prove this," said our founding mothers and fathers, "let (the) Facts be submitted to a candid world."

Not the least of the reasons for this unique aspiration for fundamental human inclusiveness, civility, and collegial justice and for the compensating checks and balances at its very heart is human being as the gospel conceives it. Is it too much of a stretch of the imagination that such a wild and crazy notion first caught fire in that encounter with the woman from Cana?

Of course, I do not mean even to imply that I believe this to be a Christian nation. Our frequent moral imbalance, our moral complexity and moral confusion in high places, our ambient puritan stigmata, our embarrassing and shameful treatment of Native Americans and enslaved Africans, let alone the plurality and freedom of expression of our many religions are evidence enough never to entertain such a notion.

But it is, I believe, true that we've inherited a residual pattern and keenness of desire that just as in Christ, there is here, as well, "neither Jew nor Greek, neither slave nor free, neither male nor female" *(Gal 3:28)* in whatever figurative way we can bring that to pass.

I don't know much if anything about Australia, but in the wake of some of our recent confusion about sex and religion, I'm mindful of an Aussie's comment on the internet. She said how grateful she is that in the distant past, the United Kingdom sent their prisoners to Australia and their Puritans to the USA.

We might even in some strange way be grateful for that, ourselves. But I am not exactly sure why.

Treasures

"Hear this," said Amos, "you who trample on the needy, and bring the poor of the land to an end… " (Amos 8:4).

A friend once said that he would like to ask God why God allows such things as war, famine, hunger, terrorism, disease, and poverty, but that he was afraid to. "Why?" I asked. "Because," he said, "God might ask me the same question."

Whether or not Amos ever wondered much about God's stewardship on such matters — and there's not much evidence that he did — God sure wondered about his. Like many of us, Amos was pretty much minding his own business, when, with no warning at all, God signed him on, and it wasn't just to teach Sunday School. Again, like many of us, Amos could think of plenty else he'd rather do, but it didn't take long for him to make the turn. Pretty soon, he had everybody running for cover, and his special target was that one percent of us with all the tax breaks, the *noblesse* who consistently disregard the *oblige*.

"Hear this," said Amos, "you who trample on the needy, and bring the poor of the land to an end…" Pretty soon the Lord will send a famine all over the place, he went on, and not the usual food and water kind which probably wouldn't bother you anyhow, but a famine of making himself so scarce that you won't even have the foggiest idea under whom you're pledging allegiance anymore *(Amos 8:4,11).*

We could use a little more of that kind of Amos and a little less of our kind of bragging and strutting. Nevertheless, all we've got is us, a church that a couple of millennia ago was called The Way, and if its present behavior speaks at all, has lost its own. But prophetic witness, you know, is not just about showing off our own treasures and threatening others to sign up. It's also about showing others the treasures they've already got and don't even know about. That could be, for the moment, the better part of our prophetic ministry.

Historian and churchman Thomas Govan spoke of our system of government as "the American political experiment." He said that it is perhaps the greatest gift we have to offer. But if any of the polls about government are correct, not a lot of people know enough about it to give it away to anybody. We churchers could find a lot less important things to do than tell them. And one way to do that is to learn about it ourselves, maybe take a course on Constitution as a second language, and then to be about in a convincing and winsome way.

Trouble is, the system's not working, and it's not just because we've failed, although there's that. Why are so many millions in poverty and without security of mind and body? Why do we seem so to revere the economy at the ultimate expense of the environment and our people? When will we learn that justice is the social equivalent and embodiment of love? Perhaps as soon as we pay attention and stop our leaders from pulling the flag over our eyes in the name of patriotism.

Among other things, God makes a covenant with us to strive for justice and peace among all people, and to respect the dignity of every human being. We've got a Constitution that has that primarily in mind. All we have to do is insist on its being employed and implemented and to stop tolerating the outrageous way that it's being mishandled and even ignored.

So what does God ask of us? God wants a loving fellowship of faith that withstands the temptation to hide behind its religion and that becomes a secure community of mutual trust and accountability that not only speaks with authority, but demonstrates it by attending to its gospel. It must ask the necessary and searching questions first of itself and then of the society in which it finds itself in service. Only then can it lead by example to become an instrument for healing, always mindful that the nature of God is more nearly shown by grace and forgiveness than by judgment and condemnation.

Then we must learn to have and lead our nation to have a serious and respectful dialogue with the Muslim world and its political leaders, for it is proven time and again that a capacity for self-criticism produces a stronger people. We must ask not only why is such engagement not tolerated today by most Muslim leaders, but why is it even less and less tolerated by our own leaders both in church and state? Surely Islam, a grand religion that never perpetrated the sort of Holocaust that Europe did, is being distorted when it is treated as a guidebook for suicide bombing. How is it that not a single Muslim leader will say that? How is that we cannot help them say it?

The church has all the gifts of grace from God with which to be nourished and energized and made secure so that it can ask such questions and model such a society, so that it can listen creatively, witness to its own resources, and to all those others, as well, that wherever the brokenness of the world is being mended and under whatever name, there is present the kingdom of God. Let not the hostile outrage provoked by the perils of this time impede us, but stir and inspire us as it did Amos in our mutual vocation and in our will to love and perfect justice as children of God. Let us pray that we may engage this challenge comforted by Paul's profound assurance "that neither death, nor life, nor angels, nor principalities, nor things present, nor things to come, nor powers, nor height, nor depth, nor anything else in all creation, will be able to separate us from the love of God in Christ Jesus our Lord."

Race

"What is your opinion? A man had two sons…" (Matthew 21:28)

A scene in an old Clark Gable movie shows him seated at a shoeshine stand getting a shine. The lad shining his shoes comments idly, "Great day for the race." Gable, wondering if he'd missed a turn at the track, anxiously asks, "What race?" The lad answers, "The human race."

Our vision, our understanding depend so very much on our perspectives. The two sons in Jesus's parable were asked by their father to work in the vineyard. One said he would and didn't. The other said he wouldn't and did. This, like a lot of Jesus's parables, begs an explanation that he doesn't always give. When he does, it's rarely the one we either want or expect.

So Jesus never said this was a parable of the kingdom until he elaborates. From a parable about two sons, Jesus segués to, "The tax collectors and the harlots go into the kingdom of God before you." He's talking to churchers, and he says that largely about the kind of folk you don't often see at prayer in their midst, the kind you'd never expect to do the will of God, not on your terms, anyway, and he says they do it anyway, even if after their fashion.

Then Jesus reminds his audience that they've already heard all this from John, the Baptiser, and how they didn't listen when he'd said it plain as day. Then he reminds them again that the last people they'd ever expect could find John's "way of righteousness" are the IRS middle management guy and the streetwalkers. They "go into the kingdom God," for they could never enter it unless they recognized it. They repent. They believe. It might be called "redundant redemption."

It's what we expect to see, what we look for, that without pausing to think, colors our perceptions. It's a common communication mistake. We hear about the race, and one thinks about horses while the other thinks about humans. What on earth we hear when we hear about Anglicanism should be clear and confusing enough for most of us.

Jesus's story is about such presumptions and intentions. Neither a church nor a nation will get very far on such a basis. We cannot and we dare not presume what a purple shirt or a religious vocabulary or a flag lapel pin or a Patriot Act alone means apart from the substance of it. Merely claiming to be an orthodox Anglican or a compassionate conservative will never reveal so much about caring or conserving as truly being and doing, for there's the test.

The kingdom of God and its electorate are probably always a surprise. For it's not a place. It's a relationship. The real litmus test is that wherever the brokenness of the world is being mended, there is present the kingdom of God. Least of all may that healing have any discernible religious labels and probably doesn't. It could be secular to the core. Jesus would sometime put it rather like this, "Wherever you did it unto one of the least of these, you did it unto me."

In the kingdom of God, it is always a great day for the race.

Rules

"I am the living bread which came down from heaven... (whoever) eats this bread will live forever." (John 6:60)

A Roman Catholic bishop up in New Jersey ruled a child's first communion invalid because the priest used bread made of rice flour. He made no exception even when he learned that the child is allergic to wheat.

I don't know of any scriptural qualifiers about the bread — or the wine — at the Last Supper. Of course, there are those who would not welch(sic) even on their death bed in their conviction that it was grape juice all along. And then there was the frenzied rapture a few decades ago when plain old bakery bread began to replace the fish food.

One other story against the grain is that the Jesuits or some other hard-nosed missionaries managed to entice a lot of Chinese into baptism over the years by providing them one of their main staples during times of drought. Maybe old +New Jersey could figure out how he might invalidate all those baptisms so he could disenfranchise a few generations of Chinese Rice Christians. Jesus said, "I am the living bread which came down from heaven... (whoever) eats this bread will live forever" *(Jn 6:60)*. It was a big saying, and it bothered a lot of people, probably still does. When he first said that, church membership dropped off noticeably to an unprecedented low leaving pretty much the original twelve.

Obviously, as if it made any difference, he never went far enough to say whether this new bread was of wheat or rice or barley or whatever, just mostly of himself which was problem enough. Leave it to the church and to its bishops like the astute Bishop from New Jersey for major theological decisions like that.

As for the rest of us, we'll keep avoiding the real bread by busying ourselves, thank you, with and about who can love whom and how and even whether.

Rescue

"There was a man, a landowner, who planted a vineyard..." (Matthew 21:33)

Vineyards get a lot of mileage in the Bible. There must be something about vines that appeals to preachers. "Meanwhile, back at the vineyard…" It's as good a metaphor as any, I suppose. And so we have today another vineyard story. But this time, the story is not about vines. At a deeper level, it's uncannily about greed.

And what could be more appropriate for our times, for this very moment, than greed? Seven hundred billion dollars worth of greed as if something that simple could bail us out. It's about greed, and being about greed, it's inevitably about violence. And we're all very familiar with those twin evils — not only in Jesus's time, but for sure in ours, for they go hand in hand. They're going hand in hand at this very moment at this here and now.

Our morning story recounts a householder who sends his servants twice to check with his sharecroppers about the status of his grapes. The croppers not only don't report, they throw out the owner's emissaries and murder them. So he sends his son. Out of their absurd overconfidence and misjudgment, they kill the son in the strange reasoning that this way, they can take possession of the entire inheritance. Greed.

Remember the scene in the 1987 movie "Wall Street" where the protagonist Michael Gekko is CEO of a major brokerage house. He's addressing the board and stockholders of a large paper company. After berating them at some length about their careless and malicious management of money, he concludes: "I am not a destroyer of companies. I am a liberator of them! The point is, ladies and gentleman, that greed — for lack of a better word — is good. Greed is right. Greed works. Greed clarifies, cuts through, and captures the essence of the evolutionary spirit. Greed, in all of its forms — greed for life, for money, for love, knowledge — has marked the upward surge of mankind. And greed — you mark my words — will not only save (your paper company), but (as well) that other malfunctioning corporation called the USA."

It is a shocking scene. The suspense is palpable, even in the theatre audience. It is as if the character Gekko has actually turned and indicted us. Perhaps it is the last place we'd ever expect to feel like we'd encountered an Old Testament prophet face to face, least of all his character. For not a one of us has not experienced at least a moment of greed or been the victim of someone else's greed. Of the seven deadly sins, greed goes by the fancier name avarice, has a most impressive staying power, and is not easily forgot.

It's not an unfamiliar pattern. But it's no longer grapes. It's oil. It's not vineyards. It's global warming. (I saw a bumper sticker. It said, "I love global warming.") It's refineries and SUVs and road rage. It's not farming. It's international chaos and poverty and genocide and corporate welfare resenting care for the poor. But at the seat of it all, it's still greed, greed issuing in violence and even more tragically in some politicized cover-up.

George Hunsinger of Princeton Theological Seminary writes that George Orwell talked about this in his famous essay on "Politics and the English Language." He spoke of how we use language to name things without calling up mental pictures of them. Perhaps it might be something like this: An invasion is engineered on false pretenses, hundreds of thousands are killed or maimed, no one is safe in the streets. It's called "collateral damage." Homes, hospitals, and mosques are blown up. Water, electricity, and other services are cut off. Civil society is destroyed. Half the population is left without any means of livelihood. Detainees are tortured and humiliated. Prisons are filled with people picked up off the streets. Cities are targeted and destroyed. And the insurgency is blamed on outside elements. All this is called "bringing democracy."

"Political language," Orwell said, "— and with variations this is true of all political parties — is designed to make lies sound truthful and murder sound respectable and to give an appearance of solidarity to pure wind." And so here we are. Somehow in the midst of all this we're to find a way to contend with it and to incarnate the covenant we made at our baptism.

It has never been easy to be a follower of that Way — the Way, that lovely word the early disciples of Jesus used to describe themselves and their purpose. After all, greed for power coupled with violence crucified their Lord and likely could easily crucify them. He made that very clear for them and for us. Every time we are signed with the cross do we take up and embrace the cross, the symbol of greed and violence and paradoxically of grace and justice. But let us recover Jesus's metaphor of the vineyard for a moment. I confess it would be difficult to find a better one. For the irony of our time is that we are the sharecroppers and also the servants sent by the householder. And we are his heirs. We not only bear the Christ, but are asked to seek and serve the Christ wherever and in whomever. Meanwhile, back at the vineyard…

Keeper

"No slave can serve two masters; for a slave will either hate the one and love the other, or be devoted to the one and despise the other. You cannot serve God and wealth." (Luke 16:13)

Apparently, there's not much all that novel about bailouts.

Luke's tale about the unjust steward from twenty centuries ago tells about bailouts by reducing debt rather than by paying off debt. The steward had got himself fired for somehow wasting his boss's goods. So he gambled on getting the boss to forgive him and at the same time presuming to make friends with the debtors who'd previously probably hated to see him coming to collect. Cutting their debts by half or more maybe also pleased the boss by providing a more reliable return than he ever had expected. It surely made friends for the steward all around, not to mention possibly saving face in a messy situation and maybe even giving him another opportunity to restore his practice. *(Lk 16:1-13)*

Funny thing on the way to the market was that his scheme worked. And best of all, it got him out of manual labor and standing on the corner with a sandwich board and a tin cup. For as it happened, the irony of it all seems to be that the boss did actually commend him for collecting at least some of what he'd maybe never have got in the first place. Faith is faith, the boss decided, whether it is in a little or a lot, so take it when you can get it, and dishonesty is dishonesty, whether it, too, is in a little or not so much, so cut your chances and take what you can get.

Anyway you look at it, it's about bailout. The unjust steward in Luke's tale was hard after some on his own even if it was with somebody else's money. And the upshot gives us the famous bonus counsel on the side that "no servant can serve two masters..." especially when they're God and wealth.

It's famous counsel alright, but you'd think the way we seem to ignore it, we're not hearing all that so well. Luke's tale is for sure a gentler way of summing up what's so much at issue in our current political malaise. It's not only about bailout, but it's also about taxes if only in a backhanded way of at least lowering one's bracket. The steward would seem right at home with the mantra of our time: "It's the economy, stupid." For somehow, the subject of taxes always appears whenever the economy shows up and in whatever way we pay them — in measures of wheat or quite coincidentally in our time even in measures of oil.

This parable is about the economy. Literally the management of a household. And what is that but the way we care for the environment and more especially the way we care for one another? Somehow to hear it from Jesus, serving God and caring for the poor obviously has always had a lot in common. Like the old song about love and marriage, you can't have one without the other. Luke's story reminds us that we are stewards of all this, some of us just, some of us unjust. But however we accept that vocation, we cannot embrace the commission God gave us in our inheritance to look after Eden in any other way. Cain asks God the question for us.

"Am I my brother's keeper?"

And God's answer is the whole of the Bible and of creation ever since. It is a resounding Yes. The Earth is for our keeping and for our keeping up.

There's a new book, a parody from the writers of The Daily Show. It's called *Earth (the Book)*. It is not so subtly conceived as a handy guide for extraterrestrials who arrive on this planet after humanity has become extinct just in case those extraterrestrials want to know what they are missing. It adopts a faux-scientific tone to explain the planet, its life forms and their quantifiable characteristics. In short, Earth is billed as the "No 1 Planet for Alien Tourists." *(cf "NYTimes" review 16ix10, pp C1&C6)*

I don't want to put theology in their mouths, and I couldn't possibly know exactly what those authors intended, but whatever, their splendid parody suggests at least that God will probably never stop looking for "stewards," just, or not so just.

Popsicle

"If they do not hear Moses and the prophets, neither will they be convinced if someone should rise from the dead." (Luke 16:31)

A two-page ad in the Washington Post magazine reports that the Sprint cellphone people are promoting what they call, "A new class of cellular luxury — the world's first $10.5 million phone — a limited-time offer for billionaires."

Apparently fearful that even this might not catch a billionaire's eye, Sprint threw in a bonus. Buy one and get a private island all of your own. Then Sprint suggested to its anticipated audience, "When you're in the business of dominating this quaint little popsicle stand called planet Earth, you need the technology that keeps you acting fast." And then, the clincher, The "Island offer is available only to the wealthiest one hundred people on planet Earth. Offer expires next Saturday."

In the light of this opportunity, the story about the rich man and Lazarus in our gospel today literally screams out the reminder from the past that the more things change, the more they stay the same. This gospel parable is a story about warning and about how the security of wealth can blind one from seeing the handwriting on the wall. In this Sprint ad, a contemporary parable in its own way, one can rarely see such a notice even on the wall of the very environment that makes so much of all that wealth possible in the first place.

The offer, preoccupied with its own tempting expiration date, did not add, of course, that this planet Earth, this "Popsicle" may well be on the verge itself of expiring, maybe not next Saturday, but a lot sooner than one might imagine. Further, had they been thinking at all, they may well have picked another metaphor than one that melts even faster than the glaciers whose disappearance themselves already shows how easily this island can become a mere sandbar.

Characteristic of many like himself, the rich man even tries to use a dead Lazarus as a servant to make his life easier. But it is not only wealth in itself that's being disdained in this parable or even in the ad. In both, it is the use of wealth and the blind false security that it can so often cause. Such wealth prevented the rich man from heeding the warning of Moses and the prophets that had been there all along and together with another two thousands years of tradition remains there for us.

The rich man in the parable ignored Moses and the prophets and, indeed, as Abraham said neither would he heed even someone "risen from the dead." Indeed, we have that "someone." We have this risen Christ in each of us and in the lives of all his faithful followers down through the centuries. How might we witness to it? Will we send Lazarus or, as it is said, will we go ourselves and tell it on the mountain?

Deed

John said to him, "Teacher, we saw someone casting out daemons in your name, and we tried to stop him, because he was not following us." But Jesus said, "Do not stop him; for no one who does a deed of power in my name will be able soon afterward to speak evil of me. Whoever is not against us is for us." (Mark 9:38-40)

Extraordinary stories about walking on water and about being swallowed by fish and about turning water into wine, at best may strike most of us not only as quaint, but perhaps even as absurd. Pity those few who feel they must accept them as part of their belief in the inerrancy of scripture. For them, these tales simply have to be absolute nightmares.

Maybe Paul had this sort of thing in mind when he called the gospel a scandal and a stumbling block to the Greeks and Jews and surely would have included us if we'd been standing around. But because we are so shocked anyway, our preoccupation with the lack of any convincing fact about these stories can lead us to risk overlooking what may be any possible convicting truth within them.

So why is it that the obvious consensus of the faithful in our spiritual genealogy down through the centuries is to tell these stories over and over and over again? What is there about them that makes a difference? What is there about them that we can believe, that somehow, we must believe? If we are to take comfort in them, how can we?

The 18th-century poet Samuel Coleridge suggested a way. He called it the "willing suspension of disbelief." He spoke of that childlike ability to believe that is born firmly in each of us, that characteristic which Jesus likened as evidence for the presence of the kingdom, but which so often withers as we grow older and are taught by some that the world of imagination is simply not all that reliable.

The power of Coleridge's phrase, the "willing suspension of disbelief," is the conviction that not only disbelief, but belief, as well, is a matter of choice. And that by virtue of God's creative imagination of us into human being, we are free so to choose. Faith, itself, is a choice. It is primarily an act of the will, a commitment. Just so is the choice to rid ourselves of what may be a clutter of disbelief.

We live in a time when few of us will to believe what we do not already understand or what we have not experienced or what does not meet our own personal criteria in order even to qualify as "experience."

Most of us have not been swallowed by a fish. Most of us have not walked on water, even if in certain moments some of us leave the impression rather that we think we could if brought to the test.

But like Jonah and Peter who were faced with these things, all of us have been afraid and more than likely will be again. All of us have eyes and hands and feet that haven't always been morally impeccable. All of us know someone whose faith we are convinced is "less" than our own, but whose faithfulness casts out demons again and again, demons that we can't even lay a hand on. Our fear to believe, to choose faith, can often be one of our special scandals and stumbling blocks.

We live also in a time when fear of almost any kind is our enemy, when to triumph over fear or even simply to hold fear at bay has become more important than to understand it. A growing part of our own beloved church is making the strangest of choices in these times, judgments clearly grounded in an obsession with being right and a profound fear of being wrong.

As a nation and as a people, we've spent billions to conquer fear, to make ourselves secure from our doorsteps all the way to outer space. This anxiety about a hostile environment without can only create in us a hostile environment within. We greet strangers with at least a mild suspicion, if not more. Addiction, a most singular form of fear, is rampant, not only addiction to chemicals, but addiction to power and to control and to fear itself. Wherever such addiction resides latent in our genes, as the evidence increasingly suggests that it can, fear inevitably drives it out of hiding and into control over us.

Perhaps, then, it may help to suspend our disbelief when we realize that these ancient stories are not so much about controlling fear, but about understanding and naming fear and about understanding the gravity of our moral behavior. We inherit these stories and hear them over and over that we might understand, not that we might better describe or define or convince or demonstrate through research, but that we might understand, that their message might have meaning for us, that it might make sense and become a part of us, that it might ultimately overcome our fear or at least cast it into a manageable perspective.

Just as the will to love precedes true loving, so can the will to suspend disbelief create an environment for believing. One can choose to free oneself of the notion that something must be demonstrably and factually clear before it can be considered true. To open ourselves to that possibility is the meaning and can be the beginning of our spiritual awakening.

Jonah and Peter were rescued because they believed God was accessible even under the most outrageous conditions. Remember the story of the stranger casting out demons even though he was not a card-carrying member of the discipleship. And remember how insulted were those on the inside. Perhaps that's the message, the answer, the understanding, even the healing value of a willing suspension of disbelief.

Perhaps it is another story at another time, but this is also a story about witnessing. Witnessing, not simply as telling our own faith, our own stories, but witnessing as pointing to wherever we see these same gospel signs by whatever name and "performed" by whomever, commissioned and ordained or no. Jesus was quite clear about that.

The New Testament scholar and Lutheran bishop Krister Stendahl once put it like this: Wherever we witness the brokenness of the world being mended, there is present the Kingdom of God.

Seeds

The apostles said to the Lord, "Increase our faith!" The Lord replied, "If you had faith the size of a mustard seed, you could say to this mulberry tree, 'Be uprooted and planted in the sea,' and it would obey you." (Luke 17:5-6)

When the apostles said to the Lord, "Increase our faith," they surely had the right idea, only they asked the wrong question.

Although his answer wasn't all that environmentally correct, they could have known from it, as well, can we. If your faith were merely the size of a mustard seed, Jesus said, you could deforest the planet.

Ironically, he answered them in their own terms — Size — to show them the results on his terms — Effect. The apostles wanted more faith, Jesus wanted more faithfulness. For so long as we put more stock by quantity than quality, by style than substance, he implied, we'll never catch the spirit. The Great Commission to baptize all nations is rendered senseless until it is grounded and motivated firmly in the Great Commandment to love.

You want faith-based, Jesus implies, I'll give you faith-based. Faith and love and hope are communal values long before they're personal possessions. Indeed, we never possess them as if to parcel them out on occasion and on demand, we live them as if to find in them a constant and consistently rewarding way of life, a pattern for ourselves and for others.

We don't *have* faith, we *do* faith. It's never about how much faith. It's about living the life of the faithful. For it is there where is the leverage that uproots the status quo, the spirit that permeates the body politic, and turns our hearts and minds unto the love of God and neighbor and self.

It is the age-old question of church and state. So long as the church remains obsessed with its size, its orthodoxy, its always "being right," its "how much," it will continue to be altogether indiscernible from any other secular institution measuring itself by the same criteria and have even less relevance. Only when it ceases accounting how much and, in turn, looks inward at how accountable, will size cease to matter and will relevance take effect.

But careful, beloved, it's gangbusters out there. As says the old Franciscan prayer, God may just bless us with enough foolishness to believe that we can make a difference in this world, so that we can do what others claim cannot be done.

Dots

He was setting out on a journey when a man ran up, knelt before him and put this question to him, "Good master, what must I do to inherit eternal life?" (Mark 10:17)

It has been said that when it is a question of money, everybody is of the same religion. But apparently that isn't so in Mark's story about the rich man and Jesus.

Actually, Mark's story about money and poverty is really not a story about money and poverty. Jesus is not condemning wealth, nor is he extolling poverty. Neither does he have it in for camels. But it is a story about what another Campbell by the name of Joseph called "following your bliss," about unloading the road blocks and doing what you truly wish with your life. To put it another way, Mark's story is really about discipleship and about sacrifice.

It reminds me of the great pianist Vladimir Horowitz who once was asked, "What is music?" (Which also reminds me how I've used this metaphor more than once and probably will again.) He answered that music is made up of little dots on a page, some black, some white. Almost anyone, he said, can render them with some instrument, a voice, a horn, or some string, rather like one can learn to use a typewriter to unravel shorthand. But, he said, that is not music.

Music, he said, is what's "behind the dots." Music is getting behind the dots and connecting them and making them yours or yours together with others, bringing the music into the present and sharing it. Music is never past, save in our memories. And it's never yet been done, save in our planning.

Thus music is a splendid analogy for life. One of the ways we, the church, read the dots, is that every week we come together here in this place and around this table for a kind of family reunion. We share a meal through which we look behind the bread and wine to remember Jesus and, in a way, to make him present in our lives and to look for him in the lives of others. We also hear stories, stories that are like the black and white dots until we make them our own, until someone tells or sings or plays them, until we not only hear them, but listen to them and for them here and beyond. These are the things family reunions are about. They share meals and they tell stories. They are concerts to which we listen and then remember, bring to life in the interim.

Our family story this morning, our spiritual genealogy about wealth and poverty and discipleship is really a story about sacrifice. To sacrifice something is not only to give it up or to give it away or to do without it. Listen to the word: to sacrifice something is to make it sacred, to make it holy. And to make something holy is to complete it, to make it whole, to heal it, to give it integrity and purpose and direction. It is to fulfill it and to help make it what it is intended to be and to become. That is what it means to remember, to "do this in remembrance…" To sacrifice is to read "behind the dots" and to embrace life the way life comes to us. When the man asked Jesus about eternal life, he knelt before him and addressed him as "Good Teacher." Jesus answered with, "Why do you call me good? No one is good but God alone." Perhaps Jesus meant something like that his life is a window to God, an icon through whom God is revealed, like the music we must read behind, through which the melody takes shape.

But often and again like the rich man in Mark's story, stuff gets in the way and keeps us from becoming whole. He asked Jesus how he could gain eternal life, how, to put it another way, he could become a citizen of the kingdom of God. Jesus answered by reminding him of the Commandments. The man said that he had "Been there and Done that" with the Commandments. Then Jesus pulled out the big guns and said for him to give away all of his wealth to the poor and to follow him, to become his disciple. Then, it was, that the man turned away, for he had great wealth. His wealth had got in his way. He was not looking behind the dots.

So what is Jesus saying to us about wealth, about money? Jesus is making no assault on wealth as such, nor does he condemn those who possess it. Further, he does not necessarily praise poverty as a virtue. The man's departure from Jesus in sadness and regret tells us that his life has been defined by his wealth and that a new life defined some other way is beyond his imagination. He cannot see behind the dots. Jesus doesn't force him or embarrass him or threaten him. He simply gives him the freedom to say "no." For if he were to say "yes," his "yes" would be hollow and meaningless and empty, it would simply display the dots and not what is behind them. Jesus's advice, of course, is for this particular man in his particular circumstance, even if his words could be expanded to include all of us who might have any similar sort of road block keeping us from a full life.

For it is through opening our own unique and infinitely important lives in this way that, as St Paul told the Roman Christians, that we let nothing "be able to separate us from the love of God in Christ Jesus our Lord." That is the way we can "read behind the dots" and really play the music.

Doors

"And will not God grant justice to his chosen ones who cry to him day and night? Will he delay long in helping them? I tell you, he will quickly grant justice to them. And yet, when the Son of Man comes, will he find faith on earth?" (Luke 18:1-8)

At its heart, most theology, like most fiction, is autobiography *(after Frederick Buechner in "The Sacred Journey," Harper Collins, 1982, p 1).*

That is, most of what we think about God or don't think about God and about what God does and doesn't do and should do and shouldn't do and about what we and God do together and don't do together, all this, when push comes to shove, is shaped and affected by the story of our lives. Plain and simple, it's autobiography.

It's a mistake, unfair, and insulting to put theology in ivory towers or behind altars where it's safe and inaccessible. Theology belongs in kitchens and bedrooms, SUVs and traffic jams, beer halls and soccer games where it's vulnerable and in-your-face. Underneath all the doctrines and liturgies and catechisms, that is, the "religious stuff," we always find an experience of flesh and blood, a human face smiling or frowning or weeping or covering its eyes for the glare.

That's one reason why it's so good to keep a constant eye out for those faces in our family history in that public library genealogy we call the *Bible*. Take these stories: Here's cousin Jacob in a dirt fight with heaven only knows whom, and here's the gutsy widow that reminds us of Aunt Maudie banging on the court house door *(Gen 32:3-8, 22-30; Lk 18:1-8a)*.

Further, the Book of Genesis makes no attempt to conceal the fact that Jacob, among other things, was a crook who twice cheated his lame-brain brother Esau out of his inheritance and at least once took advantage of his old father Isaac's blindness to play him for a sucker. We know next to nothing about the widow save that she was perhaps more enduring than endearing. We can be sure that God was rather fond of both. Knowing that may just hold out some hope for us. Knowing that is really sermon enough for any Sunday. (But we preachers often never know when to stop even if we're ahead.)

These stories and God's response to them tell us about faith, that faith, too, is radically autobiographical. Like a two-by-four between the eyes, these readings tell us that faith and perseverance are not all that different, that faith, unlike a neat system full of big words, is more like wrestling with God and banging on doors and maybe finally getting some sort of results, even if not always exactly what we wanted.

There is a collect that puts it rather much the same way if somewhat more delicately when it prays to God to help us "persevere with steadfast faith…" *(BCP p 235)*. For God does not always come to us in pillars of cloud by day or fire by night, easily recognized and free of all ambiguity. God meets us in circumstances we have to strive to explain in other terms. Without the persistence of a Jacob or a widow who would not let go, we may abandon our struggle for faith because it does not appear to be faith as we had imagined it. Jacob and the widow and even the old non-believing judge remind us that the persistence and the tenacity itself is faith.

For faith is like life. It is purpose made incarnate. It is better understood as a verb than as a noun, as a process rather than as a possession, as on-again-off-again rather than once-and-for-all, as risking being wrong, as not always having to be right or orthodox, as a journey without maps.

We remember as well to our benefit that doubt isn't the opposite of faith, doubt is a critical and essential element of faith, and that faith comes not as a result of understanding, but that faith is, itself, a way of understanding and of giving meaning to our lives.

One of the things that has hounded the church through the centuries is that it gives too much attention to its religion and not enough to its faith, not faith as doctrine, for heaven's sake, but as faithfulness. It doesn't make disciples by right belief, it wins disciples by faithful living, by being a community that people simply and finally cannot resist cozying up with.

Of course, it's easier to pay more attention to our religion than to our faith. For one thing, religion is far more simple and not nearly so risky. Religion offers the false comfort of easy answers, faith raises the discomfort of hard questions. Faith secures the vision that protects religious conviction from becoming religious delusion. Finally, faith enables an environment that is less judgmental and more forgiving and in which love can mature.

Like the widow pestering the unjust judge and like Jacob contending with God, we mumble and curse and try another path because these snares keep snagging our hems or bruising our feet. But we try another path and keep stubbing painful toes until, finally, we pay attention and then can ask the theological question, What, finally, is the message, the meaning in all this? What is there to give us understanding?

For one thing, it tells us that control is an illusion, and that perhaps we might try gratitude rather than mastery and power. I got an omelet in a restaurant one time that was as tough as shoe leather, but remotely edible. I groused about it, privately, but I'd have been better off had I simply been grateful for food and whatever nourishment there may have been in those tired eggs.

Be grateful for work. Work gives shape to the day, and many more today wish they had it. Be grateful for people. Each is interesting in his or her way and teaches us new things. Be grateful for love. How lonely it would be not to miss anyone, not to have someone to telephone or to be telephoned by or yes, even to grieve.

And be grateful for God. Distress in our homeland will not go away soon. Evil forces are arraigned against us. I hesitate to be so presumptuous as to use that word "evil," because warfare rarely pits good against evil. Warriors have values and codes and limits. Spreading weapons of mass destruction is not the act of a warrior. It is an act of an enemy of life itself. God is strong against such enemies.

Faith and love give us access to that strength and to our potential to use it. They allow us to wrestle, to pound on doors, to endure, and perhaps even to understand.

Bouquets

The tax collector, standing far off, would not even look up to heaven, but was beating his breast and saying, "God be merciful to me, a sinner!" (Luke 18:13)

"When I have arranged a bouquet for the purpose of painting it, I always turn to the side I did not plan." — Renoir, to Matisse

I came across these words as a kind of suggested "text" for a book on space photography. They were meant, I think, to emphasize the profound beauty of nature beyond earth, a beauty quite beyond anything we humans might have to do with arranging. *(Timothy Ferris, "Space Shots," Pantheon, 1984)*

Much of what we undertake today seems exceptionally preoccupied with arranging and rendering "bouquets." We classify people and institutions into molds, into systems, political or economical, social or religious, geographical, sexual, or racial. And then we exalt our own notions and constructs. We are anxious about order and authority, defining and redefining it.

In the process of such introspection, we do not often stand beyond and reach for perspective. We do so at the risk of compromising rather than appreciating the beauty of the creative gifts of God or nature or whatever, rather, I suppose, like in the story of Adam and Eve and their denying their stewardly commission in the Garden.

This does not seem to me to be the purpose of the religious life. But then, what is?

The Gospel story of the pharisee and the publican tells of two such purposes. The one is to be bound like the Pharisee into a neat and rigid and above all Religiously Correct system in which, ultimately, there is only security and no risk at all. The other is rather like the tax-collector, and that is to confront and embrace and often be overwhelmed by the devastating ambiguity of one's own human being.

To be human, we're taught to believe, is to be created in the image of God. A very important way we can look at that affirmation is not that we are visual clones of the Almighty, but that rather are we imagined into being by God. Our tradition suggests further that this means we are set free to choose, and that freedom of choice is a primary purpose of our humanity and thus our religion as we understand it.

God's imagining of us grants us the freedom to choose: to choose to love, to choose to reason, to choose to create, and to choose to live in harmony with God and all God's creation. *(BCP p 845)* Nowhere in that short litany is there the suggestion that these personal and deeply intimate choices must be right, only that they be free, untethered by "oughts" and "shoulds." That is the kind of freedom that more or less defines freedom. It is the risk that always comes with grace, both God's and ours.

I'm skeptical of the fixation with and insistence upon rightness that pervades so much of our political and religious thinking and policy-making. I am struck by the theme of those who seem to need an Anglican Covenant as if our faithful following the Way has somehow become a pejorative, a move for us to become better masters rather than better colleagues and companions on this journey, searching, stumbling, risking, adapting.

Spiritual maturity, I believe, may be assessed not by how right we are, but by how freely we live into and become our human being as

God imagines it — how well we live with change, how clearly we make our choices, how analogously imaginative we ourselves are, how vulnerable we are willing to become, and how committed we are to these goals even as they lack the clarity we might desire. It is a vain heart, I think, that wastes itself in the oxymoronic pursuit of righteousness, for righteousness, by its very nature, comes least of all when it is chased down.

Let us not overlook that both men in our parable came into the temple to pray, the one to the "amen corner" apparently just to review for God his resumé, the other to the back of the bus, as it were, to take stock of his sins. Only one seemed truly aware of why he was there and what might be found there with which to begin his healing.

I'm aware that the collect* speaks of faith and hope and charity as much as gifts, as well as goals. It speaks of God's promise as accessible only through love. Perhaps as we arrange, step by step, our lives, as did Renoir his bouquets for the purpose of ordering them, even striving to become more faithful, more loving, more hopeful, yes, even more righteous, may we not turn them around to that side of us we did not plan, that just fell into place, and there find new beauty, even new freedom, in the view beyond of the One who first imagined us.

*Almighty and everlasting God, increase in us the gifts of faith, hope, and charity; and, that we may obtain what you promise, make us love what you command; through Jesus Christ our Lord, who loves and reigns with you and the Holy Spirit, one God, now and forever. Amen. (BCP 235)

Talent

"For it is as if a man, going on a journey, summoned his slaves and entrusted his property to them…" (Matthew 25:14)

"The New Orleans poor got what they deserved." Not long after Katrina, a moderately wealthy and inordinately conservative Christian gentleman and otherwise law-abiding citizen used the Parable of the Talents to make this point to me. He implied that they had had the same opportunities as all of us and did not take advantage of them.

I suppose that for some, there may be more than an element of truth in that point of view and even some smug comfort. "Use it or lose it" is not for many an uncommon way of looking at life, nor is it always wrong. But punishing the poor for being poor strikes me as hardly consistent with Jesus's prophetic ambiance of justice and grace and love, especially for the poverty-stricken. Indeed, that Jesus, according to Matthew, was the very source of this parable is a reality that must not be overlooked, for it is integral in searching for its meaning.

This is a kingdom parable. Jesus is saying, "The kingdom of God will be" the way this story tells us it will be. Those who refuse actively to obey God and to put to use the life God has given us are not only just missing the point, they are jeopardizing that life and that freedom in peril of losing both.

When Jesus spoke this parable, the word "talent" referred to a unit of weight measurement and also to money. It did not refer, at that time, to what we might call a "gifted ability." As with all his parables, it is better that we let it speak from its own context at the time of its telling. The story is about a man who had servants. He was going on a journey. He entrusted his possessions to them as stewards, not as owners. Further, it is helpful to note that each of the varying amounts was given according to the abilities of the recipient, a condition that obviously will affect the outcome.

The Kingdom of God is not a slave state. The parable does not defend slavery in any way. Our servanthood in the Kingdom is to be modeled after Jesus and balanced, as well, with the fact that we are children of God. The parable does not state that the kingdom of God is primarily about money. The presence of money surely serves to make it more lifelike for us, but that is not what it's about.

It is not at all about what we have, but about our stewardship with what we have. Like the ordered freedom that is at the heart of our normative Anglican tradition, it is this point of commonality and of productive obedience among us all that is compared in this story. The parable challenges us to use our freedom to choose and to be obediently productive through staying open to and discerning the Holy Spirit in our lives.

My friend who was so ready to judge the poor apparently overlooked entirely any message there may be in the Parable of the Talents about our collegial stewardship as a nation. Perhaps for a moment, at least, did Katrina force us to face exactly to whom it is that our rich productivity is obedient.

Change

A poor widow came in and put in two small copper coins, which are worth a penny. Then [Jesus] called his disciples and said to them, "Truly I tell you, this poor widow has put in more than all those who are contributing to the treasury. For all of them have contributed out of their abundance; but she out of her poverty has put in everything she had, all she had to live on." (Mark 12:42-44)

There's a pleasant irony in Jesus's story of the widow's two copper coins. It keeps us mindful that the gospel's Good News is not only about change, it is also about small change.

This fact about the gospel seems forever to escape the church, and it is easy to see why. God puts the church in the world as a change-agent, but also as a "safe house" where people can come not only to worship, but to risk being themselves and talking about what really matters in their lives. To talk about change and about how hard it is to change, about why they need to learn to love and need to learn to be loved, about why some people are so mean-spirited and others so helpless, about why life is so difficult and often so unfair, about why there seems to be so much evil and so little good.

Imagine their feeling when they discover how consumed some churches are with self-preservation and with keeping the status quo. Imagine what a shock it must be to find the church's limited energy wasted in debating a part of its security system, such as whether to change its prayer book or hymnal or its scheduled hour of worship or whether to allow God to give a sacramental blessing to a deep and devoted companionship outside legal marriage. Imagine how puzzled one must be to discover all these issues held on the same level of importance and labored about seemingly without end, as if the gospel really is decided by majority opinion.

No wonder one more segment of people becomes convinced that the church is an inept and limited institution with little or no interest in risking its life for the good health of a broken world. When millions need food and medicine, when religion-based violence produces slaughter and hopelessness, when a handful profits and masses struggle even to survive, when armies itch to seize the day, yet the church so often remains beset by the small-minded and self-serving.

Reflecting on St Paul, Paul Tillich reminded us that the message of Christianity is not Christianity, but a new creation *(2 Cor 5:17)*. To risk a new creation is to risk the greatest change of all. But paradoxically, to embrace this gospel about change is the one condition that allows for the unconditional, and the unconditional love of God is the essential environment in which one can dare to risk surrendering to the frightening experience of a new creation.

For what is both Good and New about the Good News is the wild claim that Jesus did not simply tell us that God loves us even in our wickedness and folly and wants us to love each other in the same way and to love God, as well, but that if we will just get ourselves out of the way, God can and will single-handedly bring about this unprecedented transformation of our hearts.

And what is Good and New about the Good News is the mad insistence that Jesus lives on among us not just as another haunting memory but as the outlandish, holy, and invisible power of God working not just through the sacraments but in countless hidden ways to make even people like us loving and whole beyond anything we could conceivably pull off by ourselves.

And thus the gospel is not only Good and New but, if you take it in good humor, it's a Holy Terror. Jesus never claimed that the process of being changed into a human being — and that, by the way, is what conversion is all about — was going to be a Sunday School picnic. On the contrary, one of life's most painful experiences is hanging on for dear life to our refusal to change.

We think of the church as protection. We even speak of a part of its architecture as the sanctuary, but that hallowed ground was never intended to avoid change, only to nourish and enhance the onerous process of maturing spiritually. Such sanctuary is there to remind us of the widow and her gloriously pitiful offering as she majestically rubbed shoulders in the temple with the fat cats and their trickle-down economics yet gave away without question all that she had.

It is probably no accident that the liturgy gurus placed this story of the widow's mite smack dab in the middle of the fall season when most parishes have their every member canvass. Perhaps the planners hope for at least a mild twinge of conscience in the pews and in the pulpits. But that is to miss the point. For the issue, you see, is not what we do with money, but what we do with ourselves and the ministry to which we are called and which money may or may not enable.

In our story this morning, Jesus warned us about the scribes, not because they were guilty of bad doctrine or wrong-footed politics, but because they were mean, and they were small. They trivialized their positions of respect in exchange for small favors. At a time when people needed large and noble spirits, they were petty. They remind us, as well, of one kind of human behavior that has hardly changed at all.

There are small parishes which are already remarkably on the way to becoming enclaves where people can dare to wrestle productively with change. They can also be places where many of the larger church's so resistant movements can be seen as mostly theater where vagueness and shouting and religiose performances make for marginal entertainment value at best. And they can proclaim to all who would hear that the world as it really is out there beyond this ecclesiastical myopia makes such shallowness seem positively dangerous.

Note: My frequent "research" colleagues Tom Ehrich and Fred Buechner (plus a pinch of Jack Spong) again had something of a hand in this current homiletic mayhem.

Reminder

"Now he is not God of the dead, but of the living; for all live to him." (Luke 20:38)

This conversation of Jesus with the Sadducees is an encounter and reminder for our time.

How easily we impose our notions and our experiences framed by this world on what God may have in store for us in a newer age, let alone this one. Perhaps it is truly unavoidable that we do, for we would seem to have no other alternative. Even so, it is best that we not lose sight of how easy it is to risk underestimating the power and authority of God.

Jesus's encounter insists that we be open to the unexpected gifts of grace. Perhaps the key element in this story is how important it is for our time and our time's contention over the question of the authority and meaning of tradition. Jesus reminds the Sadducees in their time and us in ours that we must take care lest our understanding of the past — including our reading of scripture and tradition — makes us unable to see new manifestations of God's will in the present and — more importantly — in the future. That God is constantly making all things new seems so to unnerve us and thus constantly to defy our capacity to embrace it. As well, the story warns us against limiting the range of

God's grace as though anything or anyone could be beyond it, the so-called unforgiveable sin that God's Holy Spirit is incapable of forgiving and renewing and reconciling us. If even the dead — and what is more the seeming finality of death — are not beyond that grace, then surely no race or social or economic status or even religion can escape it, but only refuse and reject it.

This refreshing good news of the gospel in Jesus's hands can and must inform the way we live together as a society of law and order. Our systems of government — and especially of the way we church together — are consistent with that news only when they enhance and enable and inform the gospel's message of justice and peace, love and freedom. They are altogether contrary to it when they seek to restrict it by imposing our own limited understandings about who we are and the ways we must live together.

Molecules

"For the Son of man came not to be served but to serve, and to give his life as a ransom for many." (Mark 10:45)

The late Bennett Sims, one-time bishop of Atlanta, reported a strange thing in his book on servant leadership. And that is that the quantum theorists are certain that there is a caring pulse of energy that animates and interconnects all the entities in the cosmos. It's not unlike Teilhard de Chardin, the French Jesuit paleontologist, outraging his time when he said that the "molecules make love." This, of course, got his books banned as a consequence. (The notion of "making love" — who or what does it with whom and how — never seems then or now to sit all that well with book-banning orthodoxers.)

In Jesus's time, it was common knowledge and experience that the created order in all its facets always knew and recognized in its own way who and what was present amongst it. The daemons, the bread and fishes, the storms, the winds and waves, the human maladies, the fig trees, Satan itself in the wilderness, all across the universe were well onto the profound bend in cosmic history that happened when the Word became flesh.

No wonder Jesus could say on that first Palm Sunday that if the crowds turned silent, the very stones, themselves, the seemingly most inert and mute of all creation, would burst forth in adulation. Maybe it's what we now call atomic energy, but by whatever name, it remains *Benedicite, omnia opera Domini* — "O all ye works of the Lord, bless ye the Lord."

If the events we regularly celebrate around our holy tables tell us nothing more, they remind us over and over again how inseparable we are one from the other and even from the very stones along the way. Those stones may seem inert, they may seem to have no freedom at all, but when it comes to efficiency and presence and endurance and dependability — and even to praise, might we allow — we can learn a thing or two.

When James and John cozied up to Jesus and asked for a place in the catbird seat midst all this created order, they got a job description that should bring all of us to our feet. Leadership, you bet, said Jesus. But servant leadership, my hearties, "For the Son of man came not to be served but to serve, and to give his life as a ransom for many" *(Mk 10:45)*.

Christian "faith" is not always the same, if anywhere near or ever the same, as the Christian "Faith." To confuse the two is one of the more profound blunders of Christian churches. For the one is deeply subjective and freighted with risk and humility. It has no place nor need for crippling circumscriptions like "orthodoxy." The other is often so uncongenially certain and too often filled with pride. It is often in blind allegiance to orthodoxy, an obsession that has always compromised the church as, indeed, it does so in these very times.

Christian faith — that kind with the small "f" — always has to do with flesh and blood, time and space, more specifically with your flesh and blood and mine, with the time and space in which day by day we are all involved, stumbling, trying to appear as if we have good sense. The truth that Christianity claims to be true is ultimately to be found, if it is to be found at all, not in the *Bible* or the Church or Theology — the best they can do is point to the Truth — but is to be found in our own stories, yours and mine and our neighbors.

It is absolutely crucial, therefore, to stay in constant touch with what is going on in your own life's story and to pay close attention to what is going on in the stories of others' lives, for to say that faith is not some institutional doctrine is not to say that it is not corporate or communal. If God is present anywhere, it is in our stories. If God is not present there, then we might as well forget the whole thing. Our

Baptismal Covenant literally turns on our answer to that same question that stands at its center. "Will you seek and serve Christ in all persons, loving your neighbor as yourself?" That is where we find the stories, that is where we find faith.

And that is where we find what Jesus means by true greatness when he says, He who is greatest among you shall be your servant. I hope it is not lost on us in this gospel accounting that Jesus chose the religious establishment and its frequent fixation with puffery with which to contrast his words about servanthood.

From the religious standpoint, servanthood tends to mean a lofty ideal, all right for the Scout movement and isolated from the so-called real world of win/lose. From such secular perspective, servanthood is often seen only as "servitude," a condition imposed on women and racially different groups by male-dominant cultures or self-imposed by both men and women out of fear of their own power.

The kind of servanthood Jesus seems to imply is neither of these. Rather is it the way of fulfilling the human longing for peace and the planet's need for preservation as the theater of all life. It is the kind of leadership that is needed to make the world safe. It is always a two-way exchange, never as subjugating dominance and never as a unilateral and preëmptive arrogance.

It not only influences, but is also open to influence. It acknowledges and respects the freedom of another and seeks to enhance that other's capacity to make a difference. It is a paradox — for it gains by giving.

Just as God could say for us to listen to Jesus, his son in whom he is well pleased, thus could he show us what he means by being human. So might we hope Jesus can say of the church as what he means by a community of servanthood, leading others into creativity, productivity, and, best of all, bonding people into communities of caring. We can have no greater ministry to the society and to the world in which we are called.

And furthermore, my loverlies, we must never be too sure about what all those molecules are up to, not only here and in you and me, but in the farthest reaches of the Milky Way — and beyond.

Note to: Frederick Buechner and to Bennett Sims, thanks for the better parts of this preachment on faith and story and servanthood.

Recovery

This preachment is supposed to be about the Feast of Christ, the King, and something called "Recovery Sunday," a keeping new to me that I understand has been around for a while. The sermon is longer than usual, too long to suit me, but I got stuck and couldn't do much more with it no matter how I tried. Maybe you can. The opening story is a true one and has always meant much to me.

"Blessed is he who is coming as King in the name of the Lord." (Luke 19:38)

A twelve-step meeting was just concluding when a young woman suddenly blurted out her name, shouted that she was an alcoholic, then burst into tears and rushed out of the room. An older woman followed and saw her seated over in a darkened corner sobbing her heart out. She approached and embraced her and speaking gently, said, "My dear, just let us love you until you can come to love yourself."

In this simple, yet touching encounter, there is revealed what Twelve-Step programs are surely about. As well, there is witnessed, if not at all consciously, what the Gospel and the Gospel's church are surely about. It is no coincidence that we celebrate the Recovery programs on the same day we keep the annual Feast of Christ, the King, for these two events are both about the same thing.

They are both about love and, if you will, about justice and inclusion and servanthood, and about finding a safe place where we can practice and learn to risk taking these skills of grace into the world. For that is surely the most winsome and winning kind of evangelism.

There is another way to think about this being Recovery Sunday. These two events conjoined — Jesus's entry into Jerusalem as servant king and the twelve step entry into spiritual awakening — are about our recovering what it means to be human, what it means to live in the image of God, to reclaim and to live into that being which is the creative gift of God's imagination. This is where the Great Commandment to love is at work and the Great Commission to make disciples throughout the world is unfurled.

Our *Prayer Book* catechism puts it this way. To be human is to be created in the image of God, which means to be free to choose to love, to reason, to create, and to live in harmony with all of creation and with God *(BCP p 845)*, no less than the ministry of Jesus, himself. Addiction — and I'll talk more about that in a moment — addiction in all its forms cripples the very process of becoming human.

Perhaps the greatest irony of all this majestic Way and Truth and Life is that this One, this Jesus who comes into Jerusalem to be our

King, comes not to rule in the manner of empire to which we so often seem to aspire, but rather to lead in the manner of a servant.

This Jesus, this paradox of God, is God's evangel, the One to whom we as his beloved children and as his commissioned church must look for the Way. Our vocation as Christians is not to become more spiritual, for we are already that by virtue of God's creating us. Our vocation is to become more human.

But this Recovery Sunday is also about addiction.

If statistics mean anything at all, there's probably not a family or a friend represented here today that has not known its very fabric severely torn by the intrusion of addiction in one of its many and too often subtle forms. And if we are fortunate, we have also seen the creative healing which can result in the miracle of the process of recovery that so often can be the consequence of one of the many twelve-step programs.

We must broaden our understanding of addiction. Perhaps we have already learned or will soon learn, Satan to the contrary, that addiction's tentacles extend far beyond the chemicals such as nicotine, alcohol, and those other paralyzing narcotics. For addiction is any compulsive, habitual behavior that limits, that compromises the freedom of human desire, that jeopardizes our God-given vocation to become human. To come to that understanding is essential if we would fulfill our ministry as a church.

That brilliant story teller Madeleine L'Engle writes of a friend who despaired of seeking help for her addiction from the church. She had dropped out and turned to a twelve-step program. Madeleine asked her why and was startled to hear her friend's tearful reply. "Because this simple twelve-step program knows who is the enemy."

Addiction is our enemy at all levels of life, whether it be addiction to power or to greed or to war or to orthodoxy or to tradition or to whatever. It affects all our relationships. It is habitual, and it is a behavior, and it lurks. By the power of its subtlety, we may never know it, for denial is not a conscious act until it is thwarted, and even then, we'll do almost anything to deny that it exists and that we must come to terms with its demands.

When Jesus, the King of Peace, entered into Jerusalem, there was another entry into Jerusalem on that same day, an entry of which we rarely take any notice. Actually, I was not at all aware of it until I was recently reminded that I still need continuing education. It was an entry not about peace, but about war and oppression. It was the entry of Pilate, the lesser Roman satrap, not on the foal of a donkey, but with his legions on the armored stallions of cavalry. It was an entrance not to celebrate with the Jews, but to guard against and stamp the Roman boot on the possibility of any colonial insurrection at that time. And it was an entrance hurtling toward that confrontation with Jesus we know so well… about the understanding of truth and the very meaning of kingliness. Keeping this Feast today must remind us that we face a choice between defining peace in terms of war and peace in terms of justice, a choice between the servant kingly reign of God and the imperialistic and addictive compromise of our own worst selves.

This Christ, the King, shows us what must be done with the gift of recovery, that this is what God means by the "kingdom relationship." Servant leadership is the timeless story of the gospel. It is no longer possible and truly has never been possible for leadership to commend itself alone with external credentials, or with "orthodoxy" or with "churchmanship" or even with the Bible apart from the community and the tradition which it inspires for its understanding.

Without an evident depth of integrity, the authority of servant leadership can easily degenerate into mere power and thus become menaced by its ever present temptation not to lead, but to manipulate and to exploit. That this delusion is rampant in today's church may well be why those many the polls tell us cherish a belief in God no longer support or attend a church and become what some cynically call "the alumni association."

Not altogether to fear, the late Bishop Bennett Sims of Atlanta was convinced that there resides even now in the church the kind of servant leadership essential for a redemptive ministry to take hold and flourish. And we dare not presume — as so often we do — that it is relegated alone to the clergy, particularly to the episcopate. Lest we forget, our *Book of Common Prayer* affirms four orders of this ministry — laity, deacons, presbyters, and bishops — all of whom are commissioned in Baptism to the holiest of servant leadership.

Our Lord could not have put it any plainer when he said, "Everyone who is of the truth hears my voice" *(Jn 18:37)*.

The church and our congregations cannot expect the world to get the drift of that until we, ourselves, hear that same voice and become deeply committed servant leaders embracing the authority of grace and eschewing the destruction of power, modeling this Jesus ministry for all to see. Then may we dare to recover the vision into the kingdom of God that awaits us and into which Christ, the King, would lead us, into our own Jerusalems.

Encores

9/11

In these past few days, our free and open society has been wielded as a weapon against itself. Fear has immobilized us and suspended us in shock. How we respond as a nation and as a people in so vulnerable and fragile a moment could incisively redirect the entire human experience as we've come to know it.

We churchfolk of all people must now realize that religion is not the answer, even our own religion, no matter how deeply we cherish it or how proper we may deem it to be. It takes little perception to realize how easily religious conviction can become religious delusion. In such times of such fear and its ensuing anxiety and anger, we are probably no more immune to the risk of that madness than the next person.

Rather must we turn now to the deep and personal privacy of our faith and our potential faithfulness in whatever shape, strength, and maturity we are able to find it. For the greatest and perhaps even the only gift of our religion and its liturgies and sacraments is to provide an environment in which our faith can be nourished and shared and opened to God's grace, thus prompting our memories not only of who we are, but of *Whose* we are.

In such turning and by such resources can we ultimately embody what our Creator most desires of us, that we love God, that we love one another, and perhaps most importantly right now, that we love ourselves. Nobody can deny, of course, that we would not be here in this place if we were not willing to do just that.

But we must go a significant step further and not merely be *willing* to love, we must *will* to love. For that is the only way that rampant fear and hatred can be revealed for what they are and ultimately overcome. Love, unlike fear, is more than a feeling, for love, unlike fear, is a choice. Indeed, the gospel we embrace goes a step further and reminds us that we must love our enemies.

Love is the reason God creates us, and to be loving is what God imagines for us to be. But the great irony is that though we are commanded by God to love, we are also set free to love and thus also not to love. That is why being merely willing is not enough. We must choose, always mindful that the nature of God is more nearly shown by grace and forgiveness than by judgment and condemnation. To celebrate this gift with God one must also share in God's mercy.

A cartoon featured two people discussing with each other what they might like to ask if ever they were in the presence of God. One said he would like to ask why God allowed war, famine, hunger, terrorism, disease, and poverty to exist, but that he was afraid to ask. The other inquired why. His companion replied, Because I am afraid God might ask me the same question.

So what does God ask of us? That we be a loving community of faith that withstands the temptation to hide behind its religion and becomes a secure and mutually trusting community that can speak with authority... that can ask the necessary and searching questions of itself and of the society in which it finds itself. And thus can lead by example to become an instrument for healing, always mindful that wherever the brokenness of the world is mended, there is present the Kingdom of God.

In this kind of atmosphere, we must encourage open discussions on any number of questions, not because they necessarily have anything to do with religion, but because they have everything to do with faith and love, civility and respect.

Thomas Govan, churchman and one-time history professor at Sewanee's University of the South, spoke of our system of government as "the American political experiment." He said that it is perhaps the greatest gift we have to offer to the world. Why, then, we must ask, is it still not working as it is intended to work? Where have we failed? Why are millions in poverty and without security of mind and body? Why do we seem so to revere the economy at the ultimate expense of the environment? When will we learn that justice is the social equivalent and embodiment of love?

It is an often unbearable feeling to know that there are those in the world who hate us. Trapped between the world in which they were born and the confusing world of modernity in which they inescapably live, they seek a single cause for their confusion, their resentments, their frustrated ambitions, and their problems of cultural identity. It is perhaps not surprising that they would focus on the world's most powerful state as the object of their resentment and even commit suicide to bring it down.

It is no easy task to follow our Lord's command that we love God and neighbor and self. And yet, it is the choice we must will to make.

Writing as a Means of Grace

A story is told that one of the older nuns in a community was suffering from chronic confusion and loss of memory. From time to time, she would wander through the convent emptying people's mailboxes, striking up strange, but pleasant conversations, collecting items from sisters' bedrooms and giving them to others.

The community sponsored a school. One day, one of the teachers was called to the phone and left her mid-term exams and grade book on a table in the community room. When she returned, they were gone. A frantic two-day search began, notes left on the bulletin board, pleas made on the public address system.

Finally, somebody thought of the wandering collector. There, buried under her laundry, were the grade books and the tests, all studied and corrected. Everyone had got an A.

Nowadays, they say, when sister wanders the halls, passersby bow inwardly to her. Through her seemingly foolish actions, wandering and reminding all by her presence not to fear the final judgment, they discovered a new sense of themselves, that there are, finally, no record books, and everyone makes an A. "There is no end to the birth of God," wrote D H Lawrence. Perhaps, what appears most senseless can often seem most meaningful of all. Life fills to overflowing with opportunities to make the senseless meaningful to an irrationally rational world. We might but grasp the moment.

Sometimes we are senselessly poetic, and the world is charged with a moment of beauty. Sometimes we are senselessly tender, and hardened hearts begin to melt. Sometimes we are senselessly nonjudgmental, and we see through a glass darkly into the nature of life.

What if we became senselessly vulnerable and reduced the defense budget? Might the world know less fear? What if we were senselessly forgiving and abolished the death penalty? Would children then understand respect for life? What if we were senselessly generous and created a new welfare system that gave the poor a fighting chance? Might our own hearts be softened?

When Jesus forgave the adulterer, a senseless kindness brought the self-righteous to self-knowledge, a senseless grace embraced both accusers and accused and changed lives, a senseless justice confronted an oppressively sexist system and challenged all to do likewise. We are surrounded by the seemingly senseless: the mystics, the poets, the clowns, the so-called irrational and impractical, those who are "different." They are all there, writing something in the sand.

I'm not altogether sure why this parable intrigues me so, save it affirms for me in a rather indirect way the senselessness, the nonsensicalness of faith as a response to grace. The writing of the Out of Nowhere series has become for me a way of expressing that through irony and imagination, the very ways, I believe, that God creates. So, I ceased looking for the rational a while ago. It was too frustrating, and I found myself inevitably pandering. Hence, writing as a means of grace, as a means of welcoming grace.

Obviously, writing not only uses, but also develops language facility. Writer Toni Morrison claims that language makes us human. Writer John Evangelist said the Word became flesh. I think he not only meant what we call incarnation. I think he also meant that the Word enhances and suits, adorns and embellishes flesh. For example, when we discovered DNA, we discovered something like God's autograph. DNA is the language that informs, that gives shape and function to human being. It was there all the while, of course. Its discovery is one of grace's markers.

Then comes the real pleasure. If we'll let it and trust it, together with DNA, imagination moves in. Imagination is wishful thinking implementing faith and welcoming God, embodying the mind of Christ, affirming commitment, daring to be vulnerable, and just as DNA shapes us, imagination shapes our world. When we speak of being created in the image of God, we're saying that the Word is God's private system for imagining human being. For to be created in the image of God means, at least, to be imagined into being by God, to be the creature of God's imagination, to be told into being, to be God's "once upon a time."

By virtue of God's creating us, we are spiritual beings, breathed, inspired into being as was Adam. Our vocation in response to this gift is not so much to become more spiritual. Our vocation is to become more human, to fulfill God's desire for us, God's imagination for us that as our Catechism says, we be set free to choose: to create, to love, to reason, and to live in harmony with all of creation and with God. Our vocation is to embrace that freedom *ex nihilo*, Out of Nowhere.

The profound irony of our faith as Christians makes considerable demands on our imagination. As our imagination is the very instrument, the implement of our faith, it leads and opens the way for faith to reach out and see through Paul's glass, Paul's icon darkly. It serves our imaginations well. We are, indeed, ourselves, icons.

This becoming human, this fulfilling God's image for us, is, of course, and as well, a spiritual quest. It is a quest for meaning, integrity, memory; a quest to understand the mystery of vocation and to communicate it in a way that others will, if not understand, will at least respect or forgive. It may be sudden, as in a conversion, or it may merely be gradual, even gentle with a mild shock here and there. But the quest is incarnate. God created humanity, but a humanity free enough even to defy the divine will. God woos us and therefore takes her chances on winning or losing and will finally prefer to let someone be lost rather than to interfere with the sacredness of the human person.

Jaroslav Pelikan* puts it this way. In the beginning was the word. The very first act of God in the very first chapter of the very first book of the *Bible* is to speak, and in the Greek tradition, the word for "word" and the word for "reason" are the same — this declaration affirms that the act of communication is at the very center not only of human existence and its origins but of the mystery of the Divine Being itself.

He continues. Human beings, being created, according to that first chapter of the first book of the *Bible*, in the divine image of a God who has no face, participate through the divine image in the mystery of the Divine Being by themselves reflecting those capacities of the Divine Being that lie at the center of self-revelation through their own imagination analogous to God's creative imagining. And those capacities are two, but finally they are one: the capacity to love and the capacity to communicate. For in the beginning was the word.

I need to say this again for my sake if not for yours. We are not human beings whose vocation is to be or to become more spiritual; we are spiritual beings whose vocation is to be or to become more human. This is God's wish for us. It became for me an understanding not only of our vocation but of the church's, as well, as the community to enable and facilitate that vocation. It also clarified how religion as that corporate human endeavor to render faith both memorable and manageable can actually compromise that vocation by affecting the environment, the instrument, that is, the church, God gives us to bring it about.

In a 12-step meeting, a nun was talking about how difficult it had been for her in her recovery to take the third step, to turn her will and her life over to the care of God as she understood God. It was not until she realized that she was trying to make this commitment to her limited understanding of God rather than to the unlimited God who transcends her understanding. We do not often realize how our insistence on orthodoxy is such a stifling barrier for a person whose faith is pressing around the edges of her growth to fulfill God's image for her, to recover and to fulfill her humanity. Another marker for me has been Reinhold Niebuhr's so-called Serenity Prayer which is not a prayer about serenity, but a prayer about change and about choice, two more of the markers in our spiritual growth toward humanity. How well we cope with and incorporate change and choice and the courage and wisdom with which we engage them is a significant measure of our maturity. The 12-step program is thus a paradigm for anyone's life of faith leading toward spiritual awakening, it is a paradigm for the process of becoming fully human which, of course, is the goal of what is called recovery. It is a way of describing the Way.

The Baptismal Covenant is the church's five step program, the model of what it means to be a Christian, to incarnate the Christian life, to be a pilgrim on the Way. It is a spiritual quest.

One of my true joys is playing jazz. Our band was playing that grand old standard "Out of Nowhere" one night. When I got home, I sat down and started writing.

*Jaroslav Pelikan, "Writing as a Means of Grace," in Spiritual Quests: the art and craft of religious writing, ed William Zinser, Houghton Mifflin, pp 85-101, 1988.

Preachment

Being here at St Stephen's is a kind of homecoming for me. Nearly fifty years ago, two of my children started their education in your parish day school while I was chaplain at Rice and the Medical Center. Vicki and Rector Claxton Monro became our dear friends. I am a native Texan, a teasipper, a member of the founding class of 1954 at ETSS, a deacon and a priest at the hands of Mike Quin and John Hines. I am a guest here at the grace of Don Wimberly, another Bishop of Texas who stands in this grand tradition. Thank you, Bishop. There's a story about a distinguished-looking elderly gentleman standing at a street corner when an attractive young woman took him by the arm. "Young lady," he said, "are you trying to pick me up?" "No sir," she answered, "I'm just trying to keep you from falling down."

Lisa Hunt has been steadying me for over two decades since she came charging into my office one day to start her field-ed training for Vanderbilt Divinity School. She had two questions. Did she want to become an Episcopalian? And did she want to become a priest? Well, here she is. Most recently, she has kept me standing as priest associate at St Ann, Nashville, and by graciously inviting me to be here sharing this exciting new ministry with her and with my fellow communicants from St Ann, and with you all. Thank you.

♪♪ ♪♪♩ ♪○

We couldn't find a better biblical and liturgical beginning for our time together than the story of the Transfiguration *(Lk 9:28-36)*. It is one of the rarest events in the gospels. I think it more than a passing delight and to our considerable benefit that our celebration of this new ministry of rector and parish coincides on this day. For this story is a parable of the church. Just so as Peter, James, and John, we latter-day disciples often seem to want and prefer high and holy places. We want especially to find one away from the incessant, mind-numbing controversy, and we wonder why we can't just make one here with our Lord and keep it that way. Celebrate now. Pay later.

(It is interesting that our lectionary planners for some reason omit from Luke's accounting of the Transfiguration that the next day, when Jesus and the disciples came down from the mountain, they were confronted by a family whose child was being consumed by a daemon.)

But meanwhile, back at the mountain, there is always the Voice, surely the Voice of God, telling how pleased he is, indeed, with his son. (Think James Earl Jones reminding us that "this is CNN." And think, if you will, Maya Angelou) It is good to hear God smile like this. God smiled before at Jesus's baptism, and here, once again, that same Voice, "This is my Son, my Chosen."

But this time, there is more. Much has transpired since that fate-filled baptism. The Voice seems to have gained an impatient tone. "This is my Son, my Chosen," yes. But then, I imagine a dramatic pause before we hear — "Listen to him." It is enough to recharge his drowsy disciples. May it be enough, as well, to energize all of us on our Way to becoming God's church.

We're gathered here to celebrate a new ministry. In one way, of course, it is not new at all. This parish has "been there and done that" for decades. You have an impressive record of servant leadership in church and community most recently brought into focus with your outstanding rector Helen Havens.

As well, my colleague Lisa Hunt has a couple of challenging decades on her resumé. She's a well-seasoned priest, pastor, and preacher. She has led a parish once close to becoming moribund and once practically blown away by a tornado into becoming a parish caught up by another Holy Wind to become a source of nourishing service to its neighborhood, a source of singular and essential leadership for its diocese. In her wake, there continues a most impressive and informed leadership of wardens, vestry, and congregation. At St Ann, the message is unswervingly clear that absolutely all are welcome. Those who need to be loved can be loved until they can come to love themselves — and then love others. Every day, it proves that if you build it, they will come. A brief note about Lisa's preaching: As she started her sermon one Sunday, a third-grader was overheard in a stage whisper to her mother when she said, "This is my favorite part of the service." And then on another Sunday when the gospel was about Jesus exorcising a daemon. Lisa had assumed Jesus's role for a moment. You could almost feel her shaking the possessed man as she shouted, "Come out! And shut up!!" A stunned silence followed. And then there came a child's voice… "Uh oh!" But there is at least one caveat: She can be an altogether unnerving prophet for those of us of all ages, especially when her Isaiah DNA kicks in.

When two histories, two vocations such as this parish and this new rector are brought together by the obviously prayerful discernment that has so moved them both, a critical mass of explosive dimensions stands ready to unleash spiritual energy. It is good that you both, parish and new rector, have wisely followed Yogi Berra's counsel. When you came to this fork in your road, you took it. New ministry, indeed! Let us joyfully, even foolishly celebrate!

And what sort of celebration might this be? Perhaps some foolishness for Christ might help turn us into this new journey. Here's a quaint parable about just such a thing.

One of the older nuns in a community was suffering from chronic confusion and loss of memory. From time to time, she would wander through the convent emptying people's mailboxes, striking up strange, but pleasant conversations, collecting items from sisters' bedrooms and giving them to others.

The community sponsored a school. One day, one of the teachers was called to the phone and left her mid-term exams and grade book on a table in the community room. When she returned, they were gone. A frantic two-day search began, notes left on the bulletin board, pleas made on the public address system. Finally, somebody thought of the wandering collector. There, buried in her laundry, were the grade books and the tests, all studied and corrected. Everyone got an A.

Nowadays, they say, when sister wanders the halls, passersby bow inwardly to her. Through her seemingly foolish actions, wandering and reminding all by her presence not to fear the final judgment, they discovered a new sense of themselves, that there are, finally, no record books, and everyone makes an A. "There is no end to the birth of God," wrote D H Lawrence.

Many of our Anglican colleagues around the world speak now of what they are convinced is the senseless direction our beloved Episcopal Church is taking in these days. Perhaps so. But also, perhaps Sister's behavior suggests that what appears most senseless can often seem most meaningful of all. Life fills to overflowing with opportunities to make the senseless meaningful to an irrationally rational world. At a new time like this for priest and people, might we but grasp the moment and, as the voice at the Transfiguration said,

Listen, listen to my Son and listen for what it might be about him that pleasures God so.

Sometimes we are senselessly poetic, and the world is charged with a moment of beauty. Sometimes we are senselessly tender, and hardened hearts begin to melt. Sometimes we are senselessly nonjudgmental, and we see through a glass darkly into the nature of life. What if we became senselessly vulnerable and reduced the defense budget? Might the world know less fear? Can we ever recover from the generations of fear that were born in the horror of that other transfiguration at Hiroshima whose anniversary we keep on this very day, and that has enveloped the world ever since, first in that strangely named cold war and now in the continuing reign of terror that is its bad seed?

So what if we were senselessly forgiving and abolished the death penalty? Would our children then understand and have more respect for life? What if we were senselessly generous and created a new societal system that gave the poor a fighting chance? Might our own hearts be softened?

We are surrounded by the seemingly senseless. What can be more ludicrous than a church legislature called a General Convention that is so often only generally conventional, but yet in its finer moments struggles to become an instrument for grace and justice and to do so through the sometimes stifling stuffiness of canon law?

Bill Sanders, a former Bishop of Tennessee, said five years ago at a celebration of the twenty-fifth anniversary of the ordination of women that it was the greatest thing the Episcopal Church did in the twentieth century. Perhaps, however, even now, it risks becoming almost commonplace, as this little story suggests. Our church's chaplain at Vanderbilt University was having a what-do-you-want-to-do-when-you-grow-up talk with her young son. She asked, "Do you want to be a successful musician and composer like your dad?" "No," he said. "Well, would you like to be a priest like your mom?" "No," he said indignantly, "that's woman's work!"

It is no secret that this parish and this diocese have had an early and informing hand in setting a paradigm for "woman's work" in our church. Rector Helen Havens was the first woman ordained priest in Texas, and my fellow ETSS graduate Archdeacon Dena Harrison is the first woman elected Suffragan Bishop for this diocese. These two women along with your new rector have demonstrated so clearly the wisdom of Bishop Sanders's affirmation. Now, that momentum continues not only here, but as well a part of the same high-speed curve and inspiration that chose Katharine Jefferts Schori to lead the church into this challenging century shattering the church's glass ceiling and no telling how many other such restraints in our society once and for all. We'd be remiss not to celebrate her new ministry together with ours in our hearts and prayers today.

For among all these senseless things are things that are worth happening, things like being a little more passionate for our pains, a little more alive, a little wiser, a little more beautiful, a little more open and understanding, in short, a little more human. And to remember with St Paul that, "God chose what to the world seems foolish to shame the wise, God chose what is weak in the world to shame the strong, God chose what is low and despised in the world, even things that are not, to bring to nothing things that are…"

We are called to be challengers and servant leaders, out front with the mystics, the poets, the clowns, the so-called irrational and impractical people, and all those whose manner of life along with that of Jesus challenges the wider church. For only as we do so may we discover how much we are really all alike, acting out the divine comedy that involves us all. Surely this partakes of grace. And we are all there, are we not, along with our Lord, writing something in the sand. May God then say of us in our own transfigurations — These are my children in whom I am well pleased. Listen to them.

Interdependence

It has been said that to sacrifice something is to make it holy by giving it away for love.

In the Eucharist, the place at which that action is perhaps most graphic is in the moment of offering bread and wine and money. In our congregation, we call additional attention to that with two short prayers through which we ask God to join with us in making holy what we are sacrificing, what we are giving away for love. We may not always be so conscious of this, but there it is, anyway, what the church has meant to do for twenty centuries.

On Independence Day or the nearest Sunday, as an exceptional way of adding to our celebration and, indeed, to our sacrifice, we offer together with these other symbols our nation's flag, properly folded and placed in an alms basin.

There are many ways to display the flag, each with its own meaning. When it is to one's right as in the president's oval office, it symbolizes allegiance. When it is flown upside down, it is a sign of distress. When at half-mast, it is to indicate mourning. When a flag is torn, stepped on, or burned, the message is rejection and rebellion. When a flag flies at full staff, the announcement is peace, victory, rule or whatever adjective you might speak to the situation at the time. It is not our usual custom to display our nation's flag in our chancel, though such is far from uncommon in many churches.

Whatever way we incorporate our national symbol, it is well to keep in mind that Hebrew and Christian scriptures record two problems about patriotism as always having plagued the People of God. One is to become so conformed to a culture and its ways so as to merge the two, rather than bringing the culture into the ways of God. The other is to allow the rule of God to be replaced by the rule of the State. Therefore, we must exercise care how we use our national symbols. We Christians are believers in the Incarnation, and it is thus not always easy to separate the issues from the people or the symbols who embody them. Patriotism — about which these days some of us hear more than enough and others never enough — is one of those very important issues which we incarnate and which is not all that easy to separate from the person or the symbol that embraces it.

Few of us, I suspect, would deny that we are patriots. We may find it easier to say what that does not mean for us than to say what it does mean. One thing we all have in common on the subject, however, is the Declaration of Independence. It seems to me always useful — especially this time of year and in these perilous times — to read it thoughtfully as Christians, and perhaps to discover anew what our founders had in mind when they undertook this great American political experiment by which they told us what patriotism meant for them.

On the celebration of our nation's birthday each year, National Public Radio broadcasts a reading of the Declaration of Independence. Their announcers, reporters, analysts, and essayists each follow in turn reading a short, self-contained passage. The familiar voices are nameless, and one can only guess whose they are. The anonymity seems not only tantalizing, but somehow appropriate, as well. I like to imagine our founders as they wrote and shaped this great proclamation maybe having read it aloud similarly as they sought to get the feel, the rhythm, the power, and the authority of it.

Hearing it in this way even more convinces me that, for whatever and surely well-intended reason, the document seems strangely misnamed. I believe it might better have been called a Declaration of Interdependence, instead. It may be well for us to imagine it that way in these difficult times of another, newer, but not all that different national crisis.

Clearly and well, of course, the Declaration establishes us an autonomous nation among all the world's geopolitical states. That, in itself, is daring enough. But it continues uniquely and refreshingly to proclaim a new and radical political relationship not only with its own citizenry, but also boldly and courageously with all the earth's peoples who care to join in such a venture. It takes an incarnational view of the very nature of human being and of the body politic as itself a faithful way to render unto Caesar the things that are Caesar's and unto God the things that are God's.

We live in a time when independence has seemed to mean the license to run amok unilaterally. The founding sense of the Declaration seems scandalously misunderstood and to be masquerading alone as codependency here, as sexual, ethnic, and political insularity there. These distortions recklessly affect not only individuals and families and our thoughtful and creative governing system of checks and balances, but regions and nations across this entire planet, as well. We seem to be abandoning the very corporate nature of the stewardship which this founding document affirmed and for which it called.

The answer to all this is not, I believe, some blind, unquestioning loyalty which is no loyalty at all, but an out-and-out denial of one's citizenship. It is not the impudent display of flag lapel pins all the while blatantly ignoring the Constitutional systems which one has vowed to protect and defend and which that flag symbolizes. Rather is true patriotism to love our country enough to see that in a nuclear age it is not going to survive unless the world survives. True patriots are no longer champions of Democracy, Communism, or anything like that but champions of the Human Race. It is not the Homeland that they feel called on to defend at any cost, but the planet Earth as Home.

If in the interests of making sure that we don't blow ourselves off the map once and for all, we end up relinquishing a measure of national sovereignty to some international body, so much the worse for national sovereignty. For there is only one Sovereignty that matters ultimately, and it is of quite another sort altogether.

Oh, and there is a tidbit which we dare not overlook after a reading of the Declaration of Independence. It is that King George III entered into his journal on that vital July 4, 1776, "Nothing of any importance or consequence took place today."

Note: The useful reminders about ways and meanings of flag displays came my way from Pepper Marts, churchman, veteran, writer, and rattler of stained glass out in New Mexico. The splendid reflections on the meaning of patriotism belong to Frederick Buechner and appear in his "Whistling in the Dark," Harper & Row, p 93.

Homily

Good humor together with the faith which is its ironic companion are two of God's great gifts of the security to make us human. Sooner or later, I witnessed the both of them in my every encounter with Jack Gessell. It was no wonder to me that a similar ambiance surrounded him in his final clinical space as he quite literally seemed to welcome whatever with the faithful assurance and anticipation of which his choice for our Old Testament proper Lamentations speaks: "The steadfast love of the Lord never ceases, his mercies never come to an end; they are new every morning; [for] great is thy faithfulness" *(Lam 3:22f)*.

Colleague Mary Miller of his beloved Episcopal Peace Fellowship describes something like this about him as both a combination of "joy and stubbornness."

Being present there with him at such a time recalled for me a story that is told of Bob Hope on his death bed. His family was gathered around him giving him one more of the audiences which he so dearly loved. Someone asked him where he might wish to be buried and suggested several likely and prominent places. After a few moments of silence, he smiled and said..." Surprise me."

In the introductory Apologia of his collection of essays, "Grace and Obedience," Jack quoted Frederick Buechner, "that all theology, like all fiction, is at its heart autobiography, and that what a theologian is doing essentially is examining as honestly as he can... his own experience... and expressing in logical abstract terms the truths about human life and about God that he believes he has found implicit there." *(G&O, p 1)*

Jack knew early on in his life that he wanted to be a theologian. He wrote, "And so *malgré moi* [in spite of myself], I became a theologian, not out of some intellectual compulsion, not by reflective choice, but out of an existential demand to be able to make sense out of a world which would otherwise be nonsense." *(G&O, p 2)* No one knew better than Jack that faith has its own moments of nonsense.

In this same apology, he included among his roots the "liberal midwestern culture in which he grew up... Yale University, and the Episcopal Church. Socially," he wrote, "I am a classical liberal;

philosophically, a post-Kantian critical realist; theologically, I stand in the reformed tradition." *(G&O, p 3)*

Reading that, I wondered what on earth I from an altogether different culture am doing standing here, but then it dawned on me whether these roots of his might also be a part of the reason why he often scolded me for wearing bowties with button-down collar shirts.

From his University experience and as a new priest, he began serving in small parishes in Virginia and Massachusetts. He tells of a parishioner and friend there asking him to make sense of the Doctrine of the Atonement. "I found that I could not," he wrote. "I, who had received one of the best theological trainings of my time, a product of the peak achievement of the great classical period of American theological education following the war, had failed."

But "later in that same parish," he continues, "I came to confess that I after all had learned more theology living among those people than I had in all of the years of graduate training at the University. But those years had prepared the ground," he adds. "It was a training in humility" *(G&O, p 5)*.

I cannot help but believe that this realization was creative to his remarkable appreciation of life's irony that led to such rich times we all of us experienced as his colleagues and friends. Times that were also so invaluable and enduring for his students as their mentor. One of his faculty colleagues said of him, "Jack was a priest who wasn't afraid to tell the truth, who knew what the fifth baptismal promise (Will you strive for justice and peace among all people, and respect the dignity of every human being?) meant, who was a reticent but pleased mentor to so many, who taught people what it meant to care for the poor and marginalized... he was fearless, and he was my hero."

In the Journal of Jack's beloved Cumberland Center for Justice and Peace, Journalist David Bowman tells of Jack's early schooling in Minnesota and Kansas.

(He does not mention — but I will — that among Jack's earlier skills, he was a cheerleader at Topeka High School, a role he was never all that pleased to be reminded about sharing with a once-removed occupant of the White House.)

Jack's understanding of humility as essential to the theological enterprise recalls for me a story about the great pianist Vladimir

Horowitz. In an interview, Horowitz was asked to define music. He answered that music is made up of little dots on a page, some black and some white. He said that almost anyone can learn to "read the dots," then duplicate them somehow, perhaps, like an expert typist might unravel shorthand.

But this is not music, Horowitz hastened to say. For there to be music, one must first discover what is "behind the dots and even so how they are connected. Then one must not merely reproduce them, but render them in one's own way with spirit and imagination through whatever instrument — the voice, the strings, or the winds. Only then is there music," he concluded.

All theology like all fiction — and dare we add — even all music is autobiographical.

We can live our theology by the numbers and as straitlaced as possible, no matter what the cost. Many do that quite successfully with absolute certainty and want to be sure that others do the same. We can take life's great creative treasures simply and on their face. We can take its culture, its art, its poetry, its music, its languages, its liturgies, and just "read the dots." We can so take the very Holy Scripture that commissions us a church, that charges, baptizes, and claims us as its disciples of peace and justice. But in so doing, we can as well render them all as shallow as the rites on the pages of this liturgy, never reading behind the dots at all.

John Maurice Gessell, theologian, read behind the dots and threw his life into what he read there. While he served his parishes, he completed a PhD under Richard Niebuhr at Yale. As most of you know, he joined the faculty here at the School of Theology in 1961 and taught Christian Education and Pastoral Theology. From 1973 until his retirement he was the School's Professor of Christian Ethics. He was the first full-time faculty editor of The St Luke's Journal of Theology and drew up its statement of purpose that it would be "A Journal of religious thought for clergy and laity who wish to relate theological studies to contemporary issues." Later, it was my privilege to share with him the founding of *Covenant* (now *The Covenant Journal*) for which he agreed emphatically that the Baptismal Covenant would be its editorial grounding and for which he also wrote our statement of purpose that it "May provide a safe place, a place where truth can be told, a place where we can trust one another" *(TCJ #1, 1997)*.

David Bowman continues telling of Jack's service in the Peace Corps in 1967, his work with military deserters who had taken refuge in Sweden during the Viet Nam war. He was president of the Franklin County Mental Health Association. He worked in East Africa studying the problems of developing countries.

Jack was a longtime member of the Episcopal Peace Fellowship and subsequently its national chairman. He received the acclaimed John Nevin Sayre Peace Award at the 1997 Philadelphia General Convention. One of his public comments bears repetition in our time and I recommend it for all to consider. He spoke of war as "an inappropriate adolescent response to enormous frustration. War is a failure of intelligence, imagination, and politics. It is the failure of the human spirit. Justice requires that we do better than this to secure peace in today's world" *(an EPF newsletter, date unknown).*

Such celebrations as this one in memory and appreciation are singular occasions that summon us through our friendship and professional collegiality with Jack. They assemble us to honor and remember the life of one of us who has died and remind us that one day, so will we. Death confounds us, and grief breaks our hearts, but inevitably they bring us together. They instantly surpass all divisions real and artificial and remind us if only briefly of the converse into which God's Holy Spirit calls us where we can join together ourselves as a healing sacrament of love and the justice which is its great social counterpart.

John Maurice Gessell need not be idealized or enlarged in death beyond what he already was in life, but to be remembered as a good and decent man, who...

when he saw wrong, worked to make it right and just...

when he saw suffering, worked to make it well and whole...

when he saw daemons, stood in their path and barred them from passing.

And when he read in John's gospel as we just now did that "this is the will of my Father, that everyone who sees the Son and believes in him should have eternal life; and I will raise him up at the last day" *(Jn 6:40),* Jack embraced such assurance with all his heart.

Jack's ministry always brings to mind the words of Lutheran Bishop Krister Stendahl that "wherever the brokenness of the world is being mended, there is present the Kingdom of God."

His startling lack of pretense gave refreshing credibility to the academic vocation of priesthood, that it can be a practice of faith and also a "training in humility." He took the Great Commandment and its love child, the Baptismal Covenant, straight to heart as the reason God imagined us all into human being.

Perhaps the greatest tribute we could ever offer him and all whom he touched and to whom he reached out is not only to remember the joy, the service, and indeed the stubbornness we have known through him, but to turn and celebrate ourselves as instruments of that same healing toward others. Then and in this way may we read "behind the dots" and play the music we find there — the great and swelling anthems of justice and peace.

Darkly

A Geek web site (self-named) I found says that the difference between ethics and morals can seem somewhat arbitrary to many, but there is a basic, albeit subtle, difference. I always thought so, but never could quite get it straight. Subtle escapes me, especially whenever I try to be.

They say, morals define personal character, and ethics stress a social system in which those morals are applied. In other words, ethics point to standards or codes of behavior expected by the group to which the individual belongs. This could be national ethics, social ethics, company ethics, professional ethics, political ethics, or even family ethics. So while a person's moral code is usually unchanging, the ethics he or she practices can be other-dependent. I am not all that sure of this latter distinction, but that's what somebody who claims to know says, anyhow.

Some commentary on the morning news was comparing the 1964/65 Civil Rights legislation to the current health care legislation as significant high points in the "moral imperative" of our gradually fulfilling the creative intentions of a democracy, that is, of our founders and of the Constitution they gave us. That's got to be frustrating especially for those who are yet to get over 1965 or even women's suffrage and whose numbers seem to continue to be legion. For those founding intentions probably mean that the morality and any imperative it may have is personal and not social where ethics mantles the realm.

Today's *Borowitz Report* says the Tea-Party crowd's latest protest is that the government has taken over Congress, that talking, not voting was what our founders intended for Congress to do. Parody inevitably rides on truth as its undercarriage, but maybe its great usefulness is to provide some help in understanding morals and ethics. Talking is perhaps a sometimes too subtle revelation of one's morality (cf AA's insistence that we learn to walk our talk), whereas voting which is unavoidably personal is where morality hits the road and ethics somehow may begin to help shape it.

So maybe *there's* the moral imperative. Maybe there's where this neighbor loving stuff begins to abrade us around the edges. Groups of neighbors, i.e., society, Congress, political parties can ignore neighbors, even groups of neighbors who happen to need health care, even have a right to health protection like to police and fire protection and

Homeland Security, groups can't love like individuals can, they apparently can only if they will neighbor-up justfully and peacefully.

Any kind of mob rule reveals how personal morals can be sublimated, even secreted, when the "ethic" of the mob takes over. Political parties can provide such protection and even draw such membership so that the individual member's morality doesn't get so embarrassingly exposed.

The church is one place where individuals can and should learn about morality and ethics, indeed, have an ethic of its own and a way of practicing it. The church is where we can see and experience how this changes throughout the normative biblical historical tradition itself, how seeking and more nearly approaching God's will can take place and how it can be enhanced, and where further tradition and reason can so enable us. The church is where our spiritual nature, the word of God's imaginative creation of us, becomes flesh. The church is where our liturgical curricula must find its meaning and purpose and shape, then vigorously pursue its ends. Perhaps that is where our prophetic ministry to indict meets our pastoral commission to love and to work for a peaceful and just society for our individual selves, our congregations, and the societies and their governmental systems to which God calls us. Perhaps that is our moral imperative seen so clearly right here through a glass darkly.

When considering the difference between ethics and morals, it may be helpful to consider a criminal defense lawyer. Though the lawyer's personal moral code likely finds murder immoral and reprehensible, ethics demand the accused client be defended as vigorously as possible, even when the lawyer knows the party is guilty and that a freed defendant would potentially lead to more crime. Legal ethics must override personal morals for the greater good of upholding a justice system in which the accused are given a fair trial and the prosecution must prove guilt beyond a reasonable doubt.

The prosecution and court must also deal with the difference between ethics and morals. In some cases past actions of the accused might resonate with the current charge, but are kept out of evidence so as not to prejudice the jury. In a sense, the prosecutor "lies by omission" in representing the case, never revealing the prejudicial evidence. The same prosecutor, however, would likely find it reprehensible to fail to tell a friend if her date had a potentially dangerous or suspect history.

Another area in which ethics and morals can clash is at the workplace where company ethics can play against personal morality. Corporate greed that blurs its own ethical lines coupled with unreasonable demands on time can lead to having to choose between a stressful, demanding and consuming work ethic, and family obligations seen as moral obligations to spouse and children. Conversely, people lose jobs every day because of poor personal morals, employee theft being a common reason for dismissal.

In society, we are all faced with the butting heads of ethics and morals. Abortion is legal and therefore medically ethical, while many people find it personally immoral. Fundamentalists, extremists, and even mainstream theists all have different ideas about morality that impact each of our lives, even if indirectly through social pressures or legal discrimination.

In the case of homosexuality, many believe it is morally wrong, yet some of the same people also believe it is unethical to discriminate legally against a group of people by disallowing them the same rights afforded heterosexuals. This is a plain example of ethics and morals at battle. Ethics and morals are central issues as the world strives to overcome current challenges and international crossroads. Hopefully, in the coming years, a growing understanding will lead to peaceful and productive solutions.

The difference between ethics and morals can seem somewhat arbitrary to many, but there is a basic, albeit subtle, difference. Morals define personal character, while ethics stress a social system in which those morals are applied. In other words, ethics point to standards or codes of behavior expected by the group to which the individual belongs. This could be national ethics, social ethics, company ethics, professional ethics, or even family ethics. So while a person's moral code is usually unchanging, the ethics he or she practices can be other-dependent.

Recovery

The television news one evening reported an April Fool's Day celebration in Moscow's financial district. The scene was a lot like a New Orleans Mardi Gras. The camera zoomed in on the front entrance of a tall building for a close-up on the large banner displayed there. It read, "Our elevators are broken. Please use the ones across the street."

Yogi Berra also offered similar counsel when he delivered his well-known advice that when you come to a fork in the road, take it.

Irony, like most good humor, reverses events and surprises us with the familiar. Yogi's quip sums up in a simple one-liner perhaps the most commonplace of all human experiences — change and choice. It also sums up for me what addiction and spirituality are about. Perhaps one reason Reinhold Niebuhr's prayer (for the serenity to accept what cannot be changed, the courage to change what can be changed, and the wisdom to know the difference) remains so firmly rooted in the recovery experience is that it is precisely about change and choice and about how one lives a mature life (aka a spiritual life) in relation to both.

For working but certainly not exhaustive definitions of addiction and spirituality, the following have functioned very well for me. The psychiatrist Gerald May defines addiction as any compulsive, habitual behavior that limits the freedom of human desire. Addiction cripples choice. A healthy spirituality demands it. By spirituality, I mean not merely one more compartment along with mind and body and feelings, but rather the fundamental and essentially relational reality that distinguishes and motivates us as human beings. Call it what you will, but I think of it as a basic quality of life that is revealed through the processes of how we manage change and choice. Whenever or however we attempt to quantify that human spirit either religiously or pharmacologically — and there's not a lot of difference — we're in trouble. I cannot think of addiction and spirituality, however, apart from a good sense of humor.

Long ago, our forebears in the practice of medicine thought that humor was pretty much all that life was about. As you well know, they postulated four humors. Too much or too little of one or the other unseated a balanced life, and we got sick. Therefore, it was said that to be healthy was to have a good "sense of humor." Later on, the English playwrights used these theories of the humors to produce a whole literary corpus of what we might today call "sit coms." Dominance of one humor over another produced an eccentric character, hence, a more risible stage effect. So it was that humor, once specific to a medical state, came to mean, after all, something to laugh about.

A wholesome spirituality, a good sense of humor, and effective mental health are not all that far apart. Addiction is a marvelous way to dismantle the whole thing.

As medicine became more a science and less an art, it also distanced itself from these old nostrums. We suffered such a confusion about the relation between humor and health that many, especially the more straight-laced, came to see no connection at all. It took Norman Cousins and others with similar insights to start us back toward reality.

There's a widespread notion that something's wrong about being human, about having feelings, about making choices, and what is more or even worse, that nobody else has the problem. So, we think, the cure for all this must come from outside. We turn to others, to religion, to science, to work or to some other nostrum to medicate the turmoil in our souls. When we find what we think is the answer, we hang on for dear life. We want more and more, until more is never enough.

Little do we know that we've got something in reverse. We are not human beings whose goal is a spiritual experience, some euphoric panacea. Rather are we spiritual beings whose vocation is a human experience, that is, to awaken our spirits and become ourselves, and to assume the stewardship for which we are created.

May's definition of addiction as any compulsive, habitual behavior that limits the freedom of human spirit or desire strikes at the heart of what it means to be human, which is to be free to choose: to love, to create, to reason, and to live in harmony with all of creation and with the awesome mystery of why we are here in this life at all. The practice of addiction compromises that freedom. I've never met a human being who doesn't want that freedom by whatever name, and I've never met a practicing addict who has it.

It is important in the treatment of addiction that we not confuse it with the more common problem of repression. Addiction is primarily a disease of the will, not an act of the will. Nobody chooses to be an addict.

Addiction is a separate and even more destructive force that does not merely repress choice, but actually disables it. Repression stifles desire. According to May, addiction attaches desire, binds and enslaves the will, literally "nails" it to specific things, behaviors, and relationships. These objects of attachment become preoccupations and obsessions that take charge and rule our lives. It is precisely this energy of desire that must be released, this spirit that must be awakened, retrained, and put into the service of recovery.

Of course, addiction is no laughing matter, least of all for the practicing addict whose sense of tragedy is usually sufficient sustenance to avoid even the very happiest of times. A spiritual understanding of addiction suggests that like any other neurosis, it "has nothing to do with how one behaves or suffers; it has nothing to do with the fact that the psyche is infused with contradictions; it is primarily a failure of the capacity to attend to the truth about oneself, whatever it may be, with an awareness free of emotionalism, a capacity, by the way, that the great spiritual masters of early religions called sobriety." *(from a review by Don Lattin in "Common Boundary" magazine, Mch/Apr 92, pp 46ff)*

The capacity to attend to the truth about oneself is perhaps but another and better way to speak of a sense of humor or of spiritual well-being. I should think it is also a helpful way to describe the mental health and balance sought by any practitioner in the field of human relations, not only for one's client, but perhaps more importantly, also for oneself. This seems clearly what AA's 12th step means by "spiritual awakening," that is, to come upon the necessary chutzpah to confront maturely both change and choice. When we speak of "recovery," it seems that it is this wake-up call that we're reaching for, not only as the goal, but also as the evidence for extending that capacity to attend to the truth about life.

Gerald May's "in your face" definition of addiction avoids the risk of compromising the implications and meaning of the malady by limiting it only to chemicals and cautions us to remember or perhaps learn for the first time that addiction can include any number of disasters, both professional and personal, not the least of which is the religiosity so often found to be the culprit in our attempts to care for the addict.

I think we also risk compromising the meaning and, indeed, the maximum therapeutic potentials of spirituality as a resource when we shackle it to religion as nothing more than a mere synonym. Of course, few thoughtful people do that anymore; nevertheless, it is rare to find it introduced for consideration apart from some inevitable religious connection.

The Twelve Steps of AA, based as they are on widely held spiritual principles, are without question an effective guideline for recovery. Whatever other resources are brought to bear in the treatment of the addict, they would consider well to take their lead from these simple insights, complementing and not assuming to replace them. Addiction is a malfunctioning of the whole person centered in the will. We who undertake to offer care and management profit by remembering and implementing the old adage that we are "shepherds, not veterinarians."

Many who truly desire to "do something" about their addiction become leery by what they sense rightly as the overtly religious language of the Steps. They've previously seen spirituality as nothing other than a synonym for religion and certainly not as a way of describing the very essence of what it means to be human. They've experienced religion if at all as anything but freeing, but as restrictive and judgmental. They've been held accountable not only for their behavior, but for their feelings. They've found their faith, such as it may be, held in question rather than respected and nourished, and they've been accused as sinful rather than recognized as sick. They're understandably confused by any notion that addiction is primarily an infirmity of the spirit.

Some thirty years ago when Dr Elliott Newman was director of the Clinical Research Center here in the Vanderbilt Medical Center that now bears his name, his philosophy of rounding was to include either a theologian or a reasonable facsimile on the rounding team. From time to time, I enjoyed the privilege of serving in that capacity, as a facsimile, of course.

This "consultant," as it were, was offered full and equal access to the patient. When the rounding was completed, the team met for the usual reflections and decisions, and then the visitor was asked to comment specifically on the team's relationship to the patient. Dr Newman was deeply concerned that his research not lose sight of the integrity of human being, and he believed, as well, that the process of healing was every bit as relational and the work of a community as was the process of research.

Once again, perhaps few practicing addicts have ever considered the possibility that we are not human beings whose vocation is to a spiritual experience, but spiritual beings whose vocation is to a human experience, and that this is what is meant by the twelfth step's assurance of a "spiritual awakening" as both the goal and the evidence of recovery. The test of that renewed spirit reveals a release and return to precisely what addiction has enslaved — the ability to live an enhanced life, a heightened capacity for the truth about oneself, to love and accept love, and to experience the courage to be together with a sense of one's own humor and that of others, as well. We speak of "recovering" but don't often name what it is we're in the process of recovering. It should be clear by now that it is our humanity, our human being, that's what.

ACKNOWLEDGMENTS

Three people I can remember stayed after me to write this book or a reasonable facsimile. Priest colleague Herm Pomy, RIP, never let one of our encounters pass but that he didn't say something like, "How's the book coming?" Lynn Ronkainen, artist, and Rebecca Newton, writer and editor, put a first draft together for me all probably with less Te Deum than tedium. The prime and final movers of late, of course, are the Revd Mary Catharine Nelson and Dr. Susan Ford Wiltshire, publishers, scholars, editors, writers themselves, who've stayed after this effort down to its last. And then there are the blessed people, their vicar Catharine Regen and their always Senior Warden Terri Johnson of Calvary Episcopal Church, Cumberland Furnace, TN, as unsung a parish as ever there could be.

Writers, teachers, leaders who have lit the trail include Ronald deFord, Texas University geologist and graduate thesis mentor, Bishops John Hines, James Clements, and Scott Field Bailey, the Revd Bill Hawley, preachers and writers extraordinaire. I suppose no book "good or bad" I've ever read gets by without some influence on me.

Jennie Adams, wonder therapist, and Jack Gessel and George Yandell, for Godsake. And Archie Stapleton and Bill Hethcock. And Jim Pike, and Tom Govan, and John Spong, and John Worrell, and Louie Crew, and Barbara Crafton, and Will Campbell... and Count Basie, and Chet Baker, and Harry James, and the Jim Cullums, Sr. & Jr., and Del Sawyer, trumpet teacher, and, of course, the Monday Night Jazz Band.

I've a long list of dead folks I pray about. I don't know so much that I pray for them as if I need to or they (or God!) need to have me call them to God's attention. Maybe so. But it makes more sense to me to realize that praying about them is also praying about me and reminds me of how in our way, they are such an important part of my life then, here, there, and now.

There is my lifelong friend King Hopkins, RIP. There's the family I knew and know now and have yet got to know — among the many now gone of whom is a beloved son and his mother and my grandson. There're the mentors, their patience, their wisdom they left for me and with me. There're the friends through thick and thin. There're the great writers and musicians. There're the teachers and preachers. There're the national and international good guys and bad guys, some who inspire, some who anger, a kind of inspiration in itself.

And there is you, good and dear reader, for whom I never wrote a book, let alone an epilogue. Thanks for your patience. — Lane

AND A FINAL BOW

May God bless you with discomfort at easy answers, half truths, and superficial relationships, so that you may live deep within your heart.

May God bless you with anger at injustice, oppression, and exploitation of people, so that you may work for justice, freedom, and peace.

May God bless you with tears to shed for those who suffer from pain, rejection, starvation, and war, so that you may reach out your hand to comfort them and to turn their pain into joy.

And may God bless you with enough foolishness to believe that you can make a difference in this world, so that you can do what others claim cannot be done. Amen

A Franciscan Blessing

LIFE IS SHORT
and we do not have much time
to gladden the hearts of those
who make the earthly pilgrimage with us
so be swift to love.
The Blessing of the Father and of the Son and of the Holy Spirit
be with us always. Amen.

The Reverend Elizabeth Kaeton

Editor's Note

This collection has been lovingly culled from over 2,000 essays written by Lane Denson over a period of not quite seven and a half years. Duplications and mistakes in transcription are solely the responsibility of the editor, who would like to thank volunteers comprising almost every regular attendee of Calvary Episcopal Church in Cumberland Furnace, Tennessee, plus one additional reader from the congregation of St. Ann's Episcopal Church in Nashville. Especial thanks goes to our Senior Warden Terri Johnson and to my dear friend Susan Ford Wiltshire, whose wise counsel has always been gratefully received even when we didn't see eye-to-eye. And lest there be any confusion about the matter: when we didn't agree, Susan, with her unerring judgment, was inevitably right.

This book is Calvary's "stained glass window" for Lane, an icon through which we hope you will see grace shine, and this is its inscription:

For Lane Denson

Writer.
Country Preacher.
Trumpeter and Cornetist.
Beloved.

From Calvary Episcopal Church
Cumberland Furnace, Tennessee
March 13, 2011

LaVergne, TN USA
02 March 2011
218579LV00002B/3/P